Song
for My Father

Song for My Father

Memoir of an All-American Family

Stephanie Stokes Oliver

ATRIA BOOKS

New York   London   Toronto   Sydney

ATRIA BOOKS

1230 Avenue of the Americas
New York, NY 10020

Library of Congress Cataloging-in-Publication Data

Oliver, Stephanie Stokes.
    Song for my father : memoir of an all-American family / by Stephanie Stokes Oliver—1st Atria Books hardcover ed.
        p.   cm.
        1. Stokes, Charles M. (Charles Moorehead) 1903–1996. 2. Oliver, Stephanie Stokes—Childhood and youth. 3. Stokes, Charles M. (Charles Moorehead) 1903–1996—Family. 4. Legislators—Washington (State)—Biography. 5. African American legislators—Washington (State)—Biography. 6. Washington (State). Legislature—Biography. 7. Republican Party (U.S. : 1854–)—Biography. 8. African American judges—Washington (State)—Biography. 9. Washington (State)—Politics and government—1951–. 10. Seattle (Wash.)—Biography. I. Title.

F895.22.S76O44 2004
328.797'092—dc22
[B]   2004043686

ISBN-13: 978-0-7434-7404-7
ISBN-10:   0-7434-7404-X
ISBN-13: 978-0-7434-7405-4 (Pbk)
ISBN-10:   0-7434-7405-8 (Pbk)

First Atria Books trade paperback edition July 2005

10   9   8   7   6   5   4   3   2   1

ATRIA BOOKS is a trademark of Simon & Schuster, Inc.

FRONTISPIECE: *The Stokes family: Josephine, André, Stephanie, Charles, 1966.*

Unless noted otherwise, photos appear courtesy of the author.

Manufactured in the United States of America

For information regarding special discounts for bulk purchases, please contact Simon & Schuster Special Sales at 1-800-456-6798 or business@simonandschuster.com.

To my father,
Charles Moorehead Stokes

And mother,
Josephine Stratman Stokes

For my daughter,
Anique Sahara Stokes Oliver

And generations to come

CONTENTS

INTRODUCTION

On Election Day 1960, some stupid girl had the nerve to threaten to kick my butt at recess after our second-grade teacher asked in class, "If you could vote for president of the United States of America, who would you vote for—Nixon or Kennedy?" With my hand the only one up for Nixon, it was then that I realized our family was different from most black folks. I knew my parents were Republicans. But I didn't know that made us a minority within the minority.

That is the story shared within these pages. My father was born during a time when most African-Americans were still loyal to the "party of Lincoln," and he never switched when most blacks did during the twenty-year New Deal presidency of Franklin Delano Roosevelt in the 1930s and 40s. The Republican Party embraced him when he was a member of the Young Republicans attending national conventions as a representative of the state of Kansas, and they supported his campaigns when he moved to Washington state, where he ran for state representative, state senator, lieutenant governor, and district court judge. The GOP, both locally and nationally, welcomed his activism and helped fund his campaigns, and he was loyal in return.

Of course, the party became more conservative after the "Southern Strategy" nomination of Barry Goldwater in 1964. But I am jumping ahead of my story.

There were no sleepless nights in Seattle for Charles M. Stokes. He often called Seattle "God's country," a place of opportunity and possibility. Here, his American dream of a happy marriage, 2.5 children, home-ownership, religious freedom, gainful employment, and political participation came true.

Between the years of 1943 and 1978, Stokey—as he was affectionately called by family and friends—achieved extraordinary accomplishments. For a while after his arrival in Seattle from Kansas in 1943, he was the area's only black attorney in private practice. He became Seattle's first black state legislator, served as president and on the board of the Seattle branch of the NAACP, worked hard as an advocate for equal housing, and adjudicated fairly as Washington state's first African-American district court judge. In addition, in the 1970s, he enjoyed his role as justice of the peace—he loved presiding over weddings.

Yet, Stokey's modesty compelled him to feel that his accomplishments fell short. Always humbly saying that he was "born too soon," he felt trapped by America's racial quagmire but also remained firm in the belief that the country would eventually overcome it. He never admitted that he aspired to become governor of the state of Washington, but he ran for the office of lieutenant governor in 1960. Narrowly defeated in the primary for the Republican nomination, his political race helped raise the bar on what was possible for other African-Americans with similar ambitions. Stokey was delighted in 1989 when Douglass Wilder, also a lawyer, became the first African-American elected to a governorship, in Virginia. Our family was proud, knowing what challenges Wilder had had to face, because our own father had waged a comparable battle in an attempt to make a difference.

Married to Josephine Stratman Stokes for forty-five years before his passing in 1996, Stokey was also a devoted father of three. I am one of those children. This is my effort to share his life story of high ethics, hard work, achievement, and family love. Stories of pioneers, of being a "first," are celebrated as proud moments at the time, but they have a way of becoming obliterated as years go by. Hence, my desire to document what life was like for one American who was born at the beginning of the twentieth century, when lynching was at an all-time high, and who died at the end of the century, pondering the use of a computer.

It is a story also of my own life, beginning in Seattle with a happy childhood that included summers at the beaches of Lake Washington, a close-knit church community, and integrated education. "Our heir," Stokey would call me with amusement. I came into the world in the middle of the century, during the rock-and-roll 1950s era of *Brown v. Board of Education*, and am now living in the hip-hop new millennium of the Internet. What my father and I had in common was the experience of living through a period of much racial and political change in America. In the upper left corner of the country, our family was not immune to the turmoil. In fact, we participated in it, argued about it, were changed by it, and got through it with love and faith.

I call this tale a memoir of an all-American family to refute the prevailing notion that all-American means exclusively white. If there was one thing both generations of Stokeses—the Republican parents and the younger radicals—agreed on, it was this: We wanted America to be all that it could be. Born in 1903 in Kansas, smack-dab in the middle of the country, just forty years after the abolition of slavery, my father predicated his belief in his country on the total embrace of the promise of the United States Constitution. My own faith in America's promise was based on the adolescent belief that the world had just been waiting for my generation to "tell it like it is" so that the country could "get hip" to the error of its ways. I passionately believed that my peace-and-love generation's purpose was to get America on the right path to equal freedom for all. Call football teams all-American. Describe blond, blue-eyed supermodels as having all-American good looks, if you like. But only those who believe in liberty and justice for *all* are the true all-Americans.

Events of the 2000 presidential campaign encouraged me to document the story of our American family. In March of that year, as the campaign was gearing up and it began to seem apparent that the Republican Party was trying to increase African-American support from its traditional share of a mere eight percent of the vote, I happened to mention to a colleague, Frank Lalli, then editor-in-chief of *George*, that my father had been an active Republican who served in political office. Frank was nice enough to become interested in my father's story and in my own upbringing. He asked me to write an article called "Growing Up Black and Republican."

Editor-in-chief duties at the Internet magazine I was in the midst of helping to launch, NiaOnline, prohibited me from turning in the piece when he wanted it, but Frank was patient. After our Web site was up and running smoothly in October, I sat down to write the piece. With my television tuned to CNN, I was proofreading the finished story one evening when I heard then–news anchor Bernard Shaw's deep voice say, "I regret to report that *George* magazine has folded."

I could hardly believe it. I was actually sitting there with my story for *George* in my lap. I looked at Bernard Shaw. I looked down at my paper. Then I called Frank for the unfortunate confirmation, and to express my condolences.

Over lunch with my publishing agent, Victoria Sanders, during the unprecedented and uncertain days after the November 2000 election, I related the tale of the story finally written for the magazine that had abruptly closed down. Victoria took interest in the story itself, of my father's courage to be Republican against the tide of black Democratic political loyalty and what it must have been like to grow up in such a political family. She encouraged me to turn the story into a book, accurately predicting that George W. Bush would indeed become our Republican president. "When he takes office, people might be interested in the lives of black Republicans, of that particular time in history that shaped you—the 1960s—and of your father-daughter bond," she said.

I thank Victoria for the interest and enthusiasm that have motivated me to document my father's contribution to his country and his family. I pray that what follows on these pages would make my father proud, and that it will honor my blessedly alive and active mother.

Someone asked me if my father had been a celebrity. The assumption was that if he hadn't, why bother to write a book about him? Surely, in our celebrity culture, only a famed singer, actor, or athlete would merit a book. But I believe in the power of ordinary people doing extraordinary things. The main things my father did were to vote religiously, become politically active, and believe in the promise of America at a time when, in some parts of the country, those could be dangerous and courageous acts for African-Americans. As a journalist, I feel compelled to document the life of one American, and its representative story of a people.

So, no, my father was not a celebrity. But he did like to sing. No, I shouldn't say that. Does one *like* to talk? Does a person *like* to breathe? He just sang around the house in the same way one would think out loud.

"I must tell Jesus," he would begin in his unassuming baritone. Another day it might be, "I love the Lord, He heard my cry and pitied every groan," a song that went on solemnly. These were the songs of his soul, hymns of things hoped for but not seen. The ones he turned to for comfort, for stress relief. Singing was his meditation, his prayer, how he got over.

His life was no sad song, though. He lived to age ninety-three, long enough to see all but the first three and last three years of the twentieth century and witness many changes in attitudes toward African-Americans. His firm belief in the law and the promise of the Constitution was affirmed time and again. Charles M. Stokes loved life and lived it with verve, humor, style, and more jazz than blues.

Song for My Father is a story of one American family's struggles and successes, a tune full of patriotism, hope, and joy. I hope you will find it was a song worth singing.

Song
for My Father

Born in the U.S.A.

1903

I<small>N</small> A<small>UGUST OF</small> 1986, Mary Turner Henry, a middle-school librarian who had taken on an oral-history project for Seattle's Black Heritage Society, asked a longtime friend to sit down with her to tell his life story.

It was a typical sunny summer day. Contrary to popular belief, Seattle's clouds make way for beautiful July and August afternoons that Seattleites spend at the lake beaches and the waterfront on Puget Sound. On clear days when one can see the snowcapped tip of Mount Rainier, the city is covered with the lush, green grass and trees that exemplify its nickname, The Emerald City. Whenever there was no fog cover over Mount Rainier, Stokey would always notice from our home's picture

A<small>BOVE</small>: *Charles at age four.*

window that held a magnificent view of Lake Washington and the Cascade Mountains to the east, Mount Baker to the north, and Mount Rainier looking south. "Look! The mountain's out!" he frequently exclaimed, as if he'd never said it before.

On this early Thursday afternoon, Mary arrived at Stokey's law office. It was a spacious two-office suite with a receiving area in the front and a hidden kitchen in the back. Befitting his life as a retired judge, which he spent taking business from friends who might have elder law or estate questions, this place on the edge of the black community, near Seattle University, was comfortable and welcoming. In fact, when Mary arrived, she says, Stokey was holding court with some buddies who had stopped by to chat. "Now, it's time for you to leave," Mary says he told them. "I've got something to do."

The building was just a few miles from the slick, downtown law offices of his past, in the days when he had a great view of Puget Sound from his skyscraper window and a secretary to call in to take dictation. The wooden sign over the door, carved with the words on two lines, CHARLES M. STOKES/ATTORNEY AT LAW, attracted rich, poor, and in-between. The modest storefront location was a contrast to his sophisticated judge's chambers in the King County District Court downtown. Yet it was just right.

Seated in an upright red leather chair under the dulling oil portrait of Abraham Lincoln that was one of Stokey's prized possessions, Mary set up her tape recorder on the desk that Stokey had had since the beginning of his Seattle career. She sat near the electric typewriter that he was known for using, which had a ball he could insert to make the typeface look like exquisite script. He loved these gadgets that gave people the impression that he was ahead of his time.

After catching up on their friendship—begun in 1956 when Mary and her husband, Dr. John Henry, one of the first black surgeons of Seattle, had moved from Nashville—Mary asked the questions that made the life of Charles M. Stokes unfold on two cassette tapes.

STOKEY'S STORY: IN HIS OWN WORDS

My full name is Charles Moorehead Stokes, retired Judge Charles M. Stokes. I was named for my grandfather, who was Charles Garner. His middle name was Moorehead, so I was named for him.

My birthdate is February the first, nineteen-three. I was born in Fredonia, Kansas. My father was Reverend Norris J. Stokes—J. meaning Jefferson. And my mother was Myrtle Garner, before she married. But my mother died when I was about three. I don't remember one thing about her.

But then my father remarried. I had a stepmother—Josephine Stokes. And that's now my wife's name too. I tell my wife that my stepmother was such a lovely woman, I thought I'd get me a Josephine, too, like my dad did. She was a graduate of Baker College in Kansas, which was an astounding accomplishment for her, and for blacks, to graduate from college at that time.

My father was born somewhere in Kentucky. He got to Kansas, I suppose, by being a preacher. I understand he went to Macon, Georgia, to some sort of school they had down there. I don't know where my mother was born. I suppose there in Kansas.

You know, in those days they never did talk about things like that—where they were born, what schools they went to, that kind of information Alex Haley got in Roots. *And if you didn't happen to catch what your parents happened to drop sometime, you just never thought about it, and you never got it for posterity.*

I don't know how my father happened to become a preacher, with the possible exception that it was the thing to be at that time. That was before the turn of the century—it wasn't long after Emancipation—when black folks were just evolving from the cotton fields and the plantations. And I suppose one of the few professions available was being a preacher, and it was the easiest profession to obtain because you didn't need a license, you just started preaching. If he had gone to school, I'm sure he had some reason other than just saying he was going to preach, because he wouldn't have taken school as lightly as that.

I had one brother and one half-brother. I had a brother by my father and my natural mother. Named Norris, he was nearly two years older than I. I also had a half-brother by my father and my stepmother; his name is Maurice. I am eight years older than him. There were three of us. I—being the middle one—never got anything new. [Laughs]

My younger brother just left Seattle, after coming to visit me here for the first time. He had been to twenty-one countries, traveling around the world, but never had been here to see me. He'd been as near as San Francisco and never came to see me. Maurice is a retired professor of history at Savannah State College. He taught at Alabama State College before that. He now lives in our family's home in Pratt, Kansas.

My other brother is a singer, and led quartets. Norris aspired to be a Wings over Jordan type. He traveled with the Jackson Jubilee Singers, which were of quite some notoriety in Kansas. Have you heard of the Jackson Jubilee Singers? Etta Moten [Etta Moten Barnett; an actress and singer, the first to play Bess in *Porgy and Bess*] *was in that. Well, he was connected with them—if not, of that same type of gospel group. He also had his own quartet and would go to high schools and sing in Canada, places like that.*

Norris didn't get married until he was seventy-five years old. I told him at the time, "Why bother?" But he married a nice lady named Louise, and stopped traveling and settled down in Beckley, West Virginia. He's eighty-five now.

Maurice never did get married. And neither one of them had children.

My first schooling was in Paola, Kansas. My father was pastoring at a church there. My first school was a black school, as I remember it. When you got to the third grade, then you transferred to the other school, the north school, where the white and black went, in Pratt, Kansas. We were living there then.

I went through the elementary school grades very well. Then I got a little older, and I had other ideas. I started shooting craps, and chasing the women, and not doing a doggone thing. I was seventeen or nineteen when I messed up. It was during high school—an integrated school—and my older brother had gone on to college.

I was in a place all by myself, not staying at home, but in one of my dad's houses in which there was a kitchen shack. You know what a kitchen shack is, where they have a thrashing machine outfit, and they have a kitchen? Well, in Pratt, the shacks are box cars, and I had one of those on a lot that Dad owned in Pratt.

I had quit school because I went one year and flunked everything I took. I think the teachers ganged up on me. They knew that I could do better work and that I wasn't doing it. And I just didn't much care. I would go there un-

prepared, so they said, "We ought to cure his slothfulness." So every one of the teachers flunked me.

Then I said, "Well, if I'm going to flunk, I may as well quit."

So I quit and laid out of school three years—gambling, running around, kicking around, doing nothing. [Laughs] *Then I went back and finished high school.*

But I didn't go back to the high school in Pratt right away. Dad came over one day and asked me, "What are you going to do—to make of yourself?"

There was a colored school in Topeka called, at that time, Kansas Vocational School. It was run by Baptists. So Dad asked, "If I send you up there, would you go?" I said, "Yes."

Well, I thought that indicated he was going to pay for everything. He sent me up there and never paid a dime after that! [Laughs]

Well, I had to carry big rocks—to help build what they called the Trade Building. I had to carry milk from the Agricultural Department over to the cottages where the teachers were. I had to sweep out the Administration Building— all to stay in school. Then they took me out of school entirely. And I was still doing this work.

I did that, oh, about two or three weeks, and someone came to me and said, "Stokes, you're a fool. You're sitting here working, getting beans and syrup, whatever they're feeding you, and a place to sleep, and that's all. If you're not going to school, you can go out and work and get some money, and get paid for it."

So I called my brother Norris, who was then at Ottawa University. He was working at a barber shop or something. And he sent me four dollars—two dollars of which was my fare to come to where he was in Ottawa, Kansas. The other two dollars was just for incidentals or getting there, that sort of thing.

But there was a commandant named Winston there, who later went to Tuskegee Institute, and was the commandant of ROTC at Tuskegee. He heard I was leaving. And he must have thought there was some good in me, or something he wanted the school to have. So he says, "Oh, what's the matter?"

I said, "Well, I came up here to go to school. I didn't come up here to work free, like a slave or something."

He says, "Is that all?"

I said, "Yeah."

He said, "If you were in school, would you stay?"

I said, "Yes, I'll stay."

That was on a Friday. He said, "Unpack your things. I'll seat you in school Monday."

I don't know what he did, but I was back in school Monday. So I finished out the year.

It was an all-black vocational school. But I was taking regular high-school subjects—geometry, and I suppose English. But geometry is mostly what I remember. They had agriculture, tailoring, and carpentry. I was in the carpentering end of it.

I remember an eccentric, hard-nosed guy there named Burke, who was a splendid fellow. He was a teacher of carpentry who was building a hospital there on the grounds. He'd say, "Boy, if you're going to hit the nail—hit it! Don't play with it! Hit it!" [Laughs] And I'd go BAM! BAM! BAM! You can drive a nail quicker if you hit it! [Laughs]

I didn't graduate from this school, though. I was a sophomore then. I went back to Pratt, Kansas, and re-entered the high school there. Then I went on to graduate. I was the feature editor of the newspaper at school. I was reciting Paul Lawrence Dunbar poems, and all that crap. [Laughs]

There was one teacher there who taught journalism, and I was under her tutelage. I had a column in the newspaper, and called myself Sparkey. I wrote one day that the football guys did all that playing for the school and didn't get a dime, didn't get a dollar, didn't get anything but a blanket with pee on it. [Laughs]

I wanted to put that in the paper, but she said, "We can't do that, Charles."

I said, "Why not?"

She said, "Well, the school board wouldn't like that." So we didn't put that in Sparkey's column.

But she always thought I would be something. We got to talking once, and she said, "When you get to be something, I'm going to bring you a chicken." And years later, when I was in politics and had come back to Pratt, she came and brought me a chicken. [Laughs] Yeah, Lettie Little—she wrote a book about Kansas and gave me a copy. She was a lovely lady.

There was also another teacher who was important in my life. In college at Kansas University, E. C. Beauchler taught debate and speech—that sort of thing. He was very nice. He was loose and easy; he'd come in talking, and laughing, and tick you around. He'd teach you something, and make you want to please him. I always thought he was very nice.

You ask, did my father pay for college, or did I go on a scholarship? Girl, I had to work!

I waited tables. See, the Alpha Chi Omega girls would have these rush parties, and that would be a week or two before school started. And they'd have teas, and they'd give you two dollars to serve that tea. I served those things! I also played in a band, a dance band there in Lawrence, Kansas.

When school started one year, I was still working for those Alpha Chi Omega girls. Their sorority house had a furnace, which a white man was tending to, but he didn't stay there, and the girls were always complaining about being cold. So I told them, "Well, let me fire the furnace."

And they said, "Oh, Stokey, you can't fire the furnace."

I said, "Oh, yes, I can too. I can fire the furnace. I've done that kind of work before."

They said, all right, they'd let me do it. But I didn't have anyplace to live and it was a little chore for me to keep them warm if I wasn't there. So I told them, "I could do a better job if I lived here, see?"

They said, "Stokey, there's no place for you to live with the sorority."

"Oh yes, there is."

"Where?"

"In the trunk room."

In the trunk room was where they stored all the trunks of the girls coming to school. They said, "There's no place there."

"If I make a place, can I stay?" I asked.

They said, "Yes."

So I got in there and I packed all those regular trunks and wardrobe trunks on top of each other, and pushed them back and made a place for me along the wall. I had a table there on which I'd study. It had a mirror over it. I had my own wardrobe trunk for a dresser. Next to me was the lavatory and basin — no tub. If it was cold weather, I'd take a tin tub and take a bath right there. I was right on the edge of the campus and could go up to the gymnasium and take a shower. So I just made out that way.

They were paying me five dollars a week, and board and room. When you are working for your board and room, you don't lose your appetite. They had a very good, lovely cook there, a woman named Mary Harvey. She and her husband had a farm five miles outside of Lawrence. And she brought cream and milk, and eggs and chickens, and watermelons and things to the sorority. She was just a lovely old lady.

During the summer I had to stay there for summer school. There I am without any money. Herbert Duckett [a schoolmate] *and I were there together. Duckett would get money from home every Monday morning. And every Tuesday morning, he'd spend that money just like he was going to get some more the next day. So finally I told him, "Duckett, quit spending* our *money like that! You can't do that!"*

I was getting two dollars a week to cut the lawn while the Alpha Chi Omega girls were gone home for the summer. My two dollars would last longer than Duckett's money he was getting, because he would spend it all. [Laughs] *We'd starve from one Monday until the next Monday when he'd get some more money. But he cut down on it. We set it up so that we'd go to a little mom-and-pop grocery store with a dime. When one would buy something with that dime, the other one would have to steal something so we could get by.* [Nervous laughter]

There was a lady down the street from the Kappa House [his own fraternity's house] *who would charge us a quarter for a meal, and we'd have one meal in the evening between us. That was in 1931. Even then, charging us a quarter was helping us. She was being nice to us. She had children of her own and wanted to help us. A quarter didn't pay for the work she did for us to eat, but it was just a lovely thing she did. And that's the way we had it.*

What made me decide to go to law school? Well, to tell the truth, I really don't know, except people kept telling me, "The way you are, you ought to be a lawyer." That was because I liked to talk.

I didn't know about being a lawyer, but I knew I didn't want to be a preacher. I felt that had my daddy been Adam Clayton Powell's daddy, I could have been a preacher, too, because he had some money. But my daddy had nothing. And I didn't want to be a preacher and not have money, and have people giving you clothes, and food, and stuff. I didn't want to be depending on people. I didn't want to be cold all the time.

I'd seen my dad put gunnysacks on his feet to keep his feet warm while he went out in the country to cut wood in the snow. And I'd seen him lay brick making paved streets out of the dirt streets. He had to pick them up about five or six at a time and carry them up to the guy who was handling the bricks. I said to myself, I didn't want any of that.

There was a fellow named Elijah Scott in Topeka, and a fellow named William Harrison in Hutchinson, which was not too far from Pratt. They were doing pretty good as lawyers, so I said, heck, I'd try to be a lawyer.

At that time, we had to do pre-law in college. You could take the fourth year of college as the first year of law school. So I did six years.

In 1931, I graduated. I would have gotten my diploma at that time, but it would have cost me eighteen dollars to put on a robe and cap, walk down the line, and have all the folderol that goes with it. I didn't have eighteen dollars. So I skipped all that.

But I was able to take the bar because I had graduated—even though I didn't walk down the aisle. So I did take the bar, and I passed it.

I didn't get my diploma until 1946. That was because before then, I didn't quite have the money, and when I did have it, I didn't want to spend it for that. I was practicing law and really didn't need my diploma. Then later on, I said, "Well, I'll just get it." And I finally got it.

After I got my law degree, then I needed a job. In Leavenworth, Kansas, there was a noted black lawyer named T. W. Bell. He had expertise in habeas corpus. I went up to Leavenworth to work with him. To help me along, he gave me ten dollars a week. I spent five dollars a week for board and room, and I had five dollars left. I started with him in 1931 and stayed until 1934, when I opened my own office.

After I opened my own office, I picked it with the chickens. I mean, I had some hard times.

One day, the phone rang and it was Central. [The phone company] *She said, "Mr. Stokes?"*

"Yeah."

"We're going to have to turn off your phone."

"Why? You can't do that!"

She said, "Well, you know you're behind three or four months."

"Yes, I'm behind, but you can't turn it off!"

"Why can't we turn it off?"

I said, "Because if you do, nobody's going to hire a lawyer who can't even keep a telephone on! If you turn it off, you'll never get your money, and neither will I."

"Well we've got to get paid." So they turned it off until I could pay it.

I had some hard times. The principal of the school got a new car. The fellow I'd started with, T. W. Bell, got a new car. Dr. William McKinley Thomas, who got to Leavenworth about two weeks before I did, he got a new car. I—like a damn fool—said, "I need a new car." And I had a car that would just hit and miss: *Tick-a-tick-a-tick-a-tick*. But I, like a fool, got a new car. I got a Ford that had three chrome bands on it, from front to the side. A distinctive thing, it was a beauty, that car.

But the fellow I was buying my house from said, "If you can get a new car, you can pay me." I didn't pay him, so he sued me to take over my house. Then after a while, I'm sitting up in my office and a fellow came from Topeka and said, "Where's the automobile?"

"I'm not going to tell you."

He was the agent from the mortgage company. He said, "I know where it is."

"Where is it?"

"It's impounded because I picked it up."

"You couldn't have picked it up," I said, "because it was locked."

"Well, I had it towed away."

So I called up the sheriff. I said, "Jim, this guy stole my car. And I know who did it."

"Where is he?" he asked.

"He's here."

So the sheriff came and said, "Get in here!" And he put the agent in jail.

The man was hollering about getting out, and called his people in Topeka, and then they were calling me. His daddy was a Kansas meteorologist. And this guy had never been in jail before. The cockroaches bit him up. And the other inmates took his money and held kangaroo court. Oh, he was fit to be tied!

His people came calling me, saying what they were going to do to me. I said, "That's all right. I live dangerously. Go ahead."

The next day, they saw he wasn't going to get out, so they said to me, "You let him out, and we'll give you back your car."

And I said, "All right, that's what I want."

So I let him out. And we went over to the garage where he was to turn the car loose. Got there and he wouldn't do it.

I got on the phone and said, "Jim, this guy won't give me my car."

He said, "Where is he?"

"He's sitting right down here."

"I'll be right there!" In five minutes that white man was there, and he put that other white man back in the jail. Well, I got my car out that time.

The same day, I had to go to Kansas City, so I drove the car down. Coming back, driving this car with the distinctive three chrome bands on it, I could see the agent coming home. I met him going toward Kansas City. And I could see him do a double take—he recognized the car. Then I'm looking in the rearview mirror, and I see him stop and turn around, coming back. I commenced going faster and faster, faster. I commenced hitting eighty and ninety. He commenced hitting eighty and ninety behind me. Then he's driving with one hand, pulling off his coat with the other. He's going to work me over good, see? He was way bigger than I was. So I'm doing all this fast driving, speeding. But here come this sign that says, "Entering Leavenworth County." He saw that and I guess he thought, "I'd better let this bastard go on now, or he'll put me in jail again." [Laughs]

But he called me that night and said, "Don't ever come to Topeka."

And I said, "Well, I'll be there. I'll be there."

What he didn't know was that in the front seat was a prison guard, a black fellow, who had just been learning jujitsu. And in the backseat was one of my brothers-in-law. They had been lying down there sleeping, so the guy couldn't see anybody but me.

When I told them what happened, they said, "Why didn't you let him catch us?"

I said, "That man could have shot you or something! We ain't got no gun!"

And the prison guard said, "Why didn't you let me? I wanted to try my jujitsee on him!"

"Well, I'd rather outrun him," I said. "A good run's better than a bad stand."

Yeah, I had some hard times, but I eventually paid for the house and the automobile too. I got married [to first wife Evangeline Goddard] *and stayed in Leavenworth until 1939, at which time I became an assistant attorney in the Kansas Commission of Revenue and Taxation and went to Topeka.*

One day I wasn't feeling well, and the wife, Eva, came upstairs where I was and said, "A man's downstairs to see you."

"Who is he?"

She said, "I don't know—some white man."

I'm sick with a cold, not feeling good, all stuffy. I go downstairs, and there he is, the agent, knocking on the door and inviting me out.

I said, "You old fool, you!" I shut the door and went back upstairs. [Laughter]

He had told me not to come to Topeka, and there I was, see? He was going to try again to beat me up, that's what he was going to do! He lived in Topeka, his father lived there, and he was going to work me over for that jail time he did. [Laughter]

I moved to Topeka because I was going to get a regular salary. It wasn't much, but it enabled me to pay all my bills, keep ahead, and have a little left each time. Having a little security at that time was worth changing for.

But I was sitting up there in the Kansas Commission of Revenue and Taxation, and they didn't give me one damn thing to do. Not one thing. I'm not exaggerating—nothing! I just sat there and collected a check each month.

Why? Because I was black! And the white lawyers were at the other end of the floor—three of them.

What I'd do to amuse myself is that I'd go down to the law library and just start reading. I'd read anything. All I had to do was report. That's all I had to do. They'd given me a secretary. She started doing work processing the tax returns from sales tax and compensating tax, which gave her something to do rather than just sitting there looking like a bump on a log.

I made one mistake. I asked them how much they were paying me. I should have left that alone, because otherwise I would have been paid what the white boys were being paid. When I asked them that I think they realized, "Well, he's not expecting so much." So they cut me below what the white boys were getting.

I took that to get on my feet, get a little affluent, and get the feeling that I wasn't tied down or scared and all. Then I told them to raise me to what the white boys were getting or else I was going to quit. And I suppose they thought—which I have no reason to think, other than for purely personal piffle—"This man's a fool. He's not going to quit the job, because he's not doing nothing. A lot of us want a job to not do anything."

But I felt I was atrophying. The little law I knew, I was losing because I wasn't practicing it.

They didn't raise my salary.

When I told them I was going to quit, I either had to go back to Leavenworth or go somewhere else. I thought, I didn't do too good in Leavenworth. I'd be a fool to go back there. Where shall I go?

Ray and Ted Jones, and Elmo Johnson, lived across the street in Topeka. One family lived to my right, and the other to my left in the next block. They had come out here to Seattle to work for Boeing. They told me to come because there were no black lawyers here at all other than one—Johnnie Prim—and he was in the prosecutor's office. I said, "That sounds like a pretty good thing."

So in 1943, I came out here to Seattle.

Home, Home on the Range

"U<small>NCLE</small> S<small>TOKEY</small>, tell us a story about growing up poor in Kansas!"

My cousin Gloria's annual Christmas dinner request was always followed by the knowing laughter of the family.

"Oh, no, here we go again! The poor-little-Stokey stories," someone—most likely me—would say. "Dad, did you know Dorothy in *The Wizard of Oz?* She was from Kansas, right?"

It was that time of evening. Mom's turkey had been carved to smithereens. The Sock-It-to-Me, that delicious pink-Jell-O-and-cottage-cheese specialty that Mom's childhood friend Fannie had concocted, had already vanished. Aunt Katie, Gloria's mom, had come in late from her nursing job on the obstetrics ward of Harborview Hospital, and was serving her family-famous peach cobbler. Uncle King lit a Kool. My mother

<small>ABOVE:</small> *Charles as a young man.*

handed him an ashtray, the kind that was purchased more to comple-
ment the decor than for usage. No one who lived in the house smoked,
but guests were always accommodated.

It wasn't that we were rich. But Daddy's stories of growing up in
Kansas made us feel as lucky as living in Disneyland. We never knew
how old Daddy was, but we just assumed he was born in the "olden
days." My mother made it clear that his stories were all before her
time, but we had no idea she was twenty-two years his junior. She was
still a grown-up, and so it was all the same to us.

My cousin, my brother and sister, and I, on the other hand, were
lucky enough to be a part of the space age. "The Jetsons" was my favorite
television show. Seattle had hosted the 1962 World's Fair, the first in
the United States since World War II. Daddy had been on the planning
committee of the fair, which had featured, among others, exhibits prom-
ising that we'd be able to see the people we spoke to on the phone any
day now. At ten years old, I went to the fair and excitedly took my turn
going up to the top of the Space Needle and riding the futuristic
Monorail.

"You want to know about the times when we were so poor, we had
to go look for coal every day to keep us warm?" he asked.

"Yes, tell us that one."

"Well, every day when I was a child, my brother Norris and I had to
scrounge up the coal to heat up our house," he began. "My parents
had a rule that whichever one of us brought in the most coal got
rewarded by not washing the dishes."

"You boys had to wash dishes?" I interrupted, although I knew that
answer. That was asked for my brother, André, to hear. He was always
pleading his case that because he took out the garbage, he shouldn't
have to have a turn at washing dishes too.

"Yeah, we had to wash dishes," Daddy said. "We didn't have any sisters."

My quick glance to André caught his tongue sticking out at me.

"Every night, I ended up being the one to wash the dishes," Dad
continued. "That was because each and every day, Norris would beat
me at bringing in the coal. I'd look high and low. I'd go all over town,
looking on the ground, looking in the fields. We didn't have money to

just go buy some coal, so we had to find what other people had discarded. But somehow, Norris would come back home before I did, and he always had more coal than I could find. His full basket made my parents happy—and made me mad.

"It perturbed me to no end! I wondered, 'How does he do it? He's two years older than I am, but he's no smarter.'

"After months and months, I'd finally had it with washing those dishes all the time, while Norris sat around doing nothing. So I decided to secretly follow him.

"My stepmother said, 'Go on, boys, time to get the coal.' Norris ran out, and I ran out. Only this time, instead of heading toward my usual haunts, I held back and watched which way he went.

"He ran up the street. I ran up the street. He turned the corner. I turned the corner. Next thing I knew I saw him head into the railroad yard. Ol' Norris was taking the coal from the abundant supply that made the trains run! He was stealing coal from the train station!"

"Did you tell on him, Uncle Stokey?" Gloria asked as the rest of us were laughing.

"After all, your father was a minister, so he would have said, 'Thou shalt not steal,' " I chimed in.

"No, I didn't tell. But let's just say that I didn't wash the dishes so often after that!"

In 1983, I gave my father a birthday present of *The New York Times* published on the day he was born, February 1, 1903. I was surprised to see a front-page story on race. NEGROES AGAINST VIOLENCE, the headline read. "Richmond Colored Men Condemn Sentiments Credited to Hayes, but Which He Repudiated." When I mentioned this to Daddy, he said, "We were dealing with racial issues then, and we're still dealing with them now. Some things change, some things stay the same."

When Charles Stokes started elementary school, more than ninety percent of African-Americans still lived in the south. Although he was raised in the midwest, he was still colored, and wherever colored folks were, they lived with white supremacy, segregation, inequality, and unpredictable racial violence. When he was eleven, the Supreme Court made "separate but equal" the law of the land. In the entire country, with a population of ten million colored people, there was only one African-American judge, two Negro legislators, and two thousand blacks in college. The next decade would see almost two million blacks leave the south in a "Great Migration" toward the big cities of the north in search of a better life.

Stokey wasn't from the south. And he didn't go due north. In 1943, the midwesterner set out to find a better life in the Pacific northwest. It was a pattern in his life. "If everyone is going one way, I always look for another way."

He took with him his political ambitions and activism in the Republican Party. I always thought that Daddy stayed Republican because he was so old by then that he didn't want to change his ways. I figured he was loyal to a fault. Plus, after he got to Seattle, the Republicans helped him get elected. So why would he go Democrat?

In 2001, I had a phone conversation with one of his Kansas cronies that helped me to figure it all out. There was much I didn't know about the history of Kansas politics, and even more about the participation of black folks in Kansas, the state of the Missouri-Kansas Compromise and of *Brown v. Board of Education.* That board of education was in Topeka, Kansas, I was reminded by Arthur Fletcher.

I recalled Mr. Fletcher as a nice man, who was taller and stockier than my father. To be honest, just about everyone was taller than my father, but it wasn't an issue for anyone I knew. No one in our family ever referred to my father as short. No one teased him, certainly. His stature was more important than his height. His place in our community made him a big man. But Mr. Fletcher, a fellow Kansan who had also landed in Washington state, had the build of a football player. He was not a person to play with.

"When your dad practiced law in Kansas in the 1930s and 40s, blacks practically ran the Republican Party," Mr. Fletcher told me to my surprise when I called him in 2001 at his home in Washington, D.C., to reminisce. "In a state where blacks were only four percent of the population, the vice-chairman of the nineteen counties of Kansas was black. The position was elected by ward captains, and the blacks voted in a block.

"Politics in Kansas was like basketball. It was an exciting political game. We knew we could get people elected because we controlled the party. Against the odds, this taught us how to *win!*

"In Kansas, blacks voted for Republicans in the primary, because if we won the primary, we could win the general election. If you wanted to influence the state agencies to make a difference, you had to be a Republican. The blacks in the party were dynamic. Democrats couldn't get elected dogcatcher!" he said, and we laughed together.

"Black lawyers in the state of Kansas were heroes," Mr. Fletcher continued. "People didn't want to be basketball players, like they do now. They wanted to be lawyers. Most of the candidates were lawyers, and if they could win these counties they could take the state. We were used to competing against white boys, and if they were average, they couldn't beat us. They didn't even faze us.

"Your father admired those black lawyers who came before him, and wanted to be like them. He was a role model in Kansas. And when he went to Seattle, he carried that experience with him."

Mr. Fletcher concurred with Daddy's story about being an attorney in the Commission of Revenue and Taxation, sitting around twiddling his thumbs. "When your dad practiced law in Kansas, there wasn't much for a black attorney to do."

A decade after my father left for Seattle, political activity became such a hotbed that Mr. Fletcher said he was run out of town.

"*Brown v. Board* moved through the Kansas courts," Mr. Fletcher told me, explaining that black lawyers represented the family of eight-year-old Linda Brown and others in the 1954 case against segregated schools in Topeka. "It got so much national attention that Thurgood Marshall, who was the national head of the NAACP, came out from Baltimore to see what we were doing. When it hit the Supreme Court, the NAACP took over."

I hadn't thought about that. It had always been my impression that Thurgood Marshall and the NAACP had initiated the case. Who knew that local attorneys in the town in which my father had first worked as a lawyer, where he had cut his political teeth as the head of the Young Republicans, had spearheaded one of the most important legal cases in the country? I sure didn't. Then again, I was only two years old when the victory came. And none of my school classes ever taught this particular American history.

"When the court handed down the decision, the impact hit Kansas hard," Mr. Fletcher said. "They ran those of us that had something to do with it out of the state."

"Really?" I mustered. I couldn't believe it. I hadn't heard of any fallout from the *Brown v. Board of Education* case. I thought it had been all good for black folks. Nothing but celebration. How naive.

"Many families were destroyed by that decision." His voice was strong and firm. "We paid a price.

"I had a car dealership, and got run out of business and out of the state. We moved to Berkeley, but my wife couldn't accept what had happened to our lives. She jumped off the Bay Bridge and committed suicide. I raised five children by myself in California, where I had to be a teacher to make a living."

"I'm sorry, Mr. Fletcher, I had no idea," I said, but not really knowing what to say. Typical of most of the elders in my life, he wouldn't accept sympathy. He had shared the experience not to gain my pity but to provide a teaching moment.

"Yes, we paid a price, but you can't let the backlash and deeply rooted hate destroy you. If you let it, it can defeat you. That's when you get in touch with your spirit."

Then he added, "Your father was supporting us." Daddy was in Seattle by this time and had already made inroads as a legislator. Another Kansas attorney, Philip Burton, had joined him in Seattle and they shared a law office. Seattle was living up to the moniker preferred by the locals: God's country. Sure enough, and especially with all that was going down in Kansas, it must have seemed more and more like the promised land. "He was telling us to come to Seattle."

It's clichéd to say "the rest is history," but Arthur Fletcher moved to Pasco, a small college town in eastern Washington state, where he indeed made history. While teaching at a local college, he encouraged students to vote. He was a popular professor and city councilman, and his student support helped him win in a race my father had lost. In 1968 he became the first African-American to be nominated in the Washington state Republican primary for lieutenant governor. Unfortunately, he lost in the general election, but then President Nixon came calling, and in the early 1970s as assistant secretary of labor in Washington, D.C., Fletcher became the "father of affirmative action" by issuing an order for fair employment standards.

I was afraid I was taking up too much of this important man's time with my questions about the past. But before we hung up the phone, Mr. Fletcher gave me an additional piece of Kansas history.

"Black folks got to Kansas because of the Underground Railroad. The Atchison, Topeka, and Santa Fe Railroad had headquarters near Topeka. Black folks worked in the coal fields, recruited by the railroad after slavery. There were riots between the blacks and the Irish over who would work in the mines. So this railroad took the blacks to work in their coal mines. That's one reason we were accustomed to competing against whites."

And, I mused to myself, that's one reason why Uncle Norris, in his competition against Daddy not to have to wash the dinner dishes, knew that the railroad station was where to find the coal.

= 3 =

Washington, My Home

STOKEY'S STORY: IN HIS OWN WORDS

*I*N KANSAS, *I had been a bigwig Republican.*

I started out Republican because my dad was Republican. After I had been practicing law in Leavenworth, Kansas, awhile, I told my dad, "Look, the probate judge is a Democrat. The district court judge is a Democrat. The county commissioners are Democrat. The sheriff's a Democrat. The county attorney's Democrat. Say, if I'm going to be in Leavenworth, I better turn Democrat."

"Oh, son, don't do that. Don't do that," and he started that cadence, like he was going to preach. I got the message.

ABOVE: *Witnessing the signing of the Washington State Fair Employment Practices Act, 1949, by Governor Arthur B. Langlie (seated) at the state Capitol (from left to right): Charles M. Stokes, George Revelle, Jr., Thelma Dewitty, Hubert Dewitty, M. P. Dotson, Letcher Yarbrough.*

23

But if he hadn't told me that, I'd probably have become a Democrat. And had I known Franklin D. Roosevelt was going to be in office almost twenty years, I'd have become one anyhow! [Laughs]

When Dad came up, if you were black and a Democrat, that was an anathema. If you weren't a Republican, you were nothing! You were an ingrate for being anything else. Lincoln done freed your butt, and you gone on against him and all? No! It's just the opposite of what it is now. They thought you were a fool for being a Democrat. Now, they think you're one for being a Republican.

When I was a young lawyer, my boss, T. W. Bell, was quite a politician. In Leavenworth, people looked up to him, and that forced him to get into politics. That kind of forced me to get into it too. And then Dr. Thomas came to town, and he was politically minded, and the three of us formed a kind of triumvirate. The fellas who didn't like us too much called us "the wrecking crew." [Laughs]

But with Thomas's help and push, I was elected vice-chairman of the Young Republican National Federation, an important post that was on the national level. This sent me off to the Republican National Convention in 1936, when Alfred M. Landon of Kansas was nominated for president. So I was the first black vice-chairman of the Young Republican Federation. And I went to Cleveland and got a hundred dollars a week in expenses. Man, that was something.

You know, there's a hell of a lot of difference between having a hundred dollars in your pocket, and knowing it's there, and that you're going to get some more, and having about ten or twelve dollars and not knowing. You just feel different. You act different. You are different. So I was having a good time—a hundred dollars a week. And I was supposed to be somebody.

Back home, the governor had unexpected trouble being elected. He won by, I think about four-hundred-and-some votes after the absentee ballots were counted. I think some folks in the campaign were teed off with me, because I had gone to the National Convention. I thought I'd be helping Leavenworth by going to Cleveland, but I think they were Monday-morning quarterbacking. When they had a hard time, then they blamed me for not being there, see? But then, before, they'd said I should go, so there I was.

But the governor himself thought of me as helping him get elected. So through him was how I got to be assistant attorney at the Kansas Commission of Revenue and Taxation.

I left that job and landed in Seattle on August 27, 1943. I was admitted to practice law in 1944. Luckily for me, I didn't have to take the bar exam. I just got under the wire of reciprocity; it wasn't long after that that they changed it so that you had to take the exam if you came from another state. But even so, I had to get some very strenuous recommendations. I had helped another Kansas governor, Payne Harry Ratner, get elected, and I had him as a recommendation. I had clients I had worked for. Then the Washington state bar also wanted to have people you didn't work for, to get your reputation in the community.

It took me a little time to get settled politically in Seattle. I had started in politics in Kansas early in my career. And by the time I left, I was just getting in there good. That's why I was a little hesitant to come out here, because I was just getting to know the governors, just getting to know all of this, and the ins and outs of all of that.

When I came to Seattle I immediately tried to get connected into politics. I sent a letter down to Olympia, the capital, to Governor Langlie. In the letter, I told him who I was, and that I'd just come, and that I had a reference from Kansas governor Ratner. He never did answer.

But I stuck with the Republicans, and while I was waiting to get admitted to the bar, they finally got me work at the state-run liquor store on Western Avenue for a while. But that was hard work.

They had a guy in there that I don't think liked me. They wanted someone to work on Saturday. I think I said I wouldn't, or I couldn't, for some reason. This guy turned it around and said that I told the fellas not to work on Saturday. He wanted to call me a Communist or something. I got so damn mad at him! I didn't know what to do.

I told him, "I'm a lawyer. You think I'd be running around here telling people not to work?"

But later on, he got in trouble and I saw him get thrown out of there. See, he was trying to get me put out of the store, but he didn't succeed. He got put out.

I didn't stay at the liquor store for long, though. I mostly worked for what they called the Army Services Forces Depot, out on Marginal Way. I started out there on the labor pool. They had me unloading those heavy iron stoves they were sending up to Alaska to keep the troops warm. Those things were heavy as hell!

I tried that for about a week or so, and I said, "I just can't do this. My hands are soft, they're not used to this business."

And besides, Mr. Johnson, at whose house I was staying, worked in the medical department of the Depot. So, he said, "I'll get you on there."

I told them at work, "Transfer me over there or I got to quit. I got to do something else, even if it's wrong!"

So they did, and that was a hell of a lot better, because a number of times we didn't do anything but run around while the guys would bring in these palettes and place them up high. If we had something to do, we did it. If we didn't, we didn't. We worked most of the time, but it wasn't hard work like I was doing before.

Fortunately, I was admitted to the Washington state bar in about April 1944. It had taken about eight months, longer than usual because you've got to get all these affidavits, got to present them to the board of governors, and got to wait until they decide to act. And they decide to act when they want to. They may decide to let yours take longer, because they may not want a Negro too badly anyhow. Then after they told me it was all right, I had a time getting a fellow who was a member of the board of governors to stand up and introduce me to the court. To say, "Yes, you can now go." See, I didn't want to be pushy, to start out on my own and mess up to begin with. So, it was about April before I got admitted.

I got an office downtown at Second and Pike, in a place that was then called the Peoples Building. Now it's gone and that spot's a parking lot. The Peoples Building had Dr. Graves, a black chiropodist, and Dr. Allen, a black dentist, in there. I was able to get one room. And I had to partition off that one room, to have the secretary sit out there. The partition didn't do any good; you could still hear what was said, but it was a psychological thing. Your clients felt better, not having your secretary sitting right there.

For the first time, I was practicing law all by myself. Washington state had different laws than Kansas that I had to study. I had never heard about community property law. I had to pick shit with the chickens, and get it all by myself. [Laughs]

As a new arrival in Seattle, I found that a lot of black folks kind of resented newcomers because they considered you what they called a sharecropper, a country person without urban sophistication. Others accepted you for what you were. It was kind of an individual thing. Those to whom you were a friend were a friend to you, I found. Then too, being a lawyer, I think they accepted me more than they would otherwise—especially, when they didn't have a black lawyer in Seattle.

Of course, I went to church and told them about my new practice. Mount Zion Baptist Church's minister, Rev. F. Benjamin Davis, gave me a push. Rev. Fountain W. Penick was at another church in town, Peoples Institutional Baptist, and he was a friend of my dad's, so he was in my corner.

Soon, I got divorce cases from people. They were working and had money, and maybe they had come to Seattle from Tennessee, and had left the kids, and the wife didn't like it here, and they would divorce. And then people were buying real estate, and preparing papers for that was fairly good. But I liked the criminal part of legal work better, because that's more dramatic and melodramatic. So I did quite a bit of criminal work, and that kept me going. Then pretty soon, I became known and white people commenced coming to me too.

At first I lived with the Johnsons, who had lived across the street from me in Topeka. When I arrived in Seattle on the train, the Johnsons met me at the station, and took me to their upstairs residence over the Joneses, who owned the house. I stayed there until I finally got an apartment nearby at the Adelphi Apartments on Twenty-third Avenue not far from Madison, which was owned by Jessie and Lonnie Shields. When I lived with the Johnsons, I'd pass that place and say, "Oh, I'd like to be in there. I'd like to be in there." And finally, I got in there.

Then when I left there, I bought my first house in Seattle, on Twenty-fifth Avenue. Oh, I was proud of that house! It had a little fish pond in the front yard. I'd get out there cutting the lawn, and when I'd get through, that sun would drop through the trees, leaving patterns on the ground—on that good, green grass, and I loved it. I just loved that house.

One time at the fish pond, I bent down and lifted a rock out—and my back went out! My wife was gone to California at that time; I was by myself. I finally dragged myself into the house, and got upstairs to my bedroom with no more help than a broom handle keeping me along. Irene and I. D. Wells lived on Twenty-sixth at that time. So when I got in bed I called them. I said, "Irene, I don't care what people think, or nothing else. If I haven't called you by nine o'clock in the morning, you come help me get out of this damn bed!" [Laughs]

What kind of neighborhood was it? It was integrated. The neighbor next door was white. The one on the other side was black. The one across the street was black. It was mostly black, but it wasn't black enough to say it was all black. There were a few white people in there. At that time, they were trying to get out of the neighborhood. Now, they're trying to get back, see?

In 1950 I ran a campaign for state representative to the legislature. I won and took my seat in January of 1951. The newspaper articles said I was the first black person in the Washington state legislature. And I thought I was, because they said I was—until I started looking around the State House at the pictures of past legislators. I saw a black one, who was named Owen Bush, whose father, George Washington Bush, had helped settle the state. Looking at the picture, I said to myself, "That guy's got to be black—he ain't white." So that's how I knew I wasn't the first one.

But I do hold to be the first black state legislator from King County. And during the years I served, I was the only black legislator. People asked me if I found it to be a heavy responsibility. But no, I rather gloried in it, myself!

In 1951, during my first term there, actor Paul Robeson had said that we weren't going to fight in Korea. And I got up on the floor of the House and I told them we would fight.

I said, "There's never been a black man who was a traitor, or black skin that had 'traitor' on it." The gist of it was that, "We're not happy here, but we're happier here than anywhere else."

When I got through, the state representatives gave me a standing ovation. Now, they say it was the first time that ever happened there. Now, "they say," so I never know. But I felt very, very, very, very good about that. Standing ovation in the legislature, in the state of Washington—from a black guy?

Then, they carried that speech on the "Voice of America"—to soldiers all around the country. They sent that speech all around.

There was a black doctor who was a little put out about it. He said I shouldn't have said that about Robeson. He thought I should have been talking about taxes or something like that. Well, he may have been right, but who knows what's best to do at the time?

But I considered a standing ovation from the state of Washington something to be engendered. Very nice.

= 4 =
God Bless America

Holy Toledo! My father had spoken out against Paul Robeson, the great African-American actor and singer, who was an activist for racial equality. Robeson's political courage in the 1940s and 1950s had made him a figure of black history, and a hero to many for decades to come—including me. I had not yet been born in 1950, when Daddy had had his moment of glory in front of the Thirty-first Legislature of the state of Washington. I did not know he had gotten a standing ovation for opposing a major international celebrity who many thought had taken a controversial stance. Even years later, I was unaware that Daddy's statement had been broadcast on "Voice of America," the government-sponsored international radio broad-

ABOVE: *The freshman state representative takes his seat as the "first Negro" to be elected in almost one hundred years, and only the second in state history.*

cast. This had never been mentioned to me by my father or my mother.

It had happened more than a year before my parents were married, so my mother can be pardoned for not passing this on as family history. And it seems that my father did not discuss it much after it happened or before he announced it as "something to be engendered" in the telling of his life story to Mary Henry. Maybe he had tried to put it behind him after the black doctor had reproached him. Or perhaps he had compartmentalized it—what had been a triumph in the white world could have been an embarrassment in the black world. So he just let it pass as just one incident in his life of many.

But it came back to haunt *me* after his death in 1996. I found out about it by accident. While visiting my mother in Seattle, I was thumbing through her copy of the book *The Forging of a Black Community: Seattle's Central District from 1870 through the Civil Rights Era,* which was autographed with a personal note by the author, University of Washington professor and historian Quintard Taylor. I searched for my father's name in the index and turned to the first reference to him in the text, which discussed black Seattleites who had sought public office. I learned that one political pioneer, Rev. J. Richmond Harris, lost the 1942 Republican nomination for a state legislative seat by just twelve votes. "When asked by a newspaper reporter, 'To what do you attribute your defeat?' he replied, 'I attribute my defeat to the fact that I did not get enough votes to win.' "

The book goes on to state that "Finally, in 1950, Republican attorney Charles Stokes was elected to the Thirty-seventh [District] legislative seat, becoming the city's first African-American representative in Olympia. Stokes, who had arrived in Seattle in 1944, quickly gained notoriety as an NAACP president and the organization's chief lobbyist for the Fair Employment Practice Act of 1949."

I was pleased to read that, but flipping pages to the next, and last, reference, I found this: "One of Representative Stokes's first acts in the legislature was authorship of a resolution denouncing [Paul] Robeson for declaring that African-Americans would not fight in a war against the Soviet Union."

Uh-oh, I thought. That was news to me. It was hard to believe that my father would have so publicly criticized the great Paul Robeson. In recent times, I was aware of demands by whites for black leaders to denounce Louis Farrakhan for his "gutter religion" statement, or Jesse Jackson for his off-the-record "Hymietown" comment. But in this case, it seemed the public denunciation of one black man's comments by another had been unsolicited.

Of course, most figures of history become larger than life. I thought it was ironic that Paul Robeson, who was controversial and, some say, a Communist, now has a totally positive place in history. And my father, who was popular and largely uncontroversial in his political life, had this tarnished mention in a history book as the last word on him. But I feel that if Charles Stokes and Paul Robeson had known each other, they would have enjoyed each other's company and the many things they had in common.

Robeson was a contemporary of my father's. Born just five years before Daddy, in 1898, Robeson was also a preacher's son. They both lost their mothers at an early age, making their fathers the central parental figures of their childhoods. Their life tracks took them to law school, and although Robeson did not end up making his mark as an attorney, his love of the law translated into a passion for the Constitution. My father also embraced the promise of the Constitution's guarantee of equal rights for all American citizens. It was the faith in their country's promise that both men shared.

Stokey would have agreed with Robeson's opinion, quoted in the biography *Paul Robeson* by Martin Bauml Duberman, that "the promises of the Constitution and the Bill of Rights could be realized if people worked hard at it." In his role as statesman, my father loved oratory. He grew up at a time when reciting the Declaration of Independence and the Preamble to the Constitution was a required tradition of American public school education. Daddy actually believed that the United States had a desire "to form a more perfect Union, establish Justice, insure domestic Tranquility, provide for the common defence [sic], promote the general Welfare, and secure the Blessings of Liberty to ourselves and our Posterity . . ." in ordaining and establishing the Constitution for the United States of America.

Where the two men differed was evidently in their approach to holding America to its promise. In June of 1950, Paul Robeson spoke before a civil rights rally at Madison Square Garden in New York City. President Harry Truman had taken action to send troops into Korea. According to Duberman's book, the meaning of Truman's order, Robeson predicted at the rally, would not be lost on black Americans: "They will know that if we don't stop our armed adventure in Korea today, tomorrow it will be Africa. . . . I have said it before and say it again, that the place for the Negro people to fight for their freedom is here at home. . . ."

Shortly thereafter, the State Department revoked Robeson's right to travel abroad, citing that his criticism of the country's treatment of African-Americans was "detrimental to the interests of the United States government." "Un-American" was a buzzword of that McCarthy era, and those who risked speaking out against the government could be called to task and blacklisted.

It was in this climate that my father had been elected to serve his country in his state's House of Representatives, and I wanted to know exactly what my father had said in response to Robeson's nationally reported comments. So, in 2002, in a scary new climate of serious "un-American" terrorism caused by airplanes being used as weapons of mass destruction in the United States, I took a five-hour flight from my house in New Jersey to my mother's house in Seattle. I told Mom I wanted to drive down to Olympia to do some research on Daddy's legislative record.

"I'll go with you," she volunteered.

The Washington State Legislative Building is situated on a knoll overlooking the southern tip of Puget Sound. The elegant and classical style of the building is reminiscent of the United States Capitol, with its grand columns, granite steps, and crowning rotunda. On this drizzly day, we schlepped around looking for the front door and finally shook out our umbrellas in time to realize that one of that day's last tours of the House and Senate chambers was about to start.

On the third floor we were ushered into a large room that was empty of furnishings, yet full of history. "This is the State Reception Room," the guide said. He pointed out the Tiffany chandelier and one of the few flags with forty-two stars. "Idaho became a state so quickly after Washington statehood that they couldn't get the forty-two-star flags made fast enough before it became forty-three stars." He didn't mention that Washington became a state on November 11, 1889, just three *days* after Montana's statehood. So Montana had even less time to get a forty-one-star flag produced than the eight months Washington had before Idaho's statehood.

After he had finished and asked if there were any questions, my mother piped up. "Isn't this the room in which the governors give their inaugural balls?" she asked. "My husband was a legislator here, and this room looks familiar to me."

"Yes, this room and the Governor's Mansion have often been used for inaugural balls," the guide said. "What is your husband's name?"

"Charles M. Stokes."

"Well, we'll see if we can find his picture in the hall of photos of the legislators." I was not sure at first if he sounded helpful or skeptical.

I looked not only for Dad's picture, but for the very first African-American who had been a part of the legislature when that Pacific northwest territory became the only state in the Union named after a president.

History has it that an African-American man also named after the president, George Washington Bush—who now, ironically, could also be called by the same name of a more recent president, George W. Bush— took an eight-month journey west in 1844 to escape the discriminatory restrictions of his life in Missouri. This mulatto pioneer of the Washington Territory brought his wife, Isabelle, and six children, the eldest of whom was named William Owen Bush. Forty-odd years later, Owen, as the historians call him, would be in office as a legislator when the territory became a state. Thus, he was in the First Session of the state's legislature and was the state's first black representative. It would take a new century, a modern age, and over sixty years before another black person would be elected to that statewide office: my father.

In the State House corridors that surround the two legislative chambers hang small individual photos of each legislator, grouped together in frames to display the entire body of the House or of the Senate for each term. Our tour group left me behind as I examined the frames, searching for "the black guy" of the 1880s whom Daddy had said he had noticed on the wall of honor. I was pleased to come across Dad's photo, but I never did find Owen Bush, who it seems looked so white it was hard to distinguish him from his colleagues. The "one drop" of black blood rule had been enough to subject his family to the "black laws" that did not allow them to own land in Oregon, until white pioneers with whom they had traveled and who knew them well lobbied the Congress to make an exception for them. In other words, they were allowed to be treated like honorary whites. But they moved across the Columbia River to the Washington Territory anyway to be free of the discriminatory restrictions, and in so doing became some of its first settlers.

After our tour of the majestic State House, Mom and I drove across the Capitol campus to find the archives. It was a distance that we would have enjoyed walking in sunny weather, but in the interest of time, we drove to catch the archives before it closed for the day. I wanted to find the actual transcript of the remarks Daddy made about Robeson. A helpful volunteer steered us to the stacks. Patiently and pleasantly helping us to fulfill our request, the stout, dark-haired woman, who may have been Native American, presented us with dusty volumes and fragile pamphlets. There were thousands of pages to flip through to find any reference to him in the mounds of House Bills and Referendums, resolutions and memorials, discussions, and votes. It could have easily deterred even the most diligent researcher.

Mom sat down in a wooden library chair and resigned herself to commenting, "It's going to be hard to get what you're looking for in all these pages." Aware that it was near five o'clock, she hinted that we might as well leave. But for some reason, I knew I would unearth it by quitting time. "Let me look until they close," I said to her.

Determined and starting in the back, then flipping to the front of one *House Journal* that would have documented the beginning of his first term, I was, indeed, quickly rewarded. Astonished myself, I couldn't believe my good fortune. There was the name "Mr. Stokes." And incredibly, there too was the name "Paul Robeson."

In the morning session of the Washington House of Representatives, January 16, 1951, almost a year to the day before I was born, according to the *House Journal,* "Mr. Stokes" was recognized by the house speaker, Charles W. Hodde, to present a resolution. Speaking on the House floor, Dad had the attention of the full body, and it was recorded.

RESOLUTION

Resolution by Mr. Stokes:

WHEREAS, Our sons and daughters are fighting in Korea; and

WHEREAS, It is desirable to strengthen our defense program; and

WHEREAS, One Paul Robeson has publicly declared it to be his opinion that colored citizens would not fight against Russia in the event of war; and

WHEREAS, The colored citizens of our state are loyal to the United States and the state of Washington and are now fighting side by side with other citizens of our state in Korea and elsewhere;

Now, Therefore, Be It Resolved, By the House that we hereby commend all citizens of the state now engaged in the defense of the country and declare that the utterances of said Paul Robeson do not reflect the attitude of the colored people of the state of Washington;

Be It Further Resolved, That a copy of this resolution be sent to the senators and representatives in Washington from the state of Washington and the attorney general of the United States.

Mr. Stokes moved that the resolution be adopted.

Debate ensued.

The motion by Mr. Stokes was carried unanimously and the resolution was adopted.

In the basement reading room of the archives office, there were only a handful of people conducting research. Excited to find what I thought might be a long shot, I read the resolution aloud quietly but enthusiastically to my mother. But when I got to the part that read "the utterances of said Paul Robeson do not reflect the attitude of the colored people of the state of Washington," I stopped, looked up at Mom, and made a face of mock shock—or maybe it wasn't mock. She raised her eyebrows in accord.

When I finished I said to her, "Can you believe that he had the nerve to speak on behalf of all colored people!" Mom didn't reply, but her silence spoke to me. She may not have disagreed with me, but she wouldn't disrespect my father's memory by verbalizing her thoughts. After all, he was no longer with us to defend himself—as he surely would have.

It had been a brief statement, in keeping with the resolutions of the day. Yet, the few words had had an impact, giving him a mixed blessing. It was a rare positive, unanimous, and nonpartisan reception from ninety-eight legislators who otherwise may not have received him, the only Negro, with open arms. It was a blemish on his legacy to some in his home district, like the doctor, and to an African-American historian who would choose to single out this initiative many years later.

It is hard to determine what bearing such stances had on Daddy's popularity with his general constituency. On one hand, they re-elected him twice. Yet, he did lose his bid to the State Senate, and again for lieutenant governor. So who knows? In the wartime environment of the time, many blacks may have agreed with his sense of patriotism, and disagreed with Robeson's Communism. But neither of them is with us now to debate the issue. Only their mutual legacies of love of country survive.

As open-minded as my father was, it was hard to imagine that he would not have admired Paul Robeson. My father and his own political rival, Sam Smith, saw each other in church every Sunday and joked and laughed together. In those days, a difference of opinion didn't mean that one person couldn't find virtue in some other point of view of the same person. Disagreeing didn't have to equate with being disagreeable. Even Martin Luther King, Jr., and his nemesis Malcolm X had shaken hands and laughed together on the occasion of their chance meeting. Back in the day, men knew how to be gentlemen.

As fate would have it, I had a chance meeting myself with the son of Paul Robeson—Paul Robeson, Jr.—at the Harlem Book Fair, just two months after I returned to New Jersey from Washington state still pondering my findings. As he signed my copy of his book, *The Undiscovered Paul Robeson: An Artist's Journey, 1898–1939,* Paul, Jr., listened to my story of embarrassment over my father's stance against his father's. Then he graciously stated that at the time, there were many African-Americans who had held the same point of view my father had. Instantly, I felt better.

Daddy greatly admired many of his contemporaries who held more high-profile positions than his on the national political scene. Adam Clayton Powell, Jr., was a Baptist preacher's kid like Dad; he became a United States congressman. My father also admired Percy Sutton, the attorney for Malcolm X, who was elected president of the Borough of Manhattan in New York City. Like my father, Percy Sutton was a lawyer who supported and defended the activists.

"I was not particularly in the vanguard of the civil rights movement," Daddy told Mary Henry. "I was just more supportive of it and thought I could do more by helping someone who was. If you're in the vanguard, you have to be particularly attuned to know how to do that, *want* to do it, and then *will* do it. I was never one to *instigate* things, or push them out there, or be in the vanguard of them—but I was a good follower."

Like Sutton, whose Inner City Broadcasting Corporation owned WBLS and WLIB radio stations in New York, as well as the Apollo Theater, Dad had entrepreneurial leanings. He had attempted to start Seattle's first black jazz station, KZAM-FM.

However, in discussing with Daddy the fine characteristics of Powell and Sutton, I never mentioned one little detail of difference: They were Democrats. They and my dad may have been in opposing parties, but what they had in common was that they were African-American men who beat the odds to make their unique marks on the political landscape of our country.

When I mentioned Dad's disparaging remarks about our hero Paul Robeson to my brother, André, now an attorney himself in Hawaii, he reminded me, "Well, he *was* conservative. Stokey may have been liberal for a Republican, but he was conservative for a black person." True. As we had done so many times in our youth, we took him to task with the passion of a hardheaded generation, we disagreed with him, and we loved and adored him anyway. Still, it wasn't easy for me to accept that my own father had publicly challenged the wisdom of the man who had played Emperor Jones.

= 5 =

Sophisticated Lady

THINGS WERE LOOKING GOOD in 1951.

The move to Seattle from Kansas had turned out to be the right decision for the new Representative Stokes. Just a few months after taking his seat in the Washington state legislature—where he basked in the standing ovation from the Capitol floor, and enjoyed the honor of having his message broadcast over "Voice of America"—he also experienced joy in his personal life. For the last couple of years, he had been a bachelor in the aftermath of the divorce from Eva, who had moved to Los Angeles. Living alone in the spacious house with no relatives in the area to call upon, he missed family life and his baby daughter, Vicki. But fortune smiled upon him, and now he was a man in love again.

The woman of his affection was a young widow. As fate would have

ABOVE: *Josephine Stratman Stokes in 1968.*

it, she first laid eyes on Stokey in the late 1940s when she was a new-comer to Seattle and a new bride. In fact, her young husband had pointed Stokey out to her. As they were out driving one Sunday after-noon, Howard Wooten, a former Tuskegee Airman, spotted Stokey wait-ing at a bus stop and remarked with pride to his bride, "See that man over there? He's our Negro attorney and the president of the Seattle NAACP." In trying to impress her by pointing out that Seattle had promi-nent Negro residents, he also gave his blessing for an unforeseen future.

Seattle was a long way from Selma, Alabama, where my mother, Josephine Antoinette Stratman, was born. Literally, it was a lengthy four-day ride from the deep south to the Pacific northwest with a change of trains in Chicago. Figuratively, Seattle was far removed from the segregation and disenfranchisement that Selma was known for. But the Selma of Josephine's recollection was the warm hometown of lov-ing aunts and uncles, caring teachers and preachers, and oodles of male and female friends.

December 4 is the date she celebrates as her birthday, but that was in dispute because she was born so near midnight on that chilly evening in 1924. "My mother said I was born on the fifth, *after* midnight," Mom explained. "But the midwife who came to work at our house on the fourth insisted that I came on that date, and that's the date she put on the birth certificate."

Even her middle name was a subject of family confusion. Both my great-aunts had the same middle name themselves, Dorothy Mae Brown and Gertie Mae Tutt, whom we called Aunt Bootsie. They both claimed to have given my mother her middle name, but they couldn't agree on what it was.

"I named her Antoinette," said Aunt Dorothy, who was my mother's father's sister.

"I gave her her middle name," Aunt Bootsie, my mother's aunt on her mother's side, claimed. "It's not *Antoinette*—it's *Antoniette.*" What a difference a spelling of a name can make!

In the south, people were often referred to by first and middle names. When a mother called down the block for her daughter to come home for dinner, the entire neighborhood would hear "Katie Mae!" or "Bobby Jo!" or maybe "Barbara Jean!" But the middle names were usually one syllable, so that it was easily attached to the first name. My mother's longer first and middle names signified her uniqueness. Josephine was long enough. It was already the three syllables most folks had for their first and middle names. So few relatives bothered with calling her by both names. But to clarify the confusion over which name actually was her middle name, her mother, Flossie, eventually settled on the more common Antoinette—after Marie Antoinette, Queen of France.

As the naming rivalry indicated, these two aunts were major influences in my mother's life. After the premature passing of their parents, Flossie and her sister, Gertie Mae, were raised by their Aunt Sing (pronounced with the southern accent, making it sound like "sang"). Aunt Sing and her husband owned a restaurant near the railroad yard that was frequented by all the colored citizens, with a regular patronage from the men who worked on the trains.

It was there that Aunt Bootsie, at sixteen, met Elbert Tutt, who was considerably older than she—in his forties—prompting her and everyone else in the family to call him "Mr. Tutt." They married and had one child, Frank.

Mr. Tutt worked for the railroad as a fireman. This was a "good job" that gave his family homeownership, nice cars, and the benefit of free train travel anywhere in the country. In my childhood I saw my great-aunt and great-uncle at least once a year when they traveled by train from Selma to visit us in Seattle.

My mother explained to me the role of the fireman on a passenger train: "The fireman's job was to keep the coals stoked in the train's engine. The engineer, who was white, sat on one side of the cabin and the fireman, who was usually black, sat in the window on the other side. Mr. Tutt was always assigned to the same engineer, and they traveled together on the same trains, and the same routes, for many miles, over many years—fifty to be exact. They became friends over those years of working together, and even in segregated Selma, the engineer invited my uncle to his house."

Around the same time as the Tutts' wedding, Flossie married Joseph

Stratman, Jr., who had achieved the distinction of valedictorian of his Clark High School class. Now fully employed in a job delivering ice to the homes of well-to-do blacks and whites, he was a "good catch." As they used to say, the "ice man is a nice man."

In the 1920s, only the rich had refrigerators, and that was before the appliances were run by electricity. Blocks of ice were delivered daily and kept in a certain compartment of the refrigerator to keep them cold. Joseph's good grades in mathematics served him well.

"He had to keep meticulous bookkeeping of who owed him what," his daughter observed. "Because he worked for rich people, he also fired the furnaces of the luxury apartment buildings early in the mornings. After work, he went back to those places and banked the fire for the night. He was a real worker. If the people wanted something to be painted, he did that. And in return, the people were very nice to him. He had a trunk in the kitchen that was full of the gifts people gave him. We still have that trunk in the family, and inside, it still has the gifts that have never been used."

In the Stratman home, the kitchen was always warm. Not only did Joe Stratman feed his own furnace, but whenever a fire was made for cooking, it warmed the whole room. "So the kitchen was like a family room," Mom recalled. "We had bookshelves, and could read all kinds of things in there—books, magazines, the newspapers. So that's where the family gathered."

The sisters, Flossie and Gertie Mae, stayed close and raised their families in close proximity to each other. They even gave birth in the same month. In December of 1924, Josephine and her cousin Frank were born. They not only grew up living across the street from each other, but were also in the same class at school. She, not having a brother, and he, without a sister, enjoyed a siblinglike relationship, trying out the latest dances on each other and going to the movies together. "As a girl, I never had to worry about going places alone," my mother said. "If I needed an escort, I could always ask my cousin to come along."

Josephine was also close to her older sister, Katie Mae. Katie's best friend was a neighbor named Mary Scott. "I remember when your mother was born," she told me recently. "Katie and I were in the same kindergarten class, and the teacher announced that the mother of someone in the class had just had a baby. The 'someone' in the class was Katie, and the baby was your mother." Even in adulthood, my aunt Katie, now deceased, liked to refer to her sister as "my Mama's baby."

One of Mom's earliest childhood memories is of a May Day festival in Selma that featured an evening children's performance.

"I remember sitting on my Daddy's knee," she said, "and my sister came out onstage. I yelled out, 'Hi, Katie!' Everyone laughed at the little kid calling out to her sister."

At Christmastime, there was no doubt who Santa Claus was—it was Aunt Dorothy, Joseph's sister. Dorothy had also married an older man, named Bud Brown, when she was just thirteen years old. Unfortunately, family legend has it that he was physically abusive. "He was not kind to her," my mother said. "So she ran away."

I heard Aunt Dorothy tell the story that she left him, all right—but not before she knocked his front teeth out. And that whole situation led to the establishment of the "one hit rule" that was passed down through subsequent generations of Stratman women.

"If a man hits you once, you've got to go," Aunt Dorothy told my mother, my mother told me, and I told my daughter. "Because if he hits you once, he'll hit you again. So why wait? The time to leave is the first time."

When people left Selma, they often didn't come back. Some did not return because they had gone north and didn't want to be subjected to Jim Crow ever again. But Mom said, "Aunt Dorothy wouldn't come back so Bud Brown wouldn't find her. I saw him around town, and he was always nice to me, but she never wanted to see him again."

Aunt Dorothy never remarried, and since she had been a teenager when she was the bride of Bud Brown, when I knew her in her middle and elder years, it seemed that she had never been married. For her entire adult life, she lived as a child-free bachelorette. She didn't forget her family back in Selma, though.

"She left for Atlanta when I was one year old," Mom said. "Then later, she moved to Los Angeles. Every year, at Christmas, Easter, and school opening time, she sent us a box of clothes. She sent entire outfits, everything from the underwear to the gloves. She even sent the fireworks for the Fourth of July.

"My father also sent her things. One year he wanted to send her a turkey for Thanksgiving. He brought the live bird home. Somehow, the turkey got out of the crate and ran into the street. The whole neighborhood was chasing the turkey! The turkey got away and flew up in a tree. They hadn't clipped his wings, so he could fly. Our young friend had to climb the tree and get the turkey down. I couldn't figure out why my father couldn't just send his sister the money to buy a turkey."

In Alabama in the 1930s, African-Americans composed about 35 percent of the 2.6 million population. Among Selma's citizenry of about 30,000, the black community was insular. Segregation not only separated the races in public schools and churches, but limited free movement to certain areas of the town and blocked access to many parks, events, and community activities.

"We had to make our own fun in Selma," Mom told me. "So some of my classmates and I started a social club called The Sophisticated Eight and we gave parties. We had fun parties where we danced, and New Year's Day parties where we played cards and ate black-eyed peas, potato salad, and corn bread. The eight of us girls were very tight. We dressed alike in the same sweaters and skirts that we bought together. We had a male counterpart club called The Cavaliers. My male friends and my cousin Frank were in that organization."

In Selma's movie theaters, Josephine and her friends could not be seated on the main floor, which was reserved for whites only. "I saw *Imitation of Life* as a teenager in the segregated balcony of the movie house. Everyone was crying and going on." She explained further, "We black folks were sitting in the balcony and couldn't even see the white folks—and they couldn't see us." So not only were the races separated, the buildings were constructed in such a way that each group of people felt they were there without the presence of the other.

But being relegated to climbing the steep steps to the top floor of the theater didn't stop the colored kids of Selma from beating the summer heat by seeing the latest films. After all, the ceiling fans were closest to the balcony level.

Mom recalls that when she was a little girl, "One movie we saw was a musical with Martha Raye, who sang a song called 'Who's That Knocking at My Heart's Door?' Afterward, I was sitting on my front porch singing that song. I remember that I had on a pair of shorts. My mother came outside and asked me, 'What song is that?' And before I could answer, she said, 'Don't you ever let me hear you sing that again.' I didn't know why she didn't like the song. She went back into the house, and I wouldn't have dared to ask her anyway. But after I sat out there a while longer, I forgot she had scolded me, and I absentmindedly began singing it again. Mama came out there with her belt and she said, 'I told you not to sing that song!' " Well, of course the shorts were no protection against the sting of the belt on her thighs when it missed her behind and swatted her right on the skin. "I didn't see anything wrong with the song, myself. But then, I never did think my mother's whippings were justified. So I say all my spankings were over nothing."

Her father didn't mete out the spankings, but he insisted that she get straight A's in school. And Josephine's teachers reinforced his ambition for her. As a student, young Jo found that being the daughter of a valedictorian was not easy. "A lot of my schoolteachers were my father's classmates," she explained. "And some were not only his former classmates, but his former girlfriends. So they expected a lot from me."

Fortunately, segregation couldn't prevent her from preparing for college. "It was the thing in my town for those colored kids who were college-bound to go to Selma University's private high school."

Selma University, a historically black four-year college located right there in town, was founded in 1878 as the Alabama Baptist Normal and Theological School. Incorporated in 1881 under its second president, who was born a slave, it was officially named Selma University in 1908. A private elementary school and a college-prep high school were included until 1956.

"People didn't think the public school was good enough for college acceptance," Mom explained. "Those families that could afford it sent their children to Selma University's program. So my parents sent my sister there, to the private school."

This followed a family tradition. "My mother had never gone to public school at all, because her folk sent her to private school all the way through," Mom said. "Her teachers were all white. The teachers in the public schools were mainly black. All these schools were segregated, but there was still elitism within the segregation.

"When I came along, I decided I didn't want to do that. I thought, *You have to live with everybody in the world, and if you are going to do well, you could do it at any school.*"

I asked my mother how her parents responded to her feelings. "My parents were good about letting me go to school where I wanted to go," Mom said, "but I still had to get good grades."

Within segregated Selma was a microcosm of the larger American symbols of status. In addition to private school for the children of the black elite, having a stay-at-home mom signified the elevated station and financial stability of the family. It conveyed the message that the husband and father was a man able to provide for his family. For those wives who had to work to make ends meet, the options for employment were often limited to domestic work in the homes of white families.

While attending private school, my grandmother evidently learned more than reading and writing. She also took on certain values of her peers, such as the belief that proper young women did not work.

"Because my mother had gone to private school, she also never worked," my mother explained. "She didn't think nice girls should work. Her sister never worked either."

But attending public school gave Josephine a different view of things. She liked mingling with all sorts of people, and thought working—if one could find a respectable job—could give a girl some independence. Although Katie had gone to private school, she also wanted to make a little money of her own, and she got an after-school job as a retail clerk at the local women's store, Smart & Thrifty.

"When my sister left for college, I took her job, with my mother's disapproval," Mom said. "But my father backed me."

Josephine enjoyed making extra money, and she spent most of it right there in the store on clothes. But one thing she hadn't anticipated was having to quit her job over an unfortunate racial situation.

"I experienced several racial incidents while growing up in Selma, but this one stood out," she said. "Smart & Thrifty was a chain store, and while I was working there I had to pack some things and take them to the post office to send to another store. When I got back, the store manager said to me, 'Kathryn is looking for you.' Then she asked, 'Do you know who I am talking about?'

"I said, 'Yes, I know Kathryn.'

"She said, '*Miss Metzger* to you.'

"I said, 'I know Kathryn. She is my age, and she is in my grade.'

"She still insisted, 'It's Miss Metzger to you!' Then she paid me that day.

"I went home and told my parents. They told me I didn't have to go back there anymore. It was obvious that the store manager was prejudiced. Although she gave me the job, she didn't think black folks were equal to white folks.

"But it turned out okay, because that summer I got a job at the tobacco factory, cutting stems out of the cigar leaves for eight hours a day. And that paid more than the Smart & Thrifty."

What was lost, however, was a budding friendship. In spite of the societal restraints, Josephine and Kathryn had found equal ground together as teenage coworkers. "We had become friends, just like my uncle, Mr. Tutt, and his engineer. But I never saw her again," Mom said, her voice trailing off with regret.

Whenever my mother talked about the days of her childhood in the south, she often related the story of another racial incident that also had to do with how whites demanded blacks defer to them by name.

"When we needed something to eat after school, we could go to a store and put it on my father's bill," she stated. "One day, we went up there and the man in the store was being conversational. 'What's your name?' he asked me. And I told him.

" 'What's your mother's name?' he went on.

"I said, 'Mrs. Stratman.'

" 'What's your homeroom teacher's name?'

"Miss Ruby Nixon," I told him.

"He didn't say anything more to me, but the next time my father went there, he told him, 'That girl of yours is uppity!'

"He didn't want those people to be accorded titles," she said, explaining the Jim Crow rules of the use of honorifics—or rather, the lack thereof when it came to whites applying them to Negroes. "White folks didn't call colored people by their titles. They called them boy or girl. But I was taught to call all adults Mr., Mrs., or Miss. I never would have called that lady by her first name!

"My father said I didn't have to go there anymore. So I didn't go back there, and I didn't go back to Smart & Thrifty."

I noticed that both of these racial incidents she chose to share had to do with addressing a person with equal respect. This explained to me why my mother always preferred that my own friends call her Mrs. Stokes, even after they had known her for years and years. But it was not only a courtesy she felt should be extended from a child to an adult. My mother also referred to her own close friends as Mrs. Gallerson, Mrs. Caldwell, or Mrs. Horton—even when speaking casually with just me. I began to learn that since African-Americans could not count on getting respect from the larger community of whites, they overcompensated for it by extending it relentlessly to one another.

Unfortunately, after Mr. and Mrs. Joseph Stratman, Jr., raised Katie Mae and Josephine Antoinette and sent them off to college, they got divorced. After living a life of uncommon black privilege as a private school student, then as a married woman and stay-at-home mother who was free during the day to provide community service through the women's organizations of her church, my grandmother had to support herself for the first time in her life. Most of the relatives who had raised her had passed away, and so with no family financial support or inheritance, and only meager alimony and child support since the girls were now grown, she was on her own for the first time.

"The summer after I graduated from high school, my parents broke up," my mother explained, "and Mama had to get a job."

That was when Josephine decided that as an adult she would be a working woman, so that whether she was married or not, she would not be dependent on anyone. "I saw my mother's predicament and her pain, and I said to myself, *That will never happen to me.*"

My mother usually told the stories of her life in a matter-of-fact tone: This happened, then that happened. As I listened to her this time, I realized that she had never said—and I had never asked—how she *felt* about her parents' divorce. So I gathered the nerve to ask her.

"I was most unhappy about the whole thing!" she exclaimed. "I was *really* unhappy, because I was really a Daddy's girl. And my mother was bitter. She was *not* a happy camper. She allowed me to go visit my father, but she didn't want me to go live with him where he had moved to West Selma."

In 1995, on a trip to Selma, my mother had taken my daughter and me around to all her childhood haunts. I remembered some of the neighborhoods and the modest homes from my only previous visit, in 1960. This time, however, she drove us to another neighborhood, past finer homes and wider streets. She pointed out where her father had moved after the divorce—to a predominantly white neighborhood. This surprised me because I was under the impression that Selma and all the parts of the south were so segregated that they were either all black or all white. I didn't know there were any mixed neighborhoods before the time of the civil rights movement. But somehow, my grandfather moved away from the black side of town into West Selma, an affluent community of whites and a few blacks.

"He had befriended a black lady on the route of his job delivering ice," my mother began. "When my parents divorced, this lady allowed him to rent one of the rooms and live there. When she died, she left him her home."

Grandpa Joe remarried a lady named Mabel, and moved her into the white two-story house with green trim on the quiet street. Mom didn't call this lady by her first name, and she didn't call her by her last name.

"I never called her anything," Mom recalled. "I didn't have a relationship with her that was good, bad, or indifferent, although I respected her. She had a job—my mother didn't have a job. She had long hair—my mother had cut her long hair. She had all the things my mother didn't have."

When Mom mentioned hair, I recalled the story she told most often. During most of the years that my grandmother was married to my grandfather, she wore her hair long to please him. Being half Native American, half African-American, she had hair that was long and wavy, but it was thin, so she usually wore it in a bun. At one point, however, the style was a shorter bob, and she wanted to be in style. Against her husband's wishes, she cut her hair.

"And that was the end of the marriage," my mother said. Although they had grown apart over the two decades of their marriage and childrearing, "when Mama cut her hair, Daddy left her and took up with another woman with long hair."

That exemplified the way family stories were told: There would be an everyday occurrence, and then this dramatic, resultant event. For example, there was the story of my maternal great-grandmother, who "picked a corn on her foot and died." After years of trying to get to the medical reason for her demise, I finally figured out that she probably had diabetes, and what would have been a normal grooming procedure for a nondiabetic turned fatal for her when her toe became gangrenous.

There was another family tale of how Mom's grandfather Joseph Stratman, Sr., a young merchant seaman, met a woman named Ana in the West Indies, married her, and brought her back to the States. All alone with just her husband in this more prejudiced place, Ana missed her family, whom she had left forever. After giving birth to four children, including Grandpa Joe and Aunt Dorothy, she died of "a broken heart."

All these stories had lasting effects on my mother and influenced her views of life. For example, she never wanted me to cut my hair. She wouldn't pick a corn on her foot. She stayed close to her birth family.

When her parents divorced, Josephine and her mother stayed in her modest childhood home. Her sister was away at college in Atlanta. Her father and his new wife lived in the stately house in West Selma.

"After school with my friends, I would roller-skate from my end of town, up through blocks and blocks of beautiful homes and mani-cured gardens, to see him. His house was impressive compared to our house, which was clean, but not as large or as nice as his. He would have hot chocolate waiting for us. He also had a car (my mother never learned to drive) and would come to our house and teach me how to drive."

Around this time, Josephine experienced other losses too. Like her father, her paternal grandfather, Joseph, Sr., the retired merchant sea-man who also made his living in the ice-delivery business, had a com-fortable home and a late-model car. "He had told me, 'When you graduate from high school, I am going to give you an Austin.' That was the hot sports car. I looked forward to getting that car for my gradua-tion, and driving it off to college in Atlanta."

Even a family's choice of cars was a matter of racial solidarity. Mom's father believed in buying only Ford automobiles because the Ford Motor Company gave African-Americans jobs in Detroit. When southern blacks had a hard time getting gainful employment, or when they found themselves "last hired, first fired," many of them moved to Detroit, where they found jobs at Ford. So Mom's father and grandfa-ther drove practical Ford cars, but her grandfather encouraged her dreams about the sporty Austin.

"Then, my parents told me he was dying. I stopped by to see him one Sunday morning on the way to church," Mom recalled. "He was the first person I ever saw dying. I leaned over to hug him, and he held me real tight. I left and went on to church. He died that day." She paused, contemplating her grandfather's love and her loss. Then she added wistfully, "And I never got that car."

She did go off to college, however.

Several of the top black colleges in the United States were within just two hundred miles of Selma. Tuskegee Institute, founded on the Fourth of July in 1881 by its first president, Dr. Booker T. Washington, was about a hundred miles away. Mom saw the campus for the first time when her high school's basketball team played there. It was the

1940s, during World War II, and while she was there she also saw the
Tuskegee Airmen, the Black Air Force regiment, taxiing their planes.

"It was nice to see that," she said, in explaining why she and her
schoolmates were so proud of the Airmen. "We had pride in seeing a
black person pilot a plane." Little did she know that her own future
husband might have been flying one of those airplanes that day.

When it came time to choose a college, however, she decided
against Tuskegee Institute.

"I had friends who attended that school," she explained. "So I
wanted to go someplace different, where I would have a fresh start and
make new friends.

"My father wanted me to go to Tuskegee," Mom remarked. "My
mother wanted me to go to Spelman."

Spelman College, one of only two black women's colleges in the
country, was just another hundred miles farther up the road, in
Atlanta. Founded in 1882 as a seminary for formerly enslaved women,
the school was largely funded by financier John D. Rockefeller, who
was so impressed when visiting the college with his wife and mother-in-
law that he retired the debt on the property. He continued his involvement with the school's development by donating more money for the
construction of several major buildings on campus. In return, the
school was named Spelman Seminary, in honor of the family of his
mother-in-law, Lucy Henry Spelman. The Spelman family had been
activists in the antislavery movement. In 1924, the year my mother was
born, the name of the school was officially changed to Spelman College. Highly regarded, Spelman was to black women what the Seven
Sister colleges, such as Smith, Sarah Lawrence, and Wellesley, were to
white coeds. It was the cream of the colored college crop.

Josephine understood and respected the school's historic standing,
but had other ideas about what kind of college she wanted to attend. "I
didn't want to go to a girls' school because I have always been against
segregation of any kind, even of the sexes. But my mother wanted me
to go to Spelman because it was a Baptist school, and we were Baptists."

There was no option of attending a predominantly white or even
racially mixed college in the south. Jim Crow made sure of that. But

Josephine felt that even if she had to attend a "colored only" college, she could at least exercise her choice not to attend a "girls only" college.

In discussing her options with her sister, who was in nursing school at Grady Memorial Hospital in Atlanta, Josephine heard Katie mention that she knew a young man who spoke highly of the coed school he attended there, Clark College. "My sister told me about that school. So I applied there, and was accepted. And when I got to Clark, the young man she knew was the first one to come up to meet me." When she saw that "fine" young man, she knew she had made the right decision!

Although her mother was disappointed that Josephine had not gone to the elite Spelman College, she approved of Clark. "It may not have been Baptist, but at least Clark was a religious school," Mom said. "It was Methodist."

Attending a Methodist school meant that my mother and the rest of the student body were required to attend devotional services and other religious programs. Clark College was founded in 1869, just a few years after Emancipation, for the education of freed slaves by the Freedmen's Aid Society of the Methodist Episcopal Church. The school was named for Bishop David W. Clark, who was the first president of the Freedmen's Aid Society, and who became a bishop in 1864.

In 1943, when my mother entered college, the world was at war and Franklin Delano Roosevelt was the president of the United States. It was the same year that my father left Kansas for Seattle.

Mary McLeod Bethune was President Roosevelt's director of the Division of Negro Affairs of the National Youth Administration from 1935 to 1944, and developed close ties to First Lady Eleanor Roosevelt during this time. An African-American woman of great stature and strength, Bethune possessed a seriousness of purpose that led her to oppose segregation and work toward the full integration of blacks into all facets of American life.

After word spread that she once stood in defiance of the Ku Klux Klan after they tried to intimidate her from preparing blacks in Florida to vote (she was teaching citizens to read well enough to pass the literacy test, and led a procession to register to vote), Bethune became in demand nationwide as a public speaker. She also founded several institutions that still stand today, including the National Council of Negro Women and a small Florida college that later merged with Cookman Institute, creating Bethune-Cookman College. Cookman Institute had been associated with Mom's school, Clark College, during the time of the two schools' common founding by Methodist ministers.

My mother recalls that when she was a student at Clark, it was a major event when Mrs. Bethune came to speak at a school assembly. "My roommate, Della, was assigned to be her hostess, to escort her around the campus and look out for her," Mom told me. "Mrs. Bethune's speech was intended to inspire us to accomplish the same kinds of great things she had done. Her theme was that she was getting older, and we were needed to 'fill her shoes.' My roommate didn't think Mrs. Bethune's black, lace-up, oxford shoes—worn for the comfort of a woman in her seventies—were as fashionable as the high-heeled pumps we students wore. So when Mrs. Bethune asked in the course of her speech, 'Who will step in the shoes of Mary McLeod Bethune?,' Della turned to us and whispered, 'Who would want to?' And we all laughed."

Like most folks who look back fondly on their college experience, my mother recalled that she studied hard—and partied too. "I enjoyed going to Clark and had a successful time there," she said.

"For my first dance at school, I had three escorts. Two boys from my hometown assumed I didn't know anyone else, and another one who had introduced himself to me on the line at registration did the same. Without even asking me, they all had the same idea to just come over to my dorm to surprise me and escort me to the dance.

"First, the housemother announced over the loudspeaker in the hall of my dormitory, 'Miss Josephine Stratman, Mr. Lorenzo Craig is here to see you.' Then before I could get downstairs, the loudspeaker came on again: 'Miss Stratman, Mr. Maurice Anderson is here for you.' Then next thing I knew she called out to me again, 'Mr. William Bowen is here for Miss Stratman.'

"I'm sure they were all sitting there in the lobby looking at each other in bewilderment, wondering what was going to happen when I came downstairs.

"But it all turned out. All four of us went to the ball and they took turns dancing with me.

"When I got back to my dorm, the housemother said to me, 'I have been here a long time, and I've never had that happen before!' "

Ever the social butterfly, Josephine joined the school choir. She also joined the band that traveled to other schools for football and basketball games. It was always hard for me to imagine her little bitty self playing the trombone in the college band. Evidently, neither could my father, and during my childhood, this image of her caused much teasing on his part. "Can you imagine Jo playing the trombone?" he'd ask without waiting for an answer before he'd crack up.

"Why did you choose the trombone?" I asked her.

She shrugged her shoulders. "I thought it would be easier to play than other instruments. But I had to quit the band, because all that blowing of the trombone had an effect on my voice. The choir teacher said, 'You have to stop playing with the band because you are always hoarse.' So I did."

When it came to choosing a major, Josephine had to weigh her options carefully, in view of the limited career opportunities open in the 1940s to women in general, and particularly to black women. Now, she laughs as she recalls how she dared to dream.

"I was a home economics major, because I wanted to be a clothing designer and go to Paris. I didn't know how I thought I could do that, or where I thought I could get the money, but I lived in a lot of fantasy."

Still, in class she enjoyed learning to make spritz butter cookies for the teas and receptions. "And I learned a lot of social graces as a home ec major," she explained. "Because I had good professors who were nice to me, I had a really good college experience."

Then tragedy struck.

April 12, 1945, is a date my mother will never forget. Her beloved father, Joseph Stratman, Jr., a man in his early forties, died of tuberculosis. That date is also etched in history as the day the nation mourned the passing of President Roosevelt, of a cerebral hemorrhage. But Josephine will forever link the date of the death of the president to her own sudden, monumental loss. It was a time of pervasive sadness.

"I knew Daddy was sick, but it was a shock that he died," Mom said. "All the other people we knew, like our next-door neighbor who got tuberculosis, had recovered."

My aunt Katie used to tell the story about how her sister almost got suspended from college, because in her grief upon hearing the news from home of her father's unexpected passing, she forgot all about school protocol. "Your mother left that school so abruptly, she didn't even stop to inform her housemother what had happened, or where she was going," Aunt Katie would say, chuckling sadly.

"I got on the train and went home to the funeral," Mom explained. "After we buried Daddy, my aunt Bootsie tried to comfort my grief and drove me from Selma to Pensacola, Florida, to see her son, Frank, who was based in the Navy there. Then I went on back to school and finished my sophomore year."

Upon her return, she smoothed out the problem of her absence from school without permission, but soon realized that the future of her college education was in jeopardy for another reason: Her college tuition, room, board, and other expenses had always been paid by her father, who in the last few years had changed jobs and was working at the Selma courthouse. Now that he was gone, and her mother had no income, she had no sure source of funding.

Josephine prepared to find work that summer to save money for the fall term. She knew her mother would send what she could, and so would her sister and Aunt Dorothy. She told no one at school her predicament, but a kindly professor who had heard of her father's passing must have known that she would now need help, and one day he approached her.

"Mr. Fletcher told me about a one-hundred-dollar scholarship from *The New York Amsterdam News,*" Mom said. "I applied for it, and received it, which was a great help in paying my tuition."

So grateful was my mother for that scholarship that on the occasion of the fiftieth anniversary of her college graduation, she traveled to the offices of the *Amsterdam,* a black-owned weekly newspaper in

Harlem, and personally thanked the current publisher and editor, William Tatum, and his daughter, Elinor. Then Mom handed them a check for $1,000, which they contributed to the publication's continuing scholarship fund.

After the divorce, my grandmother Flossie decided to visit her former sister-in-law in California for a few months to look for a job there. On the train from Selma to Los Angeles, Flossie met and enjoyed the company of a handsome man who was on his way to Seattle. Charming, medium brown–skinned, with a stocky build reminiscent of Joe Louis, Collie Levingston kept in touch after they said good-bye on the train. He wrote her letters from Seattle, where he was based as a merchant seaman. She wrote back from Los Angeles, where she was staying with Aunt Dorothy.

"When she came home from California," Mom said, "she told Katie and me that she had met Mr. Levingston on the train, had corresponded with him, and that he had asked her to go to Seattle to marry him. We said, 'Go for it!' because we were already in college."

Flossie and Collie married in a private ceremony in a hotel off Jackson Street in Seattle's International District, and moved into a residence for newcomers nearby. Flossie enjoyed the ethnic flavor of the seaport town. With its diverse population of whites, blacks, Asians, and Native Americans, Seattle's downtown and central neighborhoods provided a racial tolerance that she had not experienced in Selma. Flossie quickly got a job that contributed to the war effort, working in the shipyard in Bremerton, Washington, a commuter-ferry ride away from Seattle.

"After that, when school was out for the summer, I came to Seattle to be with her," Mom explained. "And every year, I was lucky enough to get a job. The first two summers, I worked at Boeing. The third year, I worked at the Marine Hospital. And I made enough money to pay my entrance fees, with some left over for clothes and spending money at school."

At one point, Josephine considered becoming a doctor. "I thought maybe I wanted to be a doctor after working at the Marine Hospital, which was the most rewarding job I had had," she said. "Many of the patients were foreigners from the warships who became ill and had no one to visit them. My job was to take them their mail, and to assist the nurses. I was always smiling, and I would help people with their meals. The patients were so grateful. The nurses would tell me, 'Mr. So-and-So would not eat because you were not there.' And I would go into the patient's room and say, 'What do you mean you wouldn't eat?' And they would eat for me. So it was a rewarding job."

After the end of the summer working at the hospital, Josephine returned to college and reconsidered her major.

"I tried working toward getting a bachelor of science," she told me, "which meant I took biology, zoology, chemistry, physics—all of that science stuff—which led to being a doctor if you wanted to be a doctor. My partner in biology had me doing the gory work of dissecting the frog, but I didn't like it."

And her grades reflected the difficulty she was having.

"When I got home that summer, my grades had arrived before I did, and from my father's reaction, you would have thought I had flunked out of school. Because he had been so smart in school, he expected only top grades from me. But instead of me taking those classes, they were taking me! I hadn't flunked, but I didn't make the honor roll, because those classes were *hard*. I'm sorry that my father died before I got nothing but A's in my last two years. But he didn't live to see that," she said as her voice trailed off sadly.

Grandpa Joe didn't live to see that his daughter had changed her mind about going to medical school either. "I decided I couldn't be a doctor, because I couldn't give people shots, and I couldn't take the sight of blood."

But she said, she did like working in the school library during her four years at Clark, and she credits this job with giving her the idea of becoming a school librarian.

"I loved working in the library because that was when Frank Yerby, a black author, was big, and I would read all his books before putting them on the shelves. His novels were usually about mulattos in Louisiana and the grand way of life there."

During her summers in Seattle, Josephine was introduced to another way of life. It was wartime, and there were several Army bases in the surrounding area. South of nearby Tacoma, Washington, were Fort Lewis and McChord Air Force Base, and right in Seattle was Fort Lawton, a World War II prisoner-of-war camp. Military men serving in Japan, and a few years later, Korea, were deployed from the port of Seattle. Many of the returning black servicemen who crossed the Pacific and hit American soil in Washington state stayed right there. Not wanting to return to discrimination in their hometowns after fighting for their country abroad, many of them settled in the more racially tolerant Pacific northwest.

Howard Wooten, my mother's first husband, served the country as a Tuskegee Airman in the United States Air Force in World War II.

At United Service Organizations (USO) dances in downtown Seattle, Josephine and Katie met several of these upstanding servicemen, and other young African-American men who had relocated to Seattle when Boeing was hiring around the same time. Katie married one of them, Charles Ratliff. In January of 1947, they had a daughter they named Gloria Jean.

Soon after, Josephine met her mate too.

"I had met Howard the summer before I married him," she begins her story of courting. "At the Marine Hospital, this black lady told me she had someone she wanted me to meet. She said he was a former Tuskegee Airman who had a good job at Boeing, and she wanted him to meet me because she didn't want any white girls to get him. But I had a boyfriend who was going to college at Tuskegee Institute that I could have married. So I wasn't that interested.

"Then one day she said to me, 'If I invite you to dinner and send my husband to pick you up would you come?' I said yes, I would. When I got there, Howard was there. There were other people invited, too, but we were the only single ones, so it was obvious what she was trying to do. He asked me out, but I couldn't go because I had been invited out by someone else.

"Then my mother's friends in her circle at church had sons who had invited me to go with them to a big affair at the Eagles' Auditorium.

When I got there, Howard was there dancing with a nice-looking girl. Soon, he saw me and moved closer to where I was dancing with my date, and he stepped on my foot!

"The next day when I left my house to go to work, he was there in his car reading the paper. When we spoke, he apologized and said that because he had stepped on my foot at the dance, he felt he should offer to take me to work, so I wouldn't have to walk. I didn't need that, but he did give me a ride. And after that, he took me every day."

Josephine and Howard became friends, and then had their first date at the wedding of his sister Robbie. After church on Sundays, the two of them would go to what Jo called "nice places" in the Pacific northwest. One such rendezvous was a scenic thirty-mile drive from Seattle to the foothills of the Cascade Mountains. There, Howard showed her the spectacular and romantic Snoqualmie Falls.

After that summer of 1946, Jo went back to Atlanta to finish her senior year of college. She graduated in May of the next year with a bachelor of science degree.

Her mother was unable to attend the graduation ceremony. Katie, who had not only married but had become one of Seattle's first black registered nurses, couldn't make it either. Atlanta was too far to travel for a one-day event, and both were working. Being new to their jobs, it was difficult to get time off. Jo did have relatives at the ceremony, however, to help her celebrate and show their pride. "Aunt Bootsie came to my graduation, and a cousin and his wife, who lived near the campus, came," she said.

"Then I left for Seattle."

Howard was waiting for her return, and they got engaged. "He gave me a beautiful ring, so that other men would notice it right away and leave me alone," she recalled, laughing. "We decided I would go back to school to get my master's degree, and he would work. Then he would go back to finish his college degree, and go on to law school."

Fate had other plans. "When I got married, I got pregnant right away," she explained. "It was a difficult pregnancy, with bed rest and the fear of miscarriage the whole time. Then when the baby was born, he was in the breach position and they had to pull him out with forceps. I think he still has those marks from the forceps behind his ears."

They named the almost-seven-pound baby boy André Stratman Wooten. Since there were no other males to pass down her maiden name, Josephine gave it to her son as his middle name. Around the time of the baby's birth, April 11, 1948, she got accepted at the University of Washington Graduate School.

But before she could enter school, the unthinkable occurred.

Six months after André was born, there was a strike at Boeing Aircraft Company, where Howard worked. To make ends meet while the strike was on, Howard signed on with a construction crew to help paint a high viaduct over Twelfth Avenue.

As a child, he had been raised with eleven brothers and sisters in Lovelady, Texas, on their father's 1,000-acre cattle ranch. Enlisting in the service, he had flown planes in World War II as one of the famed Tuskegee Airmen, countering the racist notion that African-American men didn't have the intelligence, skill, or courage to be combat pilots. Now, to provide for his family, he again conquered fear to take a dangerous job at a great height. But his accidental fall from the bridge was not softened by a ballooning parachute. At age twenty-seven, Howard Wooten died.

My aunt Katie once told me about that sad and terrible time. "When Howard died, Jo remembered that he had said he wanted to be cremated when he passed away. But our mother wouldn't let her carry out his wishes. She didn't believe in cremation, and was adamant in saying, 'No, no! You can't burn up that boy!' "

And so, Howard was buried with full military honors at Seattle's Washelli Memorial Park, which was the largest veteran's cemetery in the area. It is distinguished by its more than 5,000 white marble headstones, which stand in military uniformity across the evergreen lawn. Memorial Day services have been held there every year since 1927.

Tucked away in a dusty and delicate family album is a black-and-white photo of my mother taken within a year of Howard's death. She is dressed in a black evening gown with black lace shawl, accompanied by her former brother-in-law Octavius, whom she said was so support-

ive after his brother's passing, as were all her in-laws. Even as a youngster gazing at this black-and-white photograph, I detected the gravity it
held as I studied her expression. She is standing straight and regal, but
her face is somber, serious, and sad. Although she is pictured at a formal affair, usually a favorite activity of hers, in this photograph, she is
obviously not in a festive mood.

Widowed at age twenty-three with a six-month-old baby, Josephine
had to get a job. "My first job after I was widowed was working for a
black dentist, Dr. John Browning," she told me. "And then I took the
civil service examination. Since my husband had been an officer in the
service, that gave me a higher hiring priority status. I took a job as a
clerk in the education department of the Veteran's Administration,
processing the papers of people who wanted to go to college after serving in the military."

Her Baptist faith helped her through this difficult time. She had
joined Mount Zion Baptist Church, Seattle's largest black congregation, in the summer between her junior and senior year of college. When
she returned to Seattle, she reactivated her membership. Singing in
the choir and joining the Junior Matrons religious circle kept her
active in the church. She had her infant son blessed in that church
with her good friend Thelma Dewitty, one of the city's first black public-
school teachers, and Thelma's husband, Hubert Dewitty, a former
serviceman turned bail bondsman, standing in as his godparents.

After a couple of years, bachelors in the church began to ask Josephine
out, but she was hesitant. With her time consumed by her job and her
baby at home, she didn't want to rush into a relationship. Her main
activity outside of making time for her mother and sister and the relatives of her late husband, who supported her in her time of mourning,
was to attend church every week.

"One Sunday, Reverend Davis asked all the college grads to stay
after church and plan a program called Rise Above Color," Mom said.
"This event was intended to inspire people to rise above discrimination
and have pride in themselves. We had speakers and a panel discussion.
There I met Attorney Stokes, the man who Howard had pointed out to
me a few years before he died.

"He was very friendly, and came over and introduced himself to me. He said he heard I was a widow. I said, 'Yes, I am, and I have a little boy.' In the years to come when we talked about our meeting, he used to tease me that I waved that little boy like a red flag," she said with a giggle.

But the prospect of sharing her affections with a toddler didn't deter Charles M. Stokes. He began inviting Josephine to his political events.

"It was the year he was running for the legislature, so he was busy, busy, busy," she recalled. "When he got elected, he invited me to the governor's ball."

As a politician, Stokey's entire lifestyle revolved around campaigning, voting, and serving in office. Growing up in Selma, where blacks could not vote, Josephine found this to be an exciting new world for her. Although she knew that her parents had strong feelings about particular candidates and expressed their opinions on the issues of the day as most voters would, they never discussed their disenfranchisement.

"I never heard my parents discuss voting, or the lack of being able to vote," she said.

Jo had moved to Seattle by the time she reached voting age, and was free to exercise her right to vote. "So I always could vote," she told me proudly. "And I have been voting ever since. I have hardly ever missed voting in an election."

I asked her if she started out as a Republican, or if my father's party affiliation had swayed her. "Let's see," she said, thinking back. "The first person I voted for was in the presidential election of Truman against Dewey. I voted for Dewey, the Republican, the first time, because I was impressed with him. I always voted for the person rather than the party. I have voted for more Republicans, because I knew more of them after I married Charles. But when I started out as a voter, I wasn't that political. I voted for the person who would do the most for my people and my interests. Then when Truman got elected, I voted to re-elect him because although I didn't think he did that much for blacks, he talked a good talk."

Although the difference in their ages made Stokey closer to her mother's age than her own, this was not even an issue for Josephine.

May-December marriages were common at that time, and in her own family. Josephine was a mature and sophisticated young woman, and Charles was a spirited gentleman who was young at heart. This balanced out the age gap between them.

"I liked him because he helped a lot of people," she said. "He hired blacks to be pages at the legislature, he hired a Negro secretary, he rented a house to the couple without a lot of money, and he took care of Mrs. Maxwell, a lady from the church, who had no children. He was good at aiding the people who came to him with problems."

And he was also popular among Seattle's Negro women. In 1952, Stokey was chosen to serve as the master of ceremonies for the first debutante ball of the Rhinestones Club, a Seattle social organization of African-American women. This cotillion continues to be held each year. He was also named the "sweetheart" of the Vogue Club (another black women's social group) for their fashion show fund-raiser. "They gave him presents," Mom said, "one of which was a small sculpture of an elephant, which acknowledged him as a Republican." That piece of art still stands on the living room mantel.

Daddy was what I would call a "women's man." Not the pejorative "ladies' man," but one who genuinely respected women, enjoyed their company, and was held by them in mutual regard. I asked my mother what she felt about dating a man that so many women obviously admired. "He was a good catch," she said reflectively. Then she added, "Who would want to date someone that nobody else would have wanted?"

After a respectable period of courtship, Charles asked Josephine to be his wife. "He was a romantic person, so he invited me out to dinner and asked me to marry him," she recalled. "We talked it over. We discussed his daughter, Vicki, who was living with her mother in Los Angeles. I mentioned my son. His response was that he couldn't wait to marry me so that he could get André out of those Lord Fauntleroy outfits I dressed him in! I enjoyed dressing André for church in fancy suits with short pants, like a little prince, but Charles thought he needed a man around to get him into long pants."

On March 19, 1951, they were married in the two-family home that

Josephine and her sister, by then divorced, had bought together for $10,000 on Hiawatha Place, parallel to one of Seattle's main boulevards, Rainier Avenue. Her mother, who was now separated from Collie and living with Aunt Katie in the upper duplex, hosted the wedding. Rev. Davis, the minister who had put Josephine and Charles together by planning the Rise Above Color program, performed the evening ceremony. Attended by only family and close friends, the wedding was small and intimate. The bride wore a navy blue silk dress, befitting a second marriage. Her friend Thelma Dewitty was the maid of honor, and Phil Burton, who was Charles's law partner and fellow Kansan, was his best man. "Charles gave me a Buick for a wedding present," she recalled. The newlyweds caught the ten p.m. overnight ferry with private cabins from Seattle to Victoria, Canada, for their honeymoon.

But the honeymoon at the Empress Hotel was cut short. "He got a phone call saying that the legislature had called a special session to reconvene over unfinished business," Josephine said. "So although we had intended to stay a week, we had to return home after a few days so he could go back to Olympia."

Newlyweds Josephine and Charles, in front of her wedding present.

He left for the state capital, but promised to make it up to her. "Every year for our anniversary, we went back there to make up the time we lost," she said with a chuckle.

After Charles and Josephine married, they began to have differing opinions on whether wives should work. "Charles didn't really want his wife to work." Being forty-eight, he was, like Jo's mother, of a generation that thought having a wife at home brought status to the husband and defined him as a man who could provide for his family. In later years, he would share with me that his stepmother had often told him in his youth that if he didn't make something of himself, he wouldn't be able to support a wife.

"Maybe he wanted to prove a point to her," Mom said. But she didn't want to repeat what she saw as her own mother's weakness in not being financially independent. She wanted to be able to support herself and her son should anything happen to her marriage or her husband, as it had to her first husband. Having already known the hardship of having to take care of herself and her baby unexpectedly as a widow, she didn't want to have to start from scratch in an emergency. Plus, she figured it would be better not to have to ask Charles for money to raise her son. Although she received monthly Social Security checks for André after his father's death, which helped with his childhood expenses, she also wanted to be able to save the money for his college education. And she possessed the higher education herself to be able to obtain a good job.

"I said to him, 'Well, I will be a very educated housewife.' " But her mind was made up.

"I enrolled at the University of Washington and got my teacher's certification. When I finished my school work, I heard about a job teaching school. At first, I was told that I had no experience, but then they said, 'Well, if we never give you a job, you won't get any experience.' So I was hired."

Joining the handful of black teachers who had to overcome regulations and attitudes that prohibited married women and African-Americans from becoming teachers in the state, Mom went to work at Horace Mann Elementary School in the heart of the Central District on East Cherry Street. It had a racially mixed, predominantly black student body. She was assigned to the fourth grade.

"I gave myself three years to see if teaching was for me," Mom recalled. "I taught fourth grade, and then I taught second grade for many years. I enjoyed teaching, and had good rapport with the students. A lot of teachers had trouble controlling the kids in their classroom. But I didn't."

I knew she had that right! I remember that she would come home and tell my father about her discipline problems and how she had taken care of them. I would eavesdrop on her talking about the kids in her class, some of whom I knew personally from church. Listening to her tales was like following a soap opera about colorful characters my own age. I often felt sorry for those kids, because my mother did not play. Yet she never raised a hand to them. And she took pride in seldom sending them to the principal's office. As she did at home with us, she took care of business herself!

"If someone acted up, I would look at them sternly," she said, explaining her method of child psychology, "and that worked for me. All I had to do was look at those little kids if they were doing something bad, and they calmed down."

Josephine's career as a public elementary school teacher began around the time of the groundbreaking *Brown v. Board of Education* decision. In 1954, the Supreme Court unanimously declared that the "separate but equal" educational doctrine was "inherently unequal" and, as such, violated the Fourteenth Amendment to the United States Constitution, which guarantees all citizens "equal protection of the laws." The case was even more meaningful for our family, because this battle for integration of the schools had been waged in Kansas, my father's home state. It had started as a local Topeka case that had challenged a segregated school, but now the triumph would have national ramifications. Daddy was proud that one of the black men he looked up to, NAACP special counsel Thurgood Marshall, had led the case and the cause, getting all the way to the Supreme Court—and had won.

But my mother's reaction to the victory was more guarded. When the case broke, she recalled, one of her professors at the university told her the news. "She wondered why I wasn't jumping up and down," Mom said, recalling that gym instructor was white, as were all of her professors there except one, and that she was one of only a handful of black students in the enrollment of 30,000. "I was elated about the bill, but I wasn't convinced it would change things overnight. And I was right. Following the decision, there were folks in the south who took their kids out of public schools and put them into private schools. So the schools that black children were sent to integrate got re-segregated because of that."

· · ·

Once in a while, Josephine asked her principal for permission to leave her classroom early to attend political events with her husband. When the legislature was in session and Stokey was based in Olympia, she would need to make the hour's drive to meet him.

"We were frequently invited to the governor's mansion for affairs, especially when Daniel Evans, a Republican, was governor," she told me. "I went to the governor's inaugural ball in 1952, and to every Republican election ball while Charles was in the legislature. I danced with the lieutenant governor when it was still almost unheard of for a white man to ask a black woman to dance.

"One year, Charles was chair of the Lincoln Day banquet when Vice-President Richard Nixon was the speaker. Charles was instrumental in getting him here to Seattle, and went to greet his arrival at the airport."

Mom went on to tell me about a Republican fund-raiser for President Eisenhower at the lavish Olympic Hotel. "I sat next to Henry Cabot Lodge," she said with obvious pride in having been assigned such a choice seat next to the U.S. senator from Massachusetts. "We were about the only black folk invited."

There were other prominent black Republican couples in the area— the Ponders, the Fraziers, the Penicks, the Lewises, to name a few—who not only voted Republican, but were active in state party politics. But that was a time when integration meant that one African-American couple might be invited to attend. I could tell from my mother's uneasy laugh that although she was happy to have been there, she and Daddy did not revel in being the tokens. But she understood that they were included because my father was a legislator.

"When the Rockefellers came to town, we were the tokens invited to greet them too," she recalled with a laugh. "Charles was one of the local chairs of Rocky's campaign."

There were other events besides political balls and fund-raisers to which the Stokeses were invited. "We got tickets to University of Washington football games, to the horse races, and other events where we sat in choice box seats," she explained.

"Once, your father was invited to a game at the U.," she said, talking about a University of Washington Huskies game at their stadium located at the edge of picturesque Lake Washington. "The person who invited him had a yacht, and picked him up and gave him a ride to the game by boat. There are a lot of perks in being a politician. That's why so many people want to be one."

I asked her if she thought Daddy would have liked to be president of the United States. She looked at me as though I should have known the question was absurd. I meant it in pure honesty. If race had not been a barrier, if racism had not been pervasive, and if he had been able to follow his ambitions, would he have wanted to emerge on the national scene? He seemed to have been on a track: attending all the Republican conventions, serving as a delegate and reading clerk. He ran for state representative office and won in a predominantly white district. He later politicked hard to become the country's first black lieutenant governor. Governor would have been next, I surmised. And many governors, including Richard Nixon and Ronald Reagan, went on to the presidency.

Ralph Bunche was a black man born the same year as my father, 1903. Daddy admired him greatly for his many achievements in the national and international political arenas. I thought, if Bunche could become the first African-American to win a Nobel Peace Prize in 1950, and then go on to become the undersecretary general of the United Nations, and receive an offer from President Truman to serve as assistant secretary of state (which Bunche turned down because he didn't want to live in the Jim Crow segregation of the nation's capital), didn't anything seem politically possible in the early 1950s?

Mom considered her husband's ambitions in the early days of their marriage, and spoke thoughtfully. "He wanted to go as high as he could. He thought of himself as a pioneer for his people, because he ran for these offices before anyone else black did."

I knew Mom thought it would be presumptuous, if not downright arrogant, to say that Daddy could have ever had a moment's thought about running for the country's highest office. And maybe it was my inner child envisioning my father as the first black president of the

United States of America. But I felt that if the political playing field had been level, with his statesmanship, intelligence, party loyalty, and love of country, he would have made a great senator, Supreme Court justice, or cabinet member. And perhaps those lofty offices could have led to the ultimate one. As my father often said, shrugging his shoulders, "I was just born too soon."

My mother, on the other hand, did not have political ambitions for herself. But has anyone ever aspired to be first lady? On visits to Washington, D.C., she enjoyed touring the White House. "That was always fun," she said, when I reminded her of the time while I was in college, when she made me meet her at the White House shortly after sunup so we could be first in line. Once inside, she listened to the docent's tales of the history of each room and how it was decorated. Then when the tour was over, Mom would express to me what decor *she* would have placed in the Blue Room, or the Red Room, and how she might have suggested the tables be set in the State Dining Room.

"I loved the place settings of each first lady and other decorations in the White House," she reminisced. "Every presidential wife had a chance to put her touch on the house."

I pushed the issue by telling her that she—a natural and elegant political wife who truly admired and studied first ladies such as Jacqueline Kennedy and Nancy Reagan—would have made a great one herself. I could have seen her giving one of those TV tours of the White House, maybe mentioning how African-Americans helped to build it and how they served president after president through slavery up to the present. To my surprise, she finally acquiesced for the sake of my fantasy, and I laughed when she remarked, "If I had ever been in the White House, I would have done it up!"

Decorating and entertaining in the White House may not have been my mother's destiny, but she certainly did oversee the interior design of our "Black House" with an opulent hand. And without a doubt, she was first lady of our family.

The year that Mamie Eisenhower was campaigning her husband's way into the White House, my father decided he, too, liked Ike, and my mother discovered that she was expecting. It was a bit of a shock for her to find that she was pregnant so soon after her wedding to Charles. But that was not the only astonishing thing that would occur.

"One Sunday when I was expecting, we went to church, then out to dinner," she began the story. "It was dusk when we came back. As we climbed the steep steps to our house, we saw in the fading light that the front door was open. We weren't sure we were seeing straight—and then a lady stepped into the doorway from inside as we approached!"

The couple knew who she was: a problem client of Charles's. "She had lost her husband and Charles was the executor of her estate," Mom said. "During this time, she became mentally unstable and decided that *Charles* was her husband."

When Josephine and Charles saw the woman inside their home, greeting them at the door, they hurried back to their car and drove downtown to the courthouse to report her to the police. But when they returned and the police came, the woman was gone.

Her breaking and entering had been accomplished by smashing the glass pane next to the door, which allowed her to reach in and unlock the door. The next morning, that pane was exposed, waiting for a handyman to come to replace it, when Charles had to leave for his hour-long drive to the legislature. Surely, they thought, lightning wouldn't strike twice. But just in case, Charles left the telephone number of the police headquarters next to the bed.

Eight months pregnant, Josephine went back to sleep after Charles left. When she woke up, she looked out of her second-story bedroom window and saw the deranged woman climbing the front steps. "Before I could get downstairs, she was back in the house," Jo recalled.

Still under the delusion that she was the real Mrs. Stokes, the woman threatened Josephine and told her to get out of *her* house. And then she produced a gun and waved it around as she elevated her threats.

"I said, 'Okay, let me get my little boy,'" Josephine recalled herself saying to the woman as she tried to stay calm and gently coax her outside, while feeling panic about her sleeping three-year-old upstairs. "She said to me, 'No, he is mine.'"

And that's when the stuff hit the fan.

"I knew she was crazy then, because even if I couldn't be sure about her and Charles, I knew my son was mine!"

The woman stepped farther into the foyer, and the two of them argued. "She came in, and pointed the gun at my pregnant stomach."

Then the woman looked beyond Josephine and noticed that the phone on the foyer settee was off the hook.

"I had tried to call the police and tell them someone was breaking in," Jo said. "But I didn't get a chance to hang up."

With the phone line still open, the emergency operator was able to hear what was going on, and had notified the police. Fortunately, just as the woman was about to go off about the phone being off the hook, the police got there.

They arrested "the crazy lady," as we kids always irreverently referred to her for years to come, and took her into custody. She was eventually admitted to a mental institution in a remote Washington town called Steilacoom, forty-five miles away from Seattle. Peace prevailed again in the Stokes household.

And that allowed me to get myself born.

= 6 =

This Little Light of Mine

I<small>T WAS THE THIRTEENTH OF</small> J<small>ANUARY</small>, a Sunday, in 1952, when my mother told my father it was time to take her to the hospital. She was going into labor. Daddy dropped her off at the hospital, saw that she was admitted, and went back home.

Then he made a phone call to his mother-in-law.

"Jo's in the hospital," he announced to her. "She's about to have the baby."

"Well, where are you?" his wife's mother, Flossie, asked.

"I'm at home," he replied.

"What are you doing there? You come get me so we can go to the hospital right now!"

In years to come when Dad would tell that story, he would always

<small>ABOVE:</small> *Me at age two.*

laugh at his own naiveté. "I didn't know I was supposed to stay at the hospital. I'd never had a baby before!"

Because his daughter from his first marriage had been adopted, and because no parenting classes had been offered at the hospital, he just didn't know the proper thing to do when his wife was having a baby. But his mother-in-law set him straight. He drove to her house, picked her up, and they rushed the few miles over to Seattle's Group Health Hospital on Capitol Hill.

"That's my baby!" Gran exclaimed every time she heard my mother's cries. Together she and Daddy paced the floor of the waiting room of the low-rise brick hospital building, which happened to be directly below the delivery room. Not allowed to get any closer, or to give any comfort to her twenty-seven-year-old daughter, all she could do was respond to the voice she had given birth to herself. "That's my baby up there!"

My mother's side of the story was that her usual stoicism was replaced by painful cries because she was having natural childbirth before there even was such a thing.

"I went to the hospital, but the baby wasn't ready to come out yet, so the doctor decided to induce labor," she explained. "That would have been all right, but because it was lunchtime, he decided to go to have lunch. As fate would have it, the labor began shortly after he left, and the baby started to come. And there wasn't a doctor on the floor. So I was left without any pain medication and no one to help, except for a nurse. So I always say I had natural childbirth."

Many people have no idea what time they were born, but because of the story about the doctor going off to lunch at noontime, I have always known that I was born at 12:25 p.m.

There is a photograph I cherish that captures a precious moment on a sunny Seattle day in the summer of 1952. Obviously taken after church, the photo shows Daddy kneeling on the front lawn of our house wearing a pale gray suit with white shirt, striped tie, and straw fedora. My four-year-old brother at Daddy's bended knee is a mini version of Dad, in a gray collarless Lord Fauntleroy suit with red bow tie. My sister, five, is on the other side of Dad in what looks like a brand-new two-piece

My mother took this photo in our front yard on
Father's Day 1952. From left to right: Vicki, age five;
me, six months; Daddy; André, four.

dress with a Peter Pan–collared blouse. Vicki, who lived with us each summer, is squinting from the sun in her eyes. I am six months old, dressed in a white smocked infant gown with baby-doll sleeves and white satin shoes that never touched the grass below. Comfortably seated on Daddy's lap leaning against him, I am alert and smiling at the camera. The photographer is most likely my mother. Where else would she be if not in the photo herself? Dad and André are smiling. It was a happy occasion—Daddy's first Father's Day with all his children.

When people would ask how many children my parents had, my father would reply proudly, "I had one, she had one, we had one—and they're all ours."

Like the new beginning suggested in the photograph, 1952 started off as a year of hope and promise. The two World Wars were over. The Cold War hadn't heated up yet. In Britain, Princess Elizabeth became Queen Elizabeth II upon the death of her father, King George VI, and planning began on her elaborate coronation to take place the next year. In America, it was the first year in the seventy-year history of the recording of lynching that no lynching was reported.

In 1952, author Ralph Ellison made an impact on the racial consciousness of the country with the publication of his first novel, *Invisible Man*. The book about a Negro male whose education and intellect were not enough to overcome the racial prejudice that rendered him "invisible" to American society won a place on the *New York Times* best-seller list and remained there for sixteen weeks. Ellison won the National Book Award for Fiction for the groundbreaking work.

Television was becoming more popular. About 22 million homes had televisions, up from 3.6 million just three years before. "American Bandstand" took to the tube in Philadelphia on a local station. The day after I was born, "The Today Show" debuted, airing its first broadcast on NBC-TV.

Hope loomed large in America that year. But inequality and unrest bubbled under the surface. In 1952, only twenty percent of African-Americans in the south were registered to vote, kept away by poll taxes, bigotry, and other illegal methods of intimidation. Segregated schools were prevalent across the country, legally enforced by the "separate but equal" doctrine. Jim Crow was alive and kicking.

My parents' marriage had a foundation of shared optimism. They believed that their participation—in local politics through my father's elected office, and on the national scene by his service as a delegate to the Republican National Convention—would help integrate the country. They, along with thousands of other politically active African-Americans of both parties, were trying to make a difference.

In the summer of 1952, when I was six months old, my parents left me with my grandmother and drove their green Buick for three days from Seattle to the Republican National Convention in Chicago.

"Remember when we left Steph with Gran and went off to the convention, Jo?" my father often began that story at holiday dinners. Mom would just smile.

"What was the big deal about that?" I asked. "I often stayed with Gran."

Indeed, when my brother was old enough to start school, and I was a toddler, my mother went to work, becoming one of Seattle's first Negro teachers. She arranged with her mother, who had always been a superb homemaker, to have her come to our home every weekday morning. I awoke each day to the sounds of my grandmother and her son-in-law trading jokes, witticisms, and laughter as she prepared grits, eggs, sausage, and biscuits for our family's breakfast. Then with Dad and Mom off to their jobs and André in kindergarten, Gran attended to me and kept the house immaculate. My very first memory is of Gran holding me upside down by the ankles to sprinkle baby powder on my tush.

This particular trip to the Republican convention was when I was still an infant, and my parents felt guilty about leaving me behind. At least, my father seemed to hold guilt about taking my mother away from her maternal duties to accompany him on his political mission. I imagine that my mother, leaving me in the capable, loving hands of her own mother to take up the role of political wife—one she enjoyed and performed so well—did not mind.

That was to be a big year for Dad at the RNC. In years to come, he would talk more about feeling bad for leaving me at home than he would about his achievement there. But family lore had it that he had given the seconding speech for the candidacy of Dwight D. Eisenhower for president. Or was it Nelson Rockefeller? It was one of those stories that grew with each telling, depending on the family member telling the tale.

To get to the bottom of the story, in 2002, I contacted the Republican National Committee in Washington, D.C. Did they have any record of a Charles M. Stokes from the state of Washington participating in the convention proceedings of the 1950s?

I was told that at the 1956 convention, he was elected an assistant reading clerk, which meant that he helped to record and announce the votes of the delegates. Later I received an e-mail saying that in the 1952 convention he had made a statement concerning the seating of part of the Georgia Delegation. And that was all.

Huh? What about the grandstanding for the presidential nomination? What about being the first black to speak from the Republican convention platform on behalf of a president?

My subsequent research delved into the issues of the convention of

that year. I learned that the convention's credential committee originally ruled that a contested Georgia delegation should be seated. This
delegation was in support of Ohio Senator Robert A. Taft's nomination over General Dwight D. Eisenhower, who was supported by the
traditional Georgia delegation.

Delegates were chosen to address the convention over this issue.
The official transcript of the 1952 Republican National Convention
records this exchange:

THE CHAIRMAN—The Chair now recognizes the delegate from the State of Washington, Mr. Stokes, to speak
on the substitute motion.

MR. CHARLES M. STOKES OF WASHINGTON—Mr.
Chairman, delegates to the Republican National Convention, the future of the Republican Party and of the two-party
principle of our democracy depends on all Republicans
working for a stronger regular Republican Party organization.

The Tucker group from Georgia is the group recognized by the National Republican organization. It is the
group which was seated in 1944 and 1948 by the Republican National Committee.

It is the group which has in its ranks, the National Com-
mitteeman and National Committeewoman from Georgia—
the two people who call the Republican Party in Georgia
to their meetings and conventions to choose delegates to
this Convention.

This group is the representative of the rank and file
Republicans of Georgia as well as the new blood which is
so essential to the continued growth and strength of our
Party.

Trickery plays no part in the naming of the Tucker
delegation. Their presence in Chicago was dictated by the
openly expressed will of their Republican friends and
neighbors in Georgia.

I call on this Convention to be on the side of honesty and decency—to go on record before the court of public opinion with an overwhelming vote for the permanent seating of the Tucker delegation.

There can be no question as to the right of the Tucker group to be permanently seated as the Georgia delegation. They have been legally and honestly elected.

Centuries past, there was a man named Diogenes who trod the streets of an ancient city in broad daylight, holding a lighted lantern aloft. When asked why he carried a lighted lantern in full daylight, he gave the classic answer which has echoed with hope in the hearts of man where corruption appears: "I'm looking for an honest man."

Diogenes, I have news for you. Hang up your lantern. Here are the honest men, here is the honest delegation from the State of Georgia, the Tucker group.

The transcript notes the applause that followed.

The 1952 Republican and Democratic political conventions were the first ones that the general public could see on television. It must have been an honor for my father to have addressed not only the convention floor, but the nation. Deflecting his own contribution, he would say that he was just happy that his own speech had been the set-up for the esteemed statesman who followed. It was future Supreme Court Justice Earl Warren, who was considered as a possible third candidate to settle the deadlock between Taft and Eisenhower. But the Warren deadlock strategy was not necessary. The full convention, in a 607–531 vote, overruled the committee's ruling, and seated the traditional Georgia delegation that my father had supported. As a result, all of Dwight D. Eisenhower's delegates were seated, Ike became the Republican nominee—and subsequently was elected president of the United States of America.

= 7 =

The Old Rugged Cross

MY PARENTS may have slipped away together to attend the 1952 Republican Convention, but after that year, they towed us children along with them. All family vacations centered around the conventions of their various organizations.

"Your father says that he never took a vacation to any place except the Republican convention before he met me," my mother liked to say.

"And then the vacations he took with you were to *your* conventions," I reminded her, "except for your anniversaries in Vancouver, Canada."

Each summer, family trips were planned around the national conventions of either the Links, Jack & Jill, Delta Sigma Theta sorority, Kappa Alpha Psi fraternity, or Daddy's lawyers' group, the National Bar

ABOVE: *In the family car, my father drove us*
to church and also across the country for political conventions.

Association. In later years, they also went to the conferences of my father's fraternal organization, Sigma Pi Phi, also called the Boule. From these venues, my parents might decide to take side trips to visit relatives, but the main reason for the vacation was to attend a convention.

In 1956, the Republican National Convention was in San Francisco, so my parents drove my brother and me down to Los Angeles to drop us off with my mother's aunt Dorothy while they attended the convention.

The movie *Auntie Mame* was popular in the 1950s, and I always related Aunt Dorothy to the main character played by Rosalind Russell. Like Auntie Mame, Aunt Dorothy was single, flamboyant, elegant, and lived life to the fullest. She would tell us stories about what it was like to work for actor Spencer Tracy, whose personal caterer she claimed to be. We never knew if these were tall tales or the truth, but we did know that she lived in an exquisite garden apartment, which was half of a duplex home, and that she seemed to know all about the white folks in Hollywood, and the black ones too, like Ethel Waters, who was nominated for an Academy Award in 1950 for Best Supporting Actress for her role in *Pinky*.

Ethel Waters was close to Aunt Dorothy's age, both having been born around the turn of the century. Both Aunt Dorothy and Ethel Waters practically raised themselves in Los Angeles after losing their mothers at early ages. Although Waters got more than her share of criticism from blacks for playing maids in the movies, she could agree with Academy Award winner Hattie McDaniel of *Gone with the Wind*, that at least by playing one, the difference in salary meant she didn't have to work as one. Aunt Dorothy would have related to that.

Aunt Dorothy's stories made it plain to us that she never worked as a maid. No, sir! She had left Selma as a teenager by working for a white family moving to the west coast, caring for their children as a nanny. After her brief marriage ended, she had made a living by catering fabulous parties for the rich and famous, but she never cleaned their houses. This was not snobbery on her part, but just an achievement she claimed. At a time when over sixty-five percent of Negro women who worked were forced to do so as domestics, she counted it as a blessing. For a woman who had not had benefit of the college education that her brother, gainfully employed in the ice-delivery business, had been able to afford her two nieces, it was an achievement that she had never had to get on her hands and knees to take care of herself.

And boy, she did have beautiful hands—even a child could tell that. Perfectly manicured at all times, she kept her long, strong nails meticulously painted with bright red polish.

Aunt Dorothy was tall and thin with a flawless, deep brown complexion the color of my favorite chocolate candy, Tootsie Roll. I was always tempted to lick her instead of give her a kiss.

While we visited with Aunt Dorothy, Daddy filled an important role at the Republican National Convention. Official documents of the gathering report that Charles M. Stokes served as assistant reading clerk. Helping to record the votes of the delegates, he had a prominent role that was even more rare for an African-American to fill. That year, Dwight D. Eisenhower was nominated for re-election for president. Then my parents drove back down to Los Angeles to pick up us kids, and two days later we were back home.

In the summer of 1960, Daddy bought a new, roomy, black Cadillac with distinctive tail fins that were all the rage, and drove my mother, brother, and me from Seattle to Chicago for the Republican National Convention.

It became a ritual of our car trips to leave at one a.m., when there would be no traffic on the roads. Lulled by the motor of the car while stretched out in my pajamas under a blanket in the backseat, I would become quiet before drifting off to sleep.

"Oh no, Jo!" Daddy would feign alarm to my mother after about twenty minutes. "We've got to go back home."

She would just smile and say nothing, knowing where he was taking the conversation.

"We must have left Steph at home. I don't hear a word from her!"

"Here I am!" I'd answer, and then everyone would laugh, and I'd realize the joke was on me.

My mother can't believe that I have no recollection of her taking us to greet Vice-President Nixon at the Chicago convention.

"While your father was at the convention, we went to the museum to see the dinosaurs. Do you remember that?" she asks when we reminisce.

"Nope."

"Don't you remember that as we were walking back into the hotel, everyone stopped to see Vice-President Nixon walk by?"

"Sorry," I say. Eight years old at the time, I guess I just didn't think it was my kind of memorable occasion. But I do recall that after we left Chicago, we drove down south to visit my mother's aunt Bootsie in Selma, Alabama. The local black newspaper reported that it was the first time that the former Josephine Stratman had returned to Selma since she had left thirteen years before.

For the first time, I met my cousins, her grandchildren, who were close to the ages of my siblings and me. I was happy that the pretty little girl cousin with the long, thick hair, Deborah, was exactly my age. She had a lot of personality that amused my father.

One night while we were there, my parents got all gussied up to go out for the evening. As they approached the front door to leave, Deborah stood up from our game of jacks.

"You all look so lovely tonight, Uncle Stokey and Aunt Jo," she said in her charming southern accent. She lived in Memphis when she wasn't visiting her grandmother in the summers.

"Well, isn't that nice of you!" Daddy said to her.

"Not really," she replied. "I was just trying to butter you up so we can go to the movies tomorrow."

We all laughed, and "butter you up" became a family catch phrase back in Seattle for years to come.

One day, Deborah and her brothers took André and me to a neighborhood pool. Back home, André was a member of a swim team, and we often attended his meets, where he picked up winning ribbons and trophies. I, on the other hand, was afraid of water, and only splashed around to keep cool in the heat.

Some tempers flared that day, however, in a way I'll never forget.

As were most public accommodations in Selma in 1960, the pools were segregated. This pool was in the black community and, so, was designated FOR COLORED ONLY. What I didn't realize is that such Jim Crow signs were meant to keep blacks out of white accommodations, but not necessarily to keep whites out of black-designated areas. So when three white boys climbed up the stairs of the above-ground pool, I was surprised to see them. The Selma kids didn't seem to be surprised, but they weren't pleased.

"What are you doing here?" one of the colored kids asked.

"Don't you worry about it," one white kid answered. "Just move out of my way."

"No, you go to your own pool."

"We can go to whatever pool we want to. Colored folks can't come to 'White Only' pools, but we can go anyplace in Selma or the U.S. of A. that we want to. So move!"

Well, he may have been right, but he was outnumbered. Somebody jumped him from behind and the fight was on.

"Fight! Fight!" somebody yelled. And all the kids in the pool started swimming toward the squirmish.

Segregation had a strange psychological effect. If blacks couldn't use white accommodations, then they became territorial about the ones they were limited to. They felt as if their own second-class amenities were exclusive to them.

"White kids've got better pools than we've got, but that ain't enough for them," one of the swimmers explained to us. "They gotta have their pools and our pools too!"

Eventually, the white boys ran off from the beating they were getting. André and our male cousins, Brother and Paul, who had stopped swimming to watch the excitement, jumped back into the pool and Deborah joined them. I remained on the side, thinking about how glad I was that black and white went swimming together every day at the beaches and pools in Seattle. That's not to say that there were never any racial incidents, but at least they weren't condoned by the law.

One summer, my father decided that he had too much work to do at his law office to prepare for an upcoming trial, and couldn't afford to take the time off to drive my mother to her Links convention in Dallas. So Mom and two of her sister Links, Mrs. Gideon and Mrs. Meade, packed up the car and took André and me with them on the drive from Seattle to the south.

André and I sat in the backseat, which we shared with Mrs. Gideon for the entire three-day, 2,200-mile drive. As the youngest, I sat in the middle as we passed through Oregon, Idaho, and Utah. In Wyoming, we were excited to stop for souvenirs in Cheyenne, a town we always heard the cowboys talking about on the TV westerns. We played word games together and looked for license plates of different states as we traveled on through Denver, Daddy's home state of Kansas, and on down to Texas.

The ride was so long and boring that at one point, André and I began to get giddy and giggly.

"André," I said, pointing to an insignia on his polo shirt. "What is that?"

"Fjords," he replied simply.

"Fjords?" I asked and laughed. "It looks like a pipe with a heart coming out of it to me."

"Fjords," he repeated stone-faced. He probably learned that word in school just before classes ended for the summer. Every time he said it, I laughed harder and harder. It was just a funny-sounding word to me. I had a tendency, like my father, to cry when I laughed hard. So tears rolled down my face as I cried and laughed at the same time, and I couldn't stop doing one or the other. Although our silliness may have annoyed my mother and the other ladies, they allowed us the laughter, which we kept up for most of the rest of the trip. I guess my mother preferred the giggling to our usual fighting.

But unfortunately, the drive down south was not to be remembered only for its fun and games. One evening, while Mom was driving around trying to find a motel that would accept colored folks, we got lost. As soon as we got down to Texas, it was no longer an option to stop at the nearest motel when we got tired. African-Americans knew to look out for the COLORED ONLY signs or to have their way plotted out in advance with word-of-mouth recommendations from friends who had made the trip before. Sometimes, though, those places might be fully occupied, and then you had to ride around looking for another motel or even a boarding house that was owned by Negroes.

On the dimly lit rural road with few cross streets, we couldn't find our way. But the police found their way to us.

"Oh, Lord," my mother said, looking in her rearview mirror. "The police are flashing their lights behind us. I have to pull over."

Two policemen got out of the patrol car and approached the driver's side of the car. One had a flashlight, and he pointed it in my mother's face. Then he made the light survey all the rest of us—Mrs. Meade in the front passenger seat, and Mrs. Gideon in the back with André and me. Mrs. Gideon gathered us close to her.

"Let me see your driver's license," the one with the flashlight said as he shined the light down her body.

This was no help to my mother in her search through her bag for her wallet, but she kept her cool, found the license, and handed it to him wordlessly.

"What are you people doing down here from Seattle, Washington?"

"We are on our way to Dallas to a convention," Mom said.

"This ain't exactly the highway to Dallas, lady." I thought he sounded too mean to be talking to my mama. "I think you are in the wrong place."

"Officer, we got off the main road to try to find a colored place to stay the night." Mom was using her schoolmarm voice now, the one that sounded patient, but I knew she was getting upset.

"Where'd you get this fancy car?" the other officer asked, taking the light and flashing it around the dashboard and the seats. The first officer stepped back and looked over the outside of the Cadillac. He checked the license plates in front and back, walking around the car slowly and deliberately.

"My husband, who is an attorney, bought it."

"Oh, he did, did he? Let me see the registration."

Mom handed it to him.

They looked it over, then returned it and flashed the light back into the car over every nook and cranny. After a long moment, he took the light out of the window and pointed it in the direction of the darkened street. There were no streetlights, no homes with porch lights on. Just black.

"There's a place that takes in coloreds down the street and around the corner," he said. Then they walked off and waited in their car until we pulled off.

As we drove off slowly, with the cops following us for several blocks, Mom and the ladies gave out tentative sighs of relief, as though they had been holding their breath during the whole ordeal, but still weren't sure if it was over.

"I was so nervous, I didn't know *what* to do," my mother said, in the first admission I ever heard of her not feeling in total control.

"Girl, you did the right thing," the ladies assured her. "You handled those crackers good."

Still fearful myself, I laid my head down in Mrs. Gideon's lap until we found the Jim Crow accommodations for the night.

On one hand, my parents didn't want us to have to experience the humiliation of segregation. And on the other hand, they wanted us to know what "our cousins," as Daddy called colored folks, were going through in other parts of the country, particularly the south. There was a feeling that none of us were totally free of segregation as long as some of us still experienced it. And as our travels showed us, we were not exempt from being subjected to it, even though we lived in another part of the country that did not practice such overt racism. Because of the color of our skin, if we were in the south, we had to conduct ourselves as the local blacks did in order to avoid trouble.

We were taught to say "Yes, sir," and "No, ma'am," to black and white adults when we were in the south. Whites demanded that, and blacks, in order to be addressed with respect by children, followed suit. In that way, black children could feel that it was a dictate of adults, rather than a racial thing. I tell you, segregation was outrageous.

On the way to Dallas, my mother stopped off at André's grandparents' large ranch in Lovelady, Texas. It was a tiny town near a small town called Crockett. André and I loved the great expanse of the

1,500-acre spread, and begged to be left there instead of going on to the convention. Although my mother had paid for our participation in the children's events, she allowed us to stay with Grandfather and Grandmother Wooten, who assured her it would be fine with them.

The Wootens' large family of adult children who lived throughout the country, from Seattle to Washington, D.C., customarily gathered there during the summers, where the grandchildren shed their city ways and were free to roam the ranch on any of their many horses.

One hot, muggy morning during my visit, Grandfather Wooten took me with him to a cattle auction. We drove to Crockett in the pick-up truck and entered a large building that resembled a stadium with indoor bleachers. I had seen auctioneers on television, talking so fast that you couldn't understand what they were saying. This fascinated me, and I asked if we could sit on the front row of the bleachers so that I could take it all in. I had just gotten my first pair of eyeglasses that year, and was accustomed to sitting in the front row of class in school because of my bad eyesight, so my request was made out of habit.

"No, Steph, we can't sit here," Grandfather replied. "We have to go up top where the colored folks sit. That's the colored area up there."

Sure enough, I looked up at the top of the bleachers and saw that all the brown faces were seated there. White folks were in the front. Just like on the buses of the south, the black folks were in the back.

Eventually, I had to go to the restroom. Grandfather said he would go to show me which one to use. "I can go by myself," I said, not wanting to take him away from his work of buying cattle at the auction. "I know how to read."

"No, I need to show you," he said gently, and took me by the hand.

As soon as he pointed out that I was to go into the doorway marked COLORED ONLY, I knew why he had accompanied me. He wanted to make sure I didn't make the mistake of going into the WHITE ONLY bathroom. The two doors were separated by two water fountains, one for the white folks, and the other for the blacks. I don't recall if the colored folks were given separate men's and women's restrooms. All I remember is thinking, *So, this is that horrible thing they talk about on television, that Negroes are fighting against. This isn't someone telling me about segrega-*

tion. This isn't one of my parents' stories. This is real. This is happening to me. *I see the signs with my own eyes. I see that this bathroom doesn't look as nice as the other one, yet it's the one I have to use.*

I wondered what would have happened if Grandfather had not escorted me and I had wandered into the wrong restroom. Would I have been shot on the spot? Would I have been arrested like Rosa Parks? I looked around for dogs. I was already afraid of dogs, even in Seattle, because I saw on television how nice they were to white people on "Rin Tin Tin" and "Lassie," yet the most prevalent media images of dogs with colored folks were those of vicious attacks on marchers.

That was the day that Stephanie Stokes was introduced to Jim Crow. I quickly came to understand that this American apartheid was often enforced by law officials—or worse, through random acts of intimidation and violence. And like the church song said of "the old rugged cross," it was "an emblem of suffering and shame."

Dr. David Pilgrim, Curator of the Jim Crow Museum of Racist Memorabilia at Ferris State University, explains it this way on the museum's Web site:

> The Jim Crow system was undergirded by the following beliefs or rationalizations: Whites were superior to blacks in all important ways, including but not limited to intelligence, morality, and civilized behavior; sexual relations between blacks and whites would produce a mongrel race which would destroy America; treating blacks as equals would encourage interracial sexual unions; any activity which suggested social equality encouraged interracial sexual relations; if necessary, violence must be used to keep blacks at the bottom of the racial hierarchy. The following Jim Crow etiquette norms show how inclusive and pervasive these norms were:
>
> a. A black male could not offer his hand (to shake hands) with a white male because it implied being socially equal. Obviously, a black male could not offer his hand or any other part of his body to a white woman, because he risked being accused of rape.

b. Blacks and whites were not supposed to eat together. If they did eat together, whites were to be served first, and some sort of partition was to be placed between them.

c. Under no circumstance was a black male to offer to light the cigarette of a white female—that gesture implied intimacy.

d. Blacks were not allowed to show affection toward one another in public, especially kissing, because it offended whites.

e. Jim Crow etiquette prescribed that blacks were introduced to whites, never whites to blacks. For example: "Mr. Peters (the white person), this is Charlie (the black person), that I spoke to you about."

f. Whites did not use courtesy titles of respect when referring to blacks, for example, Mr., Mrs., Miss, Sir, or Ma'am. Instead, blacks were called by their first names. Blacks had to use courtesy titles when referring to whites, and were not allowed to call them by their first names.

g. If a black person rode in a car driven by a white person, the black person sat in the backseat, or the back of a truck.

h. White motorists had the right-of-way at all intersections.

Stetson Kennedy, the author of *Jim Crow Guide,* offered these simple rules that blacks were supposed to observe in conversing with whites:

1. Never assert or even intimate that a white person is lying.
2. Never impute dishonorable intentions to a white person.
3. Never suggest that a white person is from an inferior class.
4. Never lay claim to, or overly demonstrate, superior knowledge or intelligence.
5. Never curse a white person.
6. Never laugh derisively at a white person.
7. Never comment upon the appearance of a white female.

On that sweltering Texas summer day, Grandfather must have noticed that my little hand was squeezing his much tighter than before as we returned to our seats at the top of the auction tent. Back at the ranch, I stayed close to my big brother, the rest of the family, the cattle, and the horses. Never once did I wander.

The Stokes family was to meet up with ol' Jim Crow on several other occasions, but since it happened to all of us together, I felt less humiliated. Many times, the black-owned hotels were comparable to the white ones. I recall that in 1958 we drove about five days from Seattle to New York for a Links convention my mother attended. From there, we drove about five hours down to Washington, D.C., where my father was sworn in to be able to appear before the Supreme Court, a largely symbolic tradition that attorneys enjoy. A lovely plaque is given to the lawyer to mark the occasion. Framed and official-looking, this document hung in my father's office afterward for decades.

Ironically, Daddy could get acknowledgment like any American attorney at the highest court in the land, but he couldn't stay in the choicest hotel in Washington, D.C. He checked us into the historic and segregated Dunbar Hotel not far from Howard University, and told Vicki and me that we would have to stay there because Negroes weren't allowed in the hotels downtown. I remember the Dunbar as being somewhat dingy, unlike the swanky Belmont Plaza Hotel where we had just stayed in New York, across the street from the Waldorf-Astoria.

During that visit to D.C., we were pleased to be visited by my father's brother, Uncle Norris, who traveled the country as a gospel singer, and was passing through as well. He had just been in a movie that had played on television. My father joked that his brother's part in the movie was such a quick walk-on that "if you blinked, you missed him."

On the five-day drive back from Washington, D.C., to Seattle, Washington, we stopped off in Daddy's hometown of Pratt, Kansas, and were welcomed by his stepmother, whose name was the same as my mother's, Josephine Stokes. Here, I saw the modest house in which my father grew up. There was a furnace smack-dab in the middle of the living room. I began to realize that maybe all his holiday-dinner stories about how poor he had been had not been make-believe.

"Let's stop for hamburgers," André said on one trip through the south to another convention.

"Okay," Mom agreed. "Charles, pull over. I see a drive-in burger place down the road."

We stopped at the drive-in, where we waited for the waitress to come out to the car, as they did at our favorite hamburger place in Seattle. We waited and waited. We noticed the waitress serving other people, then other cars that came after us got service. Finally, my father told André to go to the window to place our order.

He got out of the car and went to the window. We saw a man say something to him and point around the corner of the building. As André started to walk in that direction, my mother rolled down the window.

"André, where are you going?"

"That man told me to go around the back to the kitchen to—"

"You get yourself back in this car this instant!" Mom called out firmly, but just loud enough for him to hear.

He got in the backseat with me, and Daddy took off. André and I didn't understand what had happened.

"Where are you going? What about our hamburgers?" André asked.

"I'm hungry!" I began to whine, as was my expertise.

Mom was fuming. "How dare they do that to a child! What is wrong with them?"

"Do what?" we asked.

Mom was too angry to speak. Daddy tried to explain. "They don't serve Negroes at that hamburger joint."

André and I looked at each other with our eyes wide. We hadn't realized that getting something to eat had turned into something so serious. The silence was thick with tension.

Then Daddy added, "But that's okay, because we don't eat 'em!"

We all laughed as our stomachs growled. Dad had diligently arranged for our trip to be mapped out by the American Automobile Association. But AAA didn't provide colored folks with directions for finding a segregated place to eat. We rode around a nearby town, venturing miles from our charted path, stopping "cousins" we saw walking on the streets, and asking them for good places to get burgers. Eventually, we found a colored hamburger stand, where we were welcomed. And André jumped out to place our order at the front window.

One night, after a long, tiring drive, we found ourselves in a Southern town with no hotel or motel, segregated or otherwise. "Cousins" walking along the road directed us to a residence in the heart of the black community. As we drove up, we could see into the open front door. Fully clothed colored people of all ages were lying crowded over the floor in the entrance and the living room, covered in blankets and sleeping bags.

"We won't be staying here," Mom said quietly.

Daddy nodded and wordlessly drove away. He parked the car near the entrance to the highway we would take on our continuing journey home at sunrise. The four of us stretched out on the seats of our big ol' black Caddie, and slept as best we could.

On another night, in Memphis, we were happy to find a marquee informing us of rooms available at a comfy black-owned motel downtown. The art-deco sign above the marquee announced the name, LORRAINE MOTEL. This two-story structure was one of the nicer travelers' inns in the country, much like the quality of the Howard Johnson, which my parents always patronized because that was one national motel chain that accepted black folks.

At the Lorraine Motel, we had a room on the second floor. It had two double beds—one where André and Daddy slept, the other my mother and I shared. I liked that the sink was in the bedroom, not the bathroom, so if anyone was on the pot with the door locked, you didn't have to wait to wash up.

We weren't the only black folks who enjoyed staying at the Lorraine Motel. Civil rights activists often used it as their headquarters. Martin Luther King, Jr., did so just a few years after our visit, staying on the second floor, just as we had.

But my fond memory of the motel was stained forever by the gunman who made it the scene of King's assassination in 1968.

In 1991, the National Civil Rights Museum opened in the repurposed structure of the motel. In the late nineties, on a trip to Memphis for a speaking engagement, I was taken by my hosts on a tour of the museum, where Dr. King's room has been preserved. Standing on the second-floor balcony, I pondered all we had lost in the struggle, as well as what had been gained.

Leaving the historic site, I returned to my room at an upscale hotel just a few blocks away, where now anyone of any race would be graciously served.

= 8 =

Bless This House

EACH TIME WE RETURNED HOME from one of our long car trips, we had renewed appreciation for Seattle. Summers in Seattle were sunny, warm, and pleasant, without the humidity of the south or the northeast. We could swim in any YMCA pool, and we could go to any beach along Lake Washington.

The neighborhood in which I was born was predominantly black, but not "Colored Only." Our next-door neighbor was a widow named Mrs. Gist, a sweet, elderly white lady who often called us while we were playing outside to come to her front door, where she distributed nickels, dimes, and candy. One of our playmates was a blond, lanky boy named Billy, whom we girls took pleasure in nicknaming Billy Button. Living in a neighborhood in which he was a minority, Billy learned to

ABOVE: *In my parents' bedroom, showing what I learned in ballet class, third position.*

dance just as well as any of us. And we learned that race is not always the determining factor of one's abilities or talents, but that acculturation is.

Our home was the one my father had purchased shortly after his arrival in Seattle. Living in the house as a bachelor, he had made zebra-print fabrics the dominant decor. When he married Josephine, she quickly changed all the furnishings to Louis XIV.

We called the house "1615," referring to the address. It was a tall two-story home that looked like it was three stories because the basement had a walk-out door on the side under the front porch. The only home on the block with a double lot, it had an expansive yard that made a great playground for us and all the neighborhood children.

Fruit trees were in abundance—a pear tree in the front yard, our very own apple tree on the side, and a massive cherry tree in the backyard. The property was on a slope, as the block went up a steep hill behind us. Quiet as it's kept, Seattle is a hilly city that could rival San Francisco for its steep streets.

Behind the house was an alley, used for access to the detached garage. On the hilly side of the alley that separated our backyards from those of the neighbors and split our block in half grew massive vines of blackberries. I never liked blackberries, with all their "sticker bushes," as we called the thorny stems of the vines. But I did love to pick the berries when they were ripe. My brother, sister, and the neighbor children would get plastic mixing bowls from our kitchen, and then spend hours picking over the berries.

"There are snakes in there," some boy would inevitably say.

"How do you know?" I would ask, but I was so gullible that it wasn't hard for me to believe anything scary.

"Because that's snake food right there." There was an ominous-looking plant that grew near the berries. For years I thought it was poisonous, and that the name of the weed was "snake's food," just because the kids said so.

With our containers full of berries, we entered the kitchen through the back door and delivered them to Mom or Gran. My grandmother baked all kinds of delectable desserts. Gran always made an appropriate fuss with delight in receiving our backyard bounty. That was enough satisfaction for me. I never ate the blackberry pies she made—too many little seeds in the berries for me. My favorite was her homemade fudge, made with cocoa the color of my own skin, a delicacy I loved so much that I came to the conclusion that a person hadn't really lived unless one had had the pleasure of devouring Gran's chocolate fudge, warm, right out of the oven.

Our house and our yard were high up from the street. Up the six steps from the sidewalk and back toward the end of the front lawn was a fish pond. Surrounded by landscaping of boulders and stones in the front, ferns and ivy on the sides, and taller rhododendrons in back, the shallow pond could have made a nice kiddie pool for summer splashing, but Daddy took pride in the elegant ambiance the pond lent to the expansive yard, and didn't want us "young'uns" messing it up. He suggested instead that we run through the sprinklers, which were scattered below ground throughout the yard. Operated by a timer system, the sprinklers often came on without warning while we were playing in the yard, drenching us and causing us to squeal with delight as we scattered.

But the pond remained taboo. As an attorney, Daddy was mindful that someone might fall in the pond and sue us.

"Someone might get hurt in there," he told us when we begged to have a pool party in the pond.

But that didn't keep other kids out of it. One Sunday, when we returned from church, we found that all the fish in the pond were either missing or lying dead on the nearby grass. It seems that some boys in the neighborhood had dared one another to go fishing in the pond. The next day, Gran went off to Woolworth's and brought some goldfish home in a sealed plastic bag filled with water. She did this once a week until the pond was filled with fish again.

André and his friends stayed out of the pond. But not out of the trees.

"Do not climb that cherry tree, André," my mother admonished him when he was ten years old. "There are rotten limbs and if one of them breaks when you are on it, it will fall and you'll hurt yourself."

That's exactly what happened.

It was a beautiful summer day, but I couldn't go outside. I had the measles. Stuck in my bedroom, all I could do was gaze out the window to the backyard and watch André and his friends play. I was accustomed to hearing their "Bang! Bang! Bang!" noises, simulating shooting their toy guns while playing cowboys and Indians back there. Suffering miserably on my back with my malady, I occasionally heard, "Got ya! You're dead!" After a while, they quieted down. I stopped hearing anything, and went to sleep.

Because of the slope of the yard, there were stone steps leading up from the level of the fish pond beside the house to the yard behind it. About twenty feet beyond those steps were more stone stairs up to the alley level and garage. The cherry tree was to the right of the first set of steps. The boys, adventurous in their Davy Crockett imaginings, but knowing they were not supposed to be in the tree, climbed up silently so as not to attract the attention of my mother. They climbed up to branches as tall as my second-story bedroom window to get their "treasures"—the cherries, which were red, ripe, and juicy. André climbed highest, spied the ones he wanted on the end of a branch, and crawled out onto the limb. *Crack!*

Falling two storys, he hit the ground, teeth first on the stone steps.

Several kids had been playing in the tree with him, but when he fell, they all scattered, except one. Clyde, the son of family friends, who lived farther away than the others, was the only person who stayed to aid André. The other kids, knowing that Mom had told them not to climb the tree, split.

Clyde came inside and found my mother, who had been cleaning the house. She followed him outside and to her shock, found André facedown on the stone with his front teeth pushed up into his head.

Trying to keep herself and her son calm, she rushed him into the car, and on to the hospital emergency room, where he was ushered into oral surgery.

I heard all the commotion afterward, but did not see any of it when it happened, because I had been in bed asleep at the moment he fell. A week or two after the accident, our family prepared to drive cross-country to New York for a Links convention. Vicki arrived from Los

Angeles to spend her summer with us, and we all got ready for the big trip. That is, everyone but André. He had to stay home to go to the dentist. It was the start of many years of dentistry to cap the lost teeth and repair the damage from the fall. It was his turn to stay home with Gran. We were sad to leave him behind, but happy that he was alive.

In that house, 1615, my parents taught me to read and write. I couldn't wait to go to school like André and Vicki did. My grandmother took care of me during the day, and we often went either to one of her many club meetings or downtown to Woolworth's. Unlike in the south, we could eat at the lunch counter, and we did. Then it was our habit to go downstairs to the toy department to look at the dolls. I would see one I liked, and then Gran would tell me how much it was. The next day at breakfast, she would prompt me to tell my father how much the doll had cost, and after he gave her the money, Gran and I would return on the bus to purchase the doll.

Eventually, I turned five years old, and was able to go to school like the big kids. This was the best day of my life thus far. On the first day of school, Daddy accompanied me to Madrona Elementary. I thought it was the normal custom for children to be taken to school their first day of kindergarten by their fathers. No one had told me differently. I didn't realize until later that my mother could not take me and also be on time to greet the students of her own class.

Daddy and I had planned this for months. As diligently as studying for the SAT, I was prepped on how to write the entire alphabet in capital letters, and three words that Daddy had told me were critical for kindergarten admission: DOG, CAT, and STEPHANIE. On the first day of school, I was nervous about having to write my name because my siblings teased me about writing the P backward. They said it might have something to do with the fact that I was left-handed. When I got to Mrs. Foley's class, however, I was amazed to find out that very few students knew how to write their ABCs, much less their name, or to spell "dog" or "cat." Dad had fooled me again!

The first couple of years, my grandmother came to pick me up from school. Then she allowed me to walk home with other children.

Eventually, I was allowed to go home alone. Gran waited on our high front porch to watch me come into view as I turned the corner from the busy main road to walk the two short blocks down our side street.

That was the case one day when the weatherman had predicted rain to begin by the afternoon. Like most folks in the Pacific northwest, I had my share of rain paraphernalia. Determined to have me well dressed even in the rain, Mom bought me a raincoat in her favorite color, yellow, with a matching hat that I wore flipped up in the front and cocked to the side. It hung long in the back to allow the rain to drip down the back of my coat without getting my neck wet. The coat had three metal closures that snapped shut, and I played with them— *open, snap shut, open, snap shut*—every time I wore the thing. On this day, I couldn't find my matching umbrella for some reason, and my mother allowed me to take her fancy parasol. It had a curved handle like a cane that Mom said was made of bone. The off-white fabric featured a red apple motif. The umbrella was more than half as tall as I was.

I left school with my report card, which I held in my hand. I wanted to hand those good grades to Gran as soon as I hit the door. Instead, a storm hit me. As I turned down my street, the rain that had begun as a drizzle was now pouring cats and dogs. Then the wind picked up and my eyes began to water. Since I looked like I was crying, I let loose and started crying for real.

"Mommy! Gran! Mommy! Gran! Daddy!"

The wind began to whistle and I felt a push from behind as though the hand of Paul Bunyan was on my back, but I knew no one was there. The wind increased and I was forced to walk faster and faster. Soon I couldn't walk at all, and I was running against my will. Then, when I could not outrun the wind, it swept me up into the air. Like a tumbleweed, I was airborne, over the side of the nearby house, and—plop!— I landed in the midst of some squawking geese in the backyard.

I don't know how Gran found me. Maybe she came looking for me when the storm accelerated. But I figure that my big mouth was heard two blocks away.

She gathered me up and took me home to nurse a sprained elbow that had to be placed on a pillow for several days of missed school. My aunt Katie, who was a nurse, stopped by frequently to check on me. My new rain clothes were a mess, one of my red rubber boots was ruined, and to my mother's chagrin, her nice umbrella had turned inside out and blown away, never to be found. But in my hand was the prized—though battered, drenched, and torn up—straight-A report card.

In years to come, I would remember being picked up by a gargan-tuan wind. Each time I recalled it, the tale would grow as mighty as the storm had, until I began to feel that on that day, though ever so briefly, God had enabled me to fly like a bird in the sky.

My neighborhood was full of children. Across the street were Rexy and Wilhemina, in whose one-story home I loved to play "elevator" in their sliding door closets. Down on the corner was André's friend Timothy, who came over for breakfast every day, after he had already eaten his own mother's cooking. Behind us was the Young family, which had four girls, so it was always fun to play at their big house. A few doors down from them was my surrogate big sister when my own wasn't around, Olivia Gayle. Farther down on the corner and across the street, my ace-boon-coon at school, Juanita, lived with her grandparents, Mr. and Mrs. Glass.

Mrs. Glass took Juanita to school every day, and on her way she would toot her horn in front of our house to see if I was ready. Juanita was a beautiful child, whom adults adored, with round, brown eyes, and a shy, quick smile. Half black and half Native American, she was fair-skinned with freckles. The feature that garnered the most attention was her super-thick, jet-black hair, which her grandmother kept in two, sometimes three braids as big as the circle made by an adult thumb and forefinger. The braids hung down her back, almost to her waist, and Juanita got stares wherever she went, which she totally ignored. Everyone made much more fuss about her hair than she ever made herself. I always liked being at her house when her grandmother took out the braids to wash her hair. Amazed, I would just observe the process of the combing of her healthy, generous tresses. I always wanted to ask if I could comb and brush them, as we did with our dolls, but I wouldn't dare.

Juanita's father and mother lived in Los Angeles. When she turned eleven, probably because it was the age at which she could stay home by herself after school, they took her back. After going to visit her once, I never saw her again. But before our painful separation, Juanita was my around-the-corner neighbor and classmate, cared for by her loving grandfather, who was wheelchair-bound from polio, and her grandmother, who did all the driving. Often, they would take me with them to keep Juanita company in the backseat of their old, green car when Mrs. Glass took her husband on long Sunday drives to the outskirts of town.

In their family room, Mr. Glass liked to see how well I could read when we were learning to do so at Madrona Elementary.

"Stephanie, what does this say?" he'd ask, pointing out a comic strip title in the newspaper.

To see better, Juanita and I leaned over his shoulder as he was seated in his wooden wheelchair, the one he used indoors, which looked like a regular chair with wheels.

"Mis . . . ter . . . A . . . ber . . . naa . . . thee," I said, sounding out the syllables, as Mrs. Woods, our teacher, had taught us. "Mister . . . Abernathy!"

"That's right!" he said. "You are one smart little colored child!" And I would walk off beaming.

Several times a year, Juanita's parents came to visit, sometimes together, sometimes separately. Her mom, a Native American, was taller and more full-bodied than her father. She had a hearty laugh, and didn't mind playing rough and tumble with Juanita. One afternoon, I went to Juanita's house when her mother was there, and just stood in the doorway of her bedroom watching the fun as she and her mother had a pillow fight.

In those days of the early 1960s, colored folks were always claiming to be "part Indian." Some were, and some weren't. But, Juanita really was half Native American. There was no denying that. At age nine, I didn't know why people thought it was cool to have Native American blood. I didn't yet realize that the collective self-esteem of Negroes was so low that the idea of being mixed made some folks feel better about themselves. If you were dark-skinned, you might not be believed if you said you were mixed with white, but just about anyone could get away with saying they were "part Indian." Of course, there were plenty of people who could have claimed reservation rights because of their mixed heritage, but I never saw the Native American relative of any black person except Juanita.

When I observed all the fun that Juanita had with her mother, I thought the reason people wanted to be part Native American was that it was just plain more fun. So I left Juanita playing on the bed giggling her head off with her exotic-looking mother, who, unlike mine, didn't mind getting mussed up and whopped with a pillow.

I walked across the street, trudged down the steep hill on Olive Street, and made my way into my house. My mother was cooking dinner.

"Mom," I said. "Are we part Indian?"

"Why do you ask?" she replied.

"I just wonder if we have any Indian in us, like Juanita does."

My mother didn't look up from the chicken she was cleaning at the sink, but she spoke deliberately. "No, we are pure Negro."

I was so disappointed, I wanted to cry. No, worse, I wanted to run away. Why couldn't we be Indians, and have as much fun as Juanita and her mom? Maybe if we were at least part Indian, we could have pillow fights and tickling fits. My parents often seemed too serious, and being "pure Negro" must have been the cause.

In an attempt to make my mother think that I had run away at the indignity of it all, I ran outside. Instead of going down the front steps, however, I stood off to the side of the door on the end of the porch, where, if anyone looked out the window of the door, they wouldn't see me. I stood there for about twenty minutes, waiting for my mother to come out crying, calling my name, and looking for me, like Donna Reed or one of those other TV mothers might do. It began to get dark. I was supposed to be in the house whenever I saw the streetlights come on. They flashed on, but I didn't budge. No one came to the door either. Not Mom, not even André. Daddy wasn't home from work yet. Surely, he would drive in the garage, come into the kitchen through the back door, and ask Mom where I was. Half an hour went by. No one came outside. I started to get cold and hungry. Ready for that chicken I could smell Mom frying, I eased the door open.

Still in the kitchen, busy with her dinner, Mom paid me no attention. She hadn't even noticed that I had run away.

Fast forward about twenty-five years. My mother and I are visiting Washington, D.C., and looking for gifts in a bookstore. I say to her, "Mom, I'm going to get this book called *Black Indians* for Reggie." Reggie is my husband, who really does have a Native American great-grandmother, whose picture hangs in our home.

"Let's see," Mom asks, and gazes at the cover. "Did I ever tell you that my mother's father was an Indian?"

"What do you mean?" I ask incredulously. "I remember that when I was nine, you said that we were 'pure Negro.' "

"Oh, did I?" she replies nonchalantly, going back to her browsing.

"Yes, you did. Why did you do that if your own grandfather was Native American?"

"I just wanted you to be proud of being a Negro," she says. "I didn't want you to get your self-pride or identity from saying that you were mixed with anything else, like a lot of people were doing at the time."

And to think, I almost ran away from home for nothing.

When Daddy arrived in the early 1940s, there were about 5,000 African-American Seattleites. In the next fifty years, the number would reach about 50,000, or just under ten percent of the population. These numbers may not seem great, but among cities with a population over 500,000, Seattle consistently ranked higher in black population than every west coast city except Los Angeles. In the United States in general, the percentage hovered around ten percent, so we felt that the racial mix in Seattle, particularly in our Central District, was a microcosm of our numbers in our country.

In the 1950s and 1960s, the black population of Seattle was growing fast. Two of the major issues my father worked on as a state representative were the passage of the Fair Employment Practices Act (FEPC) and legislation for what was called "fair housing." To counter notions of blacks taking jobs away from whites, civil rights activists said that people just needed to treat everyone fairly. Similarly, it was only fair that Negroes should be able to live anywhere they could buy a home.

In 1961, the movie version of Lorraine Hansberry's award-winning play "A Raisin in the Sun" was released. The movie, starring Sydney Poitier, Claudia McNeil, and Ruby Dee, made America aware of the feelings and motivations of African-Americans who tried to better their living conditions by moving from predominantly black inner cities into resistant, often racist, all-white suburbs.

That same year, feeling the momentum in housing integration growing, Daddy convinced my mother that we should move to a grander home in a more upscale neighborhood. He didn't try to move us to Broadmoor, an upper-crust white community enclosed within a stone wall, and guarded by a foreboding iron gate. If he had, it wouldn't have been far from the house we lived in. Located near the Madison Beach that we sometimes frequented, Broadmoor was a gated community that looked like a prison to me—one in which the people within the gates were kept away from us good people.

My parents didn't look at houses in Sandpoint either. It was another exclusive—and, in my puerile opinion, "silly lily"—white neighborhood, near the University of Washington. Some of my parents' friends were moving farther north to Bothell, Shoreline, and other white neighborhoods, and cross burnings on the lawns of Negroes who attempted to move in provided the lead stories of the evening news.

My mother had a strong opinion about not living where we were not wanted. And Dad wanted integration, but not animosity. It happened that he heard about a house in the nearby Mount Baker neighborhood that was in litigation from a foreclosure after the white husband and wife had died within a month of each other and had left no heirs. The home was a spacious five-bedroom on a private dead-end street with only one house next door. The well-to-do couple had lived there for many years, with a maid residing in the basement bedroom. High on a hill, with an ivy-covered cliff in place of a backyard, the house had a floor-to-ceiling picture window with an awesome 180-degree view of Lake Washington, the floating bridge over the lake that connected Seattle with the suburb of Mercer Island, the Cascade Mountains beyond that, and due south on a clear day, the majestic Mount Rainier.

My parents bought the house for a price they kept top-secret from us kids for decades. Before we moved in, my parents' good friend Mr. Merriweather, who was a Howard University–trained architect (and the father of the child who had done the good deed several years before of telling my mother that André had fallen out of the cherry tree), provided plans for the total renovation of the forty-year-old house to bring it up to ultra-modern standards. My mother secured the professional services of an interior designer named Mrs. Berteaux. I was fascinated to find Mrs. Berteaux even more prim and proper than my mother. Together, these two ladies decided that the exterior of the house should be transformed from beige to my mother's favorite, yellow. Every room inside was updated to the high standards of my mother's taste under Mrs. Berteaux's direction.

The area wasn't all-white, but it wasn't all-black either. It was proudly mixed with white, black, and Asian. There were some citizens of Seattle who took pride in the city's gains in racial tolerance and equality. Many boasted that Seattle was the largest city in the nation to integrate its public schools without a federal court order.

The home at the entrance to our dead-end street was occupied by a pleasant Japanese family. There was a wealthy Italian family with a pool, which was a rarity in our foggy, rainy town. Another family across the street was Jewish. I enjoyed playing with their daughters, Stella and Bella, who were near my age.

The house closest to us was similar in architecture, size, and stature, and in it resided a childless Caucasian couple with the woman's elderly mother. The man and his mother-in-law were usually polite, if not cordial. But I got the impression that the woman of the house felt that it was beneath her to have a black family living next door. I also felt that she resented the fact that these were not poor Negroes, but a household that might even have a net worth that equaled her own. She took every opportunity to remind us that she was better than us.

She often ignored the pleasant greetings of my mother, and argued incessantly with my father over piddly little things. Ringing our door-bell whenever she pleased, she would ask us to do this, or move that, or just inform us about the country club she and her husband had joined. Like Mrs. Kravitz, the nosy neighbor on TV's "Bewitched," she was always looking beyond my mother at the door to see into our house. My mother invited her in on several occasions, and she always accepted, although she never once invited us into her house.

To the neighbor's credit, sometimes she showed efforts to make peace—however patronizing. At Christmastime it became her habit to leave on our porch a huge box full of unwrapped merchandise (none of which was marked to be given to any one of us in particular, and most of which we couldn't use) that was obviously castoffs from her own house.

My mother, whose habit it was to overlook the faults of just about anyone to whom she was not related, graciously returned the favor by presenting the family with monogrammed hand towels one year, gold tree ornaments the next—that kind of thing.

As for me, when I was twelve years old, I forgave the woman all her indiscretions and eccentricities when to my surprise I pulled out of the Christmas box a pair of costly, white leather, lace-up, high-top shoe-skates. It was an odd gift, and we weren't quite sure what to make of it. But my parents felt it would be rude not to accept her presents, whether useless or extravagant. Some we gave to charity. But I kept this one and never had to rent skates at the roller rink from then on.

Daddy named the house "Stokes Rest" against the wishes of the rest of us. To us, it seemed more corny than catchy, and we kids weren't into resting. On one of our car trips, at a souvenir outpost in Wyoming, or South Dakota, or one of those states we saw on TV westerns, Dad had a thick, wooden sign custom made and engraved with the name "Stokes Rest." It looked like the kind of sign you'd hang at the entry to the "Bonanza" ranch—not our city-slick house. But upon our return home, he pulled out the ladder and hung it up over the garage door, which was the first part of the house anyone could see when coming down our drive. We silently stood watching, shaking our heads and rolling our eyes. We had zero appreciation for "Stokes Rest." But for Daddy, the sign symbolized the culmination of his lifelong hard work. Each night that he came home from the office and sat down in his favorite black leather chair to gaze out of his picture window at the full moon luminous over the gentle lake, he was at rest.

For me, our move brought a bit of unrest. In my new school, I was the only black child in my fourth-grade class.

There is a photograph of my fourth-grade class in front of our portable, or modular, classroom. The school population was growing faster than officials could enlarge the main building, so we had class in our own little building, one of four or five on the upper playground. In the picture, kids are swinging from the poles on the porch. It shows that although I am the only black child, I am not the only person of color. There are Filipino, Japanese, and Mexican children, as well. The problem was not the students. Kids, when left without the prejudicial influences of adults, will get along with children of other races. As a matter of fact, I was relieved that the children did not seem to be as mean to me, or as bad in class, as the ones in my previous school.

It was the teachers that I had to adjust to. I had gotten along fine with the white teachers at the grade school I had attended since kindergarten. And my first-grade teacher had been my mother's kindly friend Mrs. Woods, whom I also saw at church on Sundays. At Madrona I had become accustomed to straight-A report cards. But in this school, all of a sudden, my grades included C's. I didn't feel that the work was more difficult. It just seemed harder to please my teacher, who was white and male. It was the first time I had had a man for a schoolteacher, and although he wasn't out-and-out mean to me, he obviously didn't think I qualified for the "teacher's pet" position I admit I was used to. My grades plummeted, and my self-esteem threatened to go along with them. But after a parent-teacher conference between Mr. R. and my mother, I noticed a slight change in his regard for me. A few more B's began to appear on my papers and report cards.

Although the majority of students were white, I never felt out of place. In fact, by the next year, I had a white boyfriend.

This was not an issue among the students. All the girls in the class had white boyfriends. For a fifth-grader, a "boyfriend" is someone who passes you notes in class, always chooses you for his square dance partner, or who gets mad at other boys if they hit you too hard playing dodge ball at recess. If his parents let him use the phone, he might even call you after school.

My crush, a sandy-haired son of a policeman and a housewife, lived near school, so he couldn't walk me all the way home. But he did invite me to stay after school one day to watch him at baseball practice. I immediately told "my girls" in class, and we made plans to hang around the playground when school let out instead of going right home.

Our teacher, who told us she was twenty-six, was pregnant, pretty, and adored by all the students, including me. But she evidently was not ready for an interracial case of puppy love.

In class, she was always nice to me, and treated me as well as she did anyone else. My grades were good—not back to all A's, but she graded me higher than the male teacher had the year before. I won the class spelling bee, and she seemed to be impressed by that and allowed me to be a class monitor, a coveted job that involved helping her clean erasers and allowed me to get out of class by taking papers to the principal's office, or returning books to the library.

So my little feelings were hurt the evening she called the house and told my mother that I was being a bit too "fast" by staying after school to watch a certain boy at baseball practice. My mother lit into me, mainly because as a teacher, she sided with whatever any other teacher had to say. I'm sure she was probably also embarrassed that the teacher was calling about a relationship problem—not even an academic concern. For my part, I knew that I was not the first girl to stay after school and watch the boys, but I had never heard of her calling anyone else's house at eight p.m. to tell on them! At school the next day, I asked my boyfriend if she had called his house to tell his mother that he had invited me to stay after school. But he said no, she hadn't.

My mother was mad. My teacher was prejudiced. My boyfriend didn't think it was a good idea to "like" me anymore. And I felt I had no recourse but to pout about it all. My bottom lip was stuck out for the rest of the week.

I got over it when I met the brother of my new neighbor, Renee, who invited me to her house for her tenth birthday party. Cute didn't come with a color for me—no one had told me it should. White, black, Asian—a cute boy was a cute boy. They liked me, and I liked them. My mother called me "boy crazy." I hadn't met a boy of any race who had a prejudice problem like the adults did. You never knew when adults, with their funny ways, would cop an attitude. But I eventually got the message that black would be better. It would mean less headaches and confusion for me.

Butchie Miller was one of two black boys in my grade, though not in my class. With skin the color of caramel ice cream, he had brown curly hair, a wide smile, beautiful teeth, and the deepest voice I had ever heard on a child. Best of all, he lived two blocks from me, so I could get walked home from school every day.

No one seemed to mind if I had close relationships with white *girls,* however. The most popular person in my class was a tomboy. Her super-short haircut and athletic prowess gave her favor with the boys in our class. But she could also turn on the feminine charm and talk about Barbie dolls with the girls. The weekend of her birthday, which was near mine in January, I was flattered to be invited to her girls' sleepover, which followed the raucous daytime party at which she hosted only boys. This would be the first time I ever spent the night at a white person's house. There was lots of buzz about this between my parents, I noticed. The party had a theme, and we were asked to arrive in our mother's clothes to play "dress up" before we changed into our pajamas.

"Mom, what am I going to wear to the party?"

"How about my black and white polka-dotted dress?"

My jaw dropped. Since she had never allowed me to play in her clothes before, I had expected her to drag out some tired, old garment from the Salvation Army–ready box. Instead she offered a new, stylish spaghetti-strapped number. The dress was entirely too big for me, of course, but I was excited that she dressed me up in this semiformal, with its full skirt that hit below the knee on her, but fell to the ankles on me. With no bosom or bra to hold up the bodice, the chiffon just hung on my bare chest. But I arrived looking as good as or better than any other girl there.

"Wow, you really got dressed up!" my hostess exclaimed as she met me at the door, clearly impressed. I knew she would notice. Ever since the first time she came to my house to play after school and my mother gave her a ride home, she was always teasing me about Mom, saying that she had never before seen a schoolteacher who wore designer clothes and drove a Cadillac. I always got her back by responding that before I met her, I had never known any family who were members of the elite Washington Athletic Club, which was reputed to exclude blacks.

Back at school one day we had a lesson in Social Studies that began as an intriguing exercise in learning. In an attempt to illustrate our country's motto of *E Pluribus Unum*—From Many, One—and explain that the heritage of all Americans originated from different countries, our teacher decided to lay down the textbook and use each student as a real-life example.

"If your ancestors came from England," she began, "please stand up and come to the blackboard." Several children rose from their desks and walked over toward her.

"If your last name is Swedish, come line up next to them," she continued. More students gleefully took their places in front of the class.

She went on with countries in Europe, then with the remaining third of the class she walked around the rows of our wooden desks and put her hand on top of heads, saying, "You are from Japan." "You are from China." "Ben is from Mexico." "These two are from the Philippines."

The children were lined up in groups against the walls going all the way around the classroom. Eventually, I was the only one left in my seat.

I was patient with excitement, because I believed teachers had infinite wisdom. Soon this woman was going to tell me what nobody else ever had. From what country had my ancestors originated? Surely, she had saved the best for last.

"Stephanie," she turned to me and began to speak more slowly, lowering her voice. The room got quiet. All eyes were on me now. "I am sorry to tell you that you are from Africa."

"Oh, shucks!" I muttered, with a snap of my finger, not knowing what else to say or do besides get a laugh from my classmates. It hadn't been *what* she said but *how* she said it that had disappointed me and made me feel ashamed. After observing the exuberance with which she had called out the other kids' family origins, I'd been anticipating somewhere wonderful like Timbuktu or Nubia. But although what she said was technically true, the tone of her voice and the snickering of the students reinforced her bigotry and my humiliation.

I began to learn that there were differences not only between blacks and whites but also between whites and whites—or, as we Negroes called them then, Caucasians. For example, at my house, we ate pork chops, pork sausage, ham, and good ol' bacon, my favorite meat. Since I saw Jimmy Dean on TV talking about his tasty sausage, I assumed all white folks ate breakfast links like we did. So when I invited two of my Jewish classmates, Leslie and Diane, to spend the night, I thought it was extraordinarily nice that my mother allowed us to eat in the dining room, but I had no idea that the breakfast she served of grits, eggs, biscuits, bacon, and sausage would become an issue for my guests.

"If we eat this, we could drop dead right here," declared Leslie, the beautiful brunette who was my best school friend, as she gazed at the platter of bacon and sausage.

"What are you talking about?" I asked, thinking she was joking around. "My mother's cooking is better than the food in the school's cafeteria, and you're not dead yet."

"Oh, I'm sure it's delicious. It looks good . . ." Then she hesitated, and started again, more carefully. "The grits look yummy. I've never had them, but I'm willing to try . . ."

"I haven't had them either, but I'm going to eat them too," agreed freckled-faced Diane, whose hair was red, short, and curly. She noticed that I dumped a dollop of butter on my grits and she followed suit.

"I had never eaten matzoh before I had it at your house," I volunteered. "I like it almost as much as regular crackers, now."

"But this is different, Steph," Leslie whispered, so my mother in the kitchen wouldn't hear. "It's against our *religion* to eat pork."

"I think it could kill us," Diane volunteered.

"Really?" I looked at Leslie and she seemed serious. I turned to Diane, and she was pondering her fate as well.

"Yes, and if we chose to eat it and it didn't kill us, our mothers would!" Leslie said. And then she and Diane burst out laughing.

"Yeah, my mother would definitely kill me if she even *thought* I had eaten pork," Diane said.

"I wonder what it tastes like, though," Leslie's deep brown eyes came to life under her fabulously thick lashes, as they always did when we were about to get into some trouble.

"You think it would make us sick to just taste it this once?" Diane asked. "I always wondered what bacon tasted like. I can't believe everyone eats it but us."

"Yeah, and nobody else dies," I said, trying to be helpful. I thought they were missing out on one of the fun foods of life. Was it really all that different from the beef jerky we always bought at the store after school?

My mother entered the room and called my father, who was on the enclosed deck reading his newspaper, to join us.

"Why aren't you eating?" Mom asked. "Is everything okay?"

"Mom, Jews don't eat sausage," I said authoritatively, as though I had always known what I just found out a few seconds before. Could it be that there was actually something about the world that had eluded my mother's knowledge?

"Oh, you don't have to eat it," she said quickly, with a wave of her hand and a shake of her head. Then I couldn't tell if she had known but had served it for my father and me, if she had forgotten that Jews don't eat pork, or if she really didn't know but wasn't about to admit it.

"We're sorry, Mrs. Stokes," Leslie said.

"No apology necessary," Mom said, and smiled. "Charles, please bless the food, so these girls can eat."

·   ·   ·

It was 1963, a hundred years after the Emancipation Proclamation, and the year seemed full of promise. My white friends and I felt we were doing our part to improve race relations by forging genuine friend-ships, characterized by the warm welcome I was given in their homes and that they were extended in mine. Similar in nature were my rela-tionships with the Asian girls in my class and neighborhood, such as Wendy and Elaine. We all just got along without much thought about race. What we had in common was that we were girls the same age. What all the racial hatred was about in the world was beyond us.

But we were aware that we were living in confusing, often danger-ous times, in which some people still didn't want "black and white together," as one stanza of the song "We Shall Overcome" expressed. Down south seemed like a different country, yet we were all affected when in September of that year the television news announced that four little girls had been killed in a bombing of the Sixteenth Street Baptist Church in Birmingham.

In one of the most shocking crimes of the civil rights era, three of the girls killed were fourteen years old—Cynthia Wesley, Carole Robert-son, and Addie Mae Collins. The youngest, Denise McNair, at eleven, was the same age as my friends and me.

It is less widely known that two black teen boys, Johnny Robinson, sixteen, and Virgil Ware, thirteen, were shot and killed by police in the subsequent uprising.

My mother, an Alabama native, had relatives in Birmingham, with whom she had often spent summers away from her home in Selma as an adolescent. She knew that church well; her great-aunt and her family were members. Desperately hoping they had not gone to the church they attended every Sunday, Mom called Aunt Dickerson and her daughters right away. They said they were getting dressed for church at the time, and assured her they were okay. We were relieved and grateful. But the horrendous and violent measures that it seemed some people resorted to, all because of the gains of integration, made us uneasy. Could anyone feel absolutely safe anywhere if children in church—one tying the sash of another during Sunday School—could be bombed to death?

= 9 =

Let Mount Zion Rejoice

IN MY HALF CENTURY on the planet, I have been blessed to be able to see quite a bit of it. I haven't made it to Bethlehem, Jerusalem, or Nazareth yet, but I have taken a boat down the Nile in Egypt, and have set foot on ground as far north as Greenland and as far south as Cape Town. And even though I have lived for most of my adult life on the other side of the continent from Seattle, there is no place I have found that is more religious, no place that warms my heart and feeds my soul more, than Mount Zion Baptist Church. Until the day that I walk where Jesus walked, that church, on the corner of Nineteenth and Madison in Seattle, will remain the "holy land" for me.

ABOVE: *At age four, with my grandmother,*
Flossie Levingston (behind me), and the ladies of her church circle.

Erected in 1890 by the first African-American pioneers who professed the Baptist faith, by the middle of the following century, Mount Zion was a grand, magnificent presence in the Central District of the city. The church was a towering brick structure with an outside staircase that made you feel you were already on the way to heaven before entering the building. It was like climbing Jacob's Ladder just to get to the front entrance.

The organ, with its robust sound, majestic chimes, and triple tier keyboard, could rival any in the white churches. Weddings were lovely occasions there, and the accompanying receptions were always held in the spacious church basement.

As the largest black congregation in Seattle, the church membership numbered about 2,000, and included the well-to-do, the not-doing-so-well, and those in the middle. Here, the woman who cleaned houses for a living could be president of the usher board. Here, the man who had a blue-collar job during the week could wear the white-shirt-and-tie uniform of the deacon board on Sunday.

Someone could be famous there too. People could have entire reputations and notable achievements built at church that no one in the outside world knew about.

Zeofious Cook, better known by the adults as Cookie, was well known among Mount Zionites for her solo rendition of "God Is." Her main competition for most popular soloist was her own sister, Susie Brooks. Whenever Susie sang the song about being "somewhere listening for my name," even the youngest worshippers would stop fidgeting long enough to nod their heads to the beat. The toe-tapping of the men in unison could be heard as Susie's soprano voice filled the sanctuary: "When He calls me, I will answer . . . I'll be somewhere, listening for my name . . . my name . . ."

"Sister Susie, you *sure* can sing that song! You just remember when I'm gone to sing it for me!" Daddy said to her one Sunday after the service. To say you wanted someone to sing at your funeral was the highest form of compliment. I, too, loved to hear her sing that song, but being a child, I was too shy to tell her so. I just stood there with him, hoping I looked earnest enough to let her know that Daddy was speaking for me too. She smiled graciously and deflected the compliment away from herself by saying, "Oh Stokey, you're going to outlive all of us!"

Mount Zion Baptist Church is where both sides of my family came together. And now, five generations have worshipped there. In 1943, after my father arrived in Seattle, and before he bought a home, he found a church home at Mount Zion. My maternal grandmother, Flossie Johnson Stratman, arrived from Selma, Alabama, around the same time as my father. She, too, was starting a new life. As soon as she arrived in Seattle, she joined Mount Zion.

In 1947, my mother graduated from college, moved to Seattle, and followed her mother and her older sister, Katie Mae, to their family's new church. Josephine quickly signed up for the Senior Choir, the one known for its beautiful harmony in performing spirituals and anthems, as opposed to the rollicking Gospel Choir, which really wasn't her style. Much like the Fisk University Jubilee Singers, which toured the world at the turn of the twentieth century, Mount Zion's Sanctuary Choir, under the directorship of Kenneth Stovall, was known throughout Seattle. When they made a 78 RPM record to raise funds for the church, my mother was the soloist on the spiritual "Listen to the Lambs."

In March of 1951, the *Seattle Times* ran a story that said: "Attorney Charles M. Stokes, Seattle's Republican Negro state legislator, sat in the congregation of Mount Zion Baptist Church. Josephine Stratman sang in the choir. He saw her, liked what he saw, and they were married."

This article, already a yellowing and fading newspaper clipping prominently displayed in our family album by the time I was old enough to read, had a picture of the happy couple with my brother, André, a month short of three years old, laughing between them.

The wedding took place at Gran's house. Following the strict protocol of the day, my parents did not marry in the church because it was the second marriage for both. But it was clear that Mount Zion was not only the guiding religious force for my father, my mother, my grandmother, my aunt, and practically everyone I knew in my neighborhood, but that it was also a good place to meet a mate.

.   .   .

Many of my parents' fellow church members are deceased now. But the man who had been the young pastor of Mount Zion in the 1940s was given the blessing of longevity. On the first sunny day in April 2003, I gathered my courage and called a phone number my mother had given me. It was the Indianapolis home number of Rev. F. Benjamin Davis.

The phone rang several times, and I was about to hang up when I realized someone had picked up. There was a long pause before I heard the voice.

"Hello?" I said first, and then was instantly ashamed that I hadn't given the man who was obviously elderly more time to adjust his receiver.

"Yes?" the answer came.

"Oh, hello. Have I reached Reverend Davis?" I asked, although I immediately recognized the deep timbre of his voice. I tried to put an enthusiastic tone to my voice, so that he would know it was a friend. Actually, I had reached him a couple of months before and had hinted that I wanted to fly from my home in New Jersey to Indianapolis to interview him, but he had politely discouraged me, saying he would be busy with his duties as pastor of Bethel Baptist, where he was still the minister at age ninety. I told my mother I wasn't sure he had remembered me, and I started not to call back, but in the meantime Mom had called him herself and then encouraged me to try him again by phone.

"Yes, you have," he responded. The voice was slow and guarded.

He had been away from Seattle's Mount Zion church for almost fifty years, and I had been just a toddler when he left to return to his hometown church in Indianapolis. So I couldn't blame him if he didn't remember me. Yet, I knew him because he was a favorite and legendary preacher in our family's history. He had come back to Seattle to preach many times as I was growing up. When our family drove across country for a Republican convention once, we stopped at his home, worshipped at his church, and visited with him and his lovely wife. I had always liked the fact that his wife was so dark skinned at a time when men of his stature often chose the lightest women they could find. I recalled the reverend as a tall, medium brown–toned man with wavy hair and sparkling eyes that made his face both handsome and charismatic. His dimpled smile revealed a slight gap between the front teeth that gave him a boyish charm.

I introduced myself and mentioned my mother's call and that I was working on a memoir about my father. This time he responded more warmly, asking about my mother and saying that my father was a person who greatly deserved to be remembered in a book.

My mother had told me that one of the first sermons she had heard Rev. Davis preach when she arrived in town had been called "Following the Snowplow." At the time, she hadn't met my father yet, but she recalled that the sermon was inspired by the trip from Seattle to Kansas Rev. Davis had taken with my father to the 1949 funeral of my grandfather, Rev. N. J. Stokes. This piece of information gave me the impression that he must have known my father and grandfather well. I asked him about that.

"I knew your grandfather long before I moved to Seattle at the end of World War II," he explained. "We were in the state Baptist convention together. I was a pastor in Ottawa, Kansas, before going to Seattle."

Then he added something that I had never heard before. "Your father decided to come out to Seattle after I gave a message in Ottawa and said, 'Ethiopia should stretch forth your hands under God.' And that inspired him to go to Seattle."

At that time, blacks around the world identified with the Biblical Ethiopians, or African peoples. Haile Selassie was the popular emperor of Ethiopia who claimed to be a direct descendant of King Solomon and the Queen of Sheba. He was admired by African-Americans for his suppression of slavery in Ethiopia, and for his Pan-African initiatives against oppression and poverty on the continent. A slight, delicate, fair-skinned man with a receding hairline and bright eyes, Selassie had visited Seattle once, and my mother says she and Daddy were among those who hosted him. Selassie's handshake was one Mom never forgot. "He had the softest hands I had ever touched on a man," she recalled.

Those were the types of experiences moving to Seattle gave both my parents. Rev. Davis said he also found the Pacific northwest to be a place of opportunity.

"I ran for office the year before your father did to show black folks they could do it," he told me. I replied that I heard he had run for Washington state representative before my father had, and I complimented him on being a trailblazer. "I ran and got nominated, but I didn't want the office. As the pastor of Mount Zion, I was there to lead the church. But at the end of the war, blacks were getting out of the service and coming to the Seattle area. My basement was open to servicemen who needed a place to stay until they could get established. I was inspiring them to be involved in politics if they were going to stay. After I ran, I said to your father that he should do it."

I heard him laugh when he recalled that my father had not wanted to run for office. I was glad that he seemed to start to enjoy reminiscing.

"Why did you think he should be the one to run?" I asked.

"He had political experience in Kansas," he said a bit impatiently, as though the answer should have been obvious to me. "He was a lawyer, so he could talk well and put his point across. But when I told him to run, he said, 'Oh, I don't think we could make it.' So then I ran and got nominated, and didn't want it. So he said to me, 'If you can get that close maybe we *can* make it.' And he did."

I thanked Rev. Davis for being a mentor to my father. He brushed off the compliment and continued talking about Daddy. "He made an outstanding contribution."

Before I hung up, I wanted to know if he remembered traveling by car the 3,600-mile roundtrip to my grandfather's funeral in 1949 with my father and my father's friend from home, Philip Burton, who was also his Seattle law partner.

"Oh, yes," he said. "That was so many years ago . . . I would have to think for a minute." He paused only momentarily. "We rode in the car from Seattle to Kansas. When we left and were on our way back, we hit a snowstorm. It was so bad that we had to pull under a shelter, and we had to stay there until the next day. But then, although the snow had stopped, it had accumulated so high that we couldn't get out until the snowplow came. So I preached about following the snowplow. By that I meant following God. We couldn't get out by ourselves. We couldn't get through without the plow to dig us out. Then we followed the plow a long way. . . . Let's see, we went from Route 75 to 30 to Grand Island, then up to Seattle."

While he was trying to figure out if they had gone through one of the Dakotas, I clicked online to MapQuest and found that Grand Island was indeed a city on Highway 30 in Nebraska, the state just north of Kansas. His mind was still pretty sharp, I noted. I'd never heard of Grand Island, which happened to be the fourth largest city in the state.

"But we couldn't go anywhere until they cleared the road," he continued. "In life, we want to go places but we are blocked. So we have to stand by the road and wait for God to help us."

I got the message. I thanked him for it, for his time with me on the phone, and for his spiritual influence on our family.

A warm feeling came over me as this special elder—who, half a century before, had inspired my father to take two life-changing risks, had attended my paternal grandfather's funeral before I was born, had married my maternal grandmother and her second husband, had performed the wedding of my parents, and later christened me as a baby—spoke words of blessing to me now as we hung up. "May the Lord bless you and keep you."

I thanked him and prayed that God would do the same for him.

That month, he celebrated his ninety-first birthday. The month after that, in May of 2003, the current minister of Mount Zion, Rev. Leslie Braxton, and several members of the church flew to Indianapolis for the funeral of the good reverend.

Rev. Davis had mentioned that his contribution to Mount Zion had been to make it a family-oriented church, with emphasis "not on the individual, or just on the church itself," but on family members worshipping together and passing down through generations the traditions of the church.

He certainly succeeded with the Stokes family. My parents believed the creed that "the family that prayed together stayed together." Daddy always chose for us to sit on the far right end of the first row of the middle section under the balcony. Seated between my parents, I was not allowed any squirming. I was taught from the beginning that during church service, there may be times when the minister would lead the congregation to let out a laugh, but generally we were not there to play. Banishment to the church nursery was the punishment for repeat offenders. A child was never too young to be taught the appropriate, reverent behavior.

When hymns were sung, my mother's finger followed the words in the hymnal that I could not yet read. I was expected to pay attention and sing along if I knew the song. If I got bored during a sermon, I was allowed to fall over to the left to quietly nap on my mother's lap. If my mother was singing in the choir on a particular Sunday, I would lean to the right to hug up against my father's arm.

As my mother tells the story, at a very young age I could remain so still and quiet for the duration of the two-hour service that afterward people would ask, "Doesn't she speak?"

"Yes, she speaks, all right," Mom answered. "You should see her at home!"

It's true that I was never innately quiet or particularly shy, but I did learn from my parents at an early age that there was a time and place for everything. At church, talking and acting up was strictly forbidden, and I preferred my parents' approval to their ire. Plus, I always thought the drama in the arena before my eyes was more intriguing than anything I could cook up. Why fidget when the deaconess who usually shushed us at Sunday School was now in church "getting the spirit," shouting "Yes, Lord!" "Thank You, Lord!" and falling out in the front pew? Why holler when the preacher was already making more noise by the end of his sermon than my pipsqueak voice could ever summon? Their performance was accepted. Mine would not have been tolerated.

My mother allowed her children only three things in church: praying, singing, and sitting still. That was it. You couldn't clap; you didn't "get happy." André, Vicki, and I also learned tremendous bladder control, refraining from even *thinking* about going to the bathroom until the service was over. This behavior at church was one of the earliest things I learned. How disciplined one's children were reflected on the family. Even I knew which kids were prone to weekly misbehavior.

Our family's tradition of disciplined church children started with my grandmother. If we, her grandchildren, sat with her during the service, we knew that any infraction would risk us being whipped into shape—that is, with just a bat of her eye. It was just one of her many fine parenting skills that was passed down from generation to generation.

Around the time that Gran passed away, I was going into the second grade and was now old enough to attend and participate in Junior Church. This service, conducted in the sizable basement of the church directly under the sanctuary, duplicated the order of service for the adults, except the sermons were, thankfully, much shorter. There could easily be up to a hundred children in attendance on any given Sunday, sitting in the beige aluminum folding chairs, arranged with a center aisle, facing the stage. During Junior Church, the Children's Choir sat facing the other young worshippers, behind the assistant minister, who was assigned to preach to us. A few deacons and deaconesses sat or paced outside of the rows, silently watching each child's every move— that is, until someone misbehaved and needed a good talking to.

Like the adult service, Junior Church, for children ages five to fifteen, was considered worship, and pious behavior was expected at all times. We had our own printed programs that helped many a child learn to read. The service usually began with the choir marching out from the "choir room," which was actually just a storage area under the stairs, in their short blue cotton robes and satin over-the-head sashes, singing "All Hail the Power." Then a rotating group of children led the service, under the supervision of the adults, by reading Scripture or saying, "We will now have the Responsive Reading, found in the back of your hymnal."

My mother was the Children's Choir director for most of my childhood, and she enlisted André, Vicki, and me to sing every Sunday. I was taught to sing alto, she said, because I knew how to read music from my piano lessons, and could therefore provide the harmony that any decent church choir had to have. It just wasn't good enough to have all the kids singing in unison. Four-part harmony was the order of the day: The girls sang soprano and alto, and the boys sang tenor. Few of them were old enough for their voices to have changed, so some faked a deep bass. But we did sound good!

I particularly liked the song called "We Are Soldiers." It had a marching rhythm that would have been nice to clap along to if we had been allowed. But no clapping, or swaying, or moving at all was permitted. That all changed later when I became a teenager and moved upstairs to the Chapel Choir.

My mother had a very strong voice, and although she didn't mean to, she often drowned out us kids. My father enjoyed teasing her about this when he would come to visit Junior Church or when we would sing for all-choir concerts. "Jo, why don't you be quiet and let the kids sing?" he would ask with mischief in his eyes. She would just ignore him, and the next Sunday she would sing as loud as she pleased.

One Mother's Day, however, we were singing a song that began "M is for the million things she gave me." Mom began the song fortissimo as she always did. Then after a few bars, while staring down at my sheet music, I realized that my mother's voice was fading.

"O means only that she's growing old . . ." we continued, unaccustomed to actually carrying a tune.

I couldn't hear Mom at all, so I looked up from my front row position to her left and saw that she was still moving her hands to direct us, but her head was down and her mouth was closed.

"T is for the tears she shed to save me . . ."

And then I noticed a tear fall from my mother's eyes for the first time in my life. "H is for her heart of purest gold . . ."

Now, Mom was silently weeping.

"E is for her eyes with love light shining . . ."

Gran had died the June before of kidney failure in her late fifties, and this was Mom's first Mother's Day without her. At thirty-five years old, she was a mother who missed her own Mama. I saw her tears and began to cry myself. In the prism of my teardrops, her delicate brown hands moved in a blur of bright red nail polish.

Then Deacon Fleeks noticed that I was crying, since I was facing the kiddie congregation. When he realized that my mother, whose back was to the crowd, was no longer singing along, but that something was wrong, he tiptoed up to the stage. Gently and wordlessly, he led her to her chair behind the post. Joan Allen, the teenage pianist, kept playing. All choked up, the Junior Church Choir plodded through the song and sat down.

Mom took a lace-trimmed white handkerchief from her black patent-leather purse and pulled herself together quickly. But I never knew her to attend church on Mother's Day after that. Still heeding her mother's admonishment in her childhood that if you didn't go to church, you shouldn't go anywhere else that day, she was in a habit of attending service religiously, every Sunday. But on this day of each year, it just became too risky for her to think she might lose control of her emotions and weep again in church. Mother's Day took on new meaning as her annual day of rest.

The next February, my father was asked to deliver the Junior Church sermon for Negro History Week. I thought this was a splendid idea. Daddy was funny, never boring, and difficult to make fun of—unlike our regularly assigned minister, who was a kindly and lovely man, but whom we kids mocked mercilessly whenever his accent from who-knows-where prompted him to pronounce words like "childring" or "idear."

Since my mother was the choir director, my father was the guest speaker, and my brother and I were in the choir, I thought it would be a good Sunday to join the church. This meant that when it was time for us to sing the invitation, the song near the end of the service that encouraged you to give yourself to Jesus, I would do just that. The day before, at choir rehearsal, I told my neighbor Diane, who was also in the choir, that I was going to join church and that she should do it with me.

"You know, it's about time we joined," I told her. It was expected that sometime between age eight and age twelve, a child would be baptized by being submerged in the pool that was under the pulpit of the "big church" upstairs. When children joined the church, I noticed that their parents were usually quite happy, sometimes even crying tears of joy. Since both my parents would be participating in Junior Church, I thought this would be my big opportunity. I wouldn't have to join by walking up the aisle in the big church in front of all those intimidating grown-ups; I could do it here with my family to witness what the minister said would be the greatest decision of my life.

Dad had prepared his lesson using a thick, brown-jacketed book we had at home that was coauthored and autographed in dramatic penmanship by Langston Hughes. It was titled *A Pictorial History of the Negro in America.* In his sermon, Dad not only talked about how God leads African-Americans to achievements in slavery and in freedom, but showed pictures from the book of slave auction bills, runaway slave WANTED posters, and signs from segregated facilities. The children, who rarely learned anything about our people in school, were fascinated by the show-and-tell. And I was proud.

After Daddy's sermon, the young congregation began the song "I Surrender All." I could hear my mother's soprano over everyone else's, and during the chorus my father's baritone rose to sing the male refrain that was usually missing from the little kids' service. When we got to the second stanza, I put my hymnal down on my seat behind me and started walking to my right, to the steps on the end of the stage. As I passed Diane, I gave her a quick gesture with my right hand to motion to her that it was time to do our thing. She came as she had agreed, and we both approached Daddy and the two deacons, one on each side of him. With a handshake from each, I had officially made clear my intentions to join the church. Then Diane and I were led aside to a Sunday School classroom to get signed up and obtain instruction on how we should come for weekly baptismal classes for a month before the big day.

My parents were quite subdued about my actions. I thought maybe they would "get happy" or do *something* out of the ordinary, since this was supposed to be an extraordinary thing I had done. But they said little.

After we got home from church, my mother went into the kitchen to cook brunch. I changed into my playclothes and was about to go over to Diane's until time to eat, when Mom called me into the room.

"Why did you join church today, Stephanie?" she asked.

Quickly, I attempted to size up the situation. Was I in trouble? I couldn't detect her feelings, so I decided to try to make her laugh.

"Oh, I just thought it would be cool to be able to use the church envelopes to put my collection money in the plate, instead of having everyone see how much I put in," I mustered, looking down. My new, green corduroy tennis shoes never looked so interesting.

Mom ignored my feeble attempt at humor.

"Do you accept Jesus Christ as your Lord and Savior?"

She spoke evenly, without a hint of anger, joy, or presumption. It was just a straightforward question.

Avoiding her gaze, I glanced past her toward the back door that I wished I could run out of, and then my eyes shifted ever so slightly to the left, looking out the kitchen window, my sight settling on the swingset in the yard that I would rather be airborne on than standing there. I might have been embarrassed, but I knew Mom was not playing.

I nodded and replied in all honesty, "Uh-huh."

That seemed to satisfy her and I was allowed to leave.

A few weeks later, just before my solemn evening baptismal ceremony in the Mount Zion sanctuary, I stood in my best white, ruffled Sunday-go-to-meeting undies in the grown-ups' choir room as one of the deaconesses tucked my bangs into a white swim cap, then draped a white cloth around me. She gave me a hug and said I looked like an angel; I believed her and felt close to God. At that moment, I knew I was doing the right thing.

I was lined up with Diane and other children and adults ready to be baptized that winter night. Finally, it was my turn. As my parents lit a candle for me and the congregation sang "Take Me to the Water" in full a cappella harmony, our minister, Rev. Dr. Samuel Berry McKinney, prayed for me. Then he declared in his booming voice of authority, "I baptize you, Stephanie Jo Stokes, in the name of the Father, the Son, and the Holy Ghost."

For all of my young life, I had been so afraid of water that I'd never even put my head under in an attempt to swim before. But with my parents, my church family, and my pastor surrounding me in this most religious of moments, my fear vanished. I closed my eyes and held my breath. With the help of the assistant minister and with deacons standing by, Rev. McKinney held both my prayerfully clasped little hands in his left hand. Plunging me backward with his right hand around the back of my head and neck, he immersed me in the pool and just as quickly brought me back up.

I was baptized.

When I turned fourteen, my mother drafted me to play the piano for Junior Church. This weekly routine of choir rehearsal at ten a.m. on Saturday and then playing for the 10:45 service on Sunday morning became my first paying job. I was given a check for twenty dollars a month, nine months of the year. During the summer, after singing upstairs for the adults on Children's Day in June (usually the Sunday after school let out), there was no Junior Church, and I didn't get paid. But the twenty dollars I received was pretty generous for the mid-1960s. I could buy a mini-dress at Lerner's for $19.99 every month—or, I should say, every *other* month, because my mother made sure I deposited half the money in the bank.

The Junior Church service was shorter than the adult service upstairs, so we had plenty of time—often an hour, if they were serving Communion on First Sunday—to play while waiting for our parents. Waiting for my father, my mother often tidied the music cabinet where she kept the sheet music for our songs, or she would hang up the choir robes we dropped on the floor in our haste to hightail it out of there to hit the burger joint across the street on Madison. A hamburger was nineteen cents, and you could get French fries, too, for the grand total of a quarter. If all you had was a dime, you could order a soft-swirl ice-cream cone. I liked to order a cone, and then dip my big, fat fries into it, experiencing the double-delicious, simultaneous sensation of freezing cold and steaming hot. After choir rehearsal on the Saturday before Children's Day, my mother always treated the entire choir to ice-cream cones.

As I got into my teens, the older kids from Junior Church would often sneak upstairs into the balcony of the church where we couldn't be well seen by the adults and sit through the tail end of the sermon, passing notes and giggling with the boys. On other occasions, usually Easter, we would head up Madison, then down the other side of the hill to the First African Methodist Episcopal Church. This church rivaled ours in size and community stature, and because my parents knew Rev. John Adams and many members of the church, I still had to be on my best behavior. But here, my friends and I could find out what was happening that day after church. Was the drill team going to have a skating party at Ridge Rink? Or was everyone going to meet at the movies at two p.m. to laugh it up at a Jerry Lewis flick? The activities of the church and the after-church bonding formed the social fabric of my Sunday life.

In the world outside my insular church community, racial upheaval swirled around us. Because people could be rallied together most easily after church, many a movie date or skating party was either canceled or preceded by protests against housing segregation, or marches in support of school integration. We learned terms that were not taught in school, such as de jure segregation, the kind that was enforced not only by custom, but by law, in the south. Then there was de facto segregation, the northern brand, which was practiced, although not set down by the law. It was this kind of segregation that the black churches in Seattle banded together to protest. Sermons often rose to an emotional pitch in citing the wrongs of de facto segregation.

"It's just *wrong* for our children to have substandard textbooks!" any one of the city's black preachers might say from the pulpit. "It's just *wrong* for the school board never to hire a Negro principal for our predominantly Negro Garfield High School! It's just *wrong!*"

And elders scattered throughout the congregation would say, "Amen!"

That would encourage the minister to continue. "The song says, 'Jesus *loves* the little children. *All* the children of the world. Red and yellow, black and white . . .' "

Then he would pause, wipe the sweat from his brow with a white handkerchief, and luxuriate in our attention, while a male voice from the congregation would help him out: "Well?"

"They are *all* precious in His sight!" The minister's voice would rise.

"Preach!" A deacon's exclamation would come right on cue.

"Jesus loves the little children of the *world!* Not just the *white* world—of the whole world!"

Clapping was not permitted in our church, but the minister did expect a vocal response. If he didn't get one, he just might ask, "Are you all 'sleep out there?" and look into faces in the congregation.

That would get the attention of our group of teenagers in the balcony, where I was playing footsie in the back row with Walker Ellison, my first church boyfriend.

"Nah, sir!" another deacon spoke out for all of us.

"Can I get a witness?"

"Yes, sir!"

"Does the Bible say 'A *child* shall lead them?' "

"Yes, Lord!"

"Well, then, you better wake up, people. There's a time to sleep, and a time to *act!*"

Then the minister would slowly speak into the mike in almost a whisper for effect. "Just because the school board is wrong, things don't have to *stay* wrong. Just because the school board is wrong, *we* don't have to be wrong."

"No, we don't, Reverend!" a woman would call out.

"But we do have to get right with Jesus! And then, what a friend we'll have! We'll have a friend in *high* places. We'll have a friend like *no* other. We'll have a friend with higher authority than the school board . . ."

"Amen!" someone interrupted.

"With *higher* authority than the superintendent . . ."

"Higher!" was the response.

"*Higher* than the governor . . ."

"All right, now!"

"That even the *president* has to obey!" He was on a roll now, and the congregation was with him.

"*Yes!* We have a friend that is more supreme than the Supreme Court, ah!" He began to punctuate his sentence for emphasis, as if he were catching his breath.

"More mighty than the most mighty man, ah! What a *friend* we have, ah! What a mighty *good* friend we have, Church. Good God! What a friend we have in *Jesus.*"

The congregation would respond to that familiar phrase with delight. Many would come to their feet. The turnout for the rally would be assured. Pausing for the shouting to quell, the minister would mop his forehead, then lower his head.

"Let us pray."

Everyone in the church, including distracted teenagers and fidgety babies, would sense the spirit and get quiet.

"God who knows our fears, God who has seen our tears, we pray that you would lead us into the light with your heavenly might. As you have brought us thus far with the faith of our fathers and the love of our mothers, guide us to do the right thing to bring justice and equality to all in our city, our state, our beloved country, for the sake of our children, and our children's children. We do this to bring the ultimate honor to you, Lord. To serve you and glorify your name, now and forevermore." He paused. "Let the church say 'Amen.' "

"Amen."

My favorite part of church activism was choir exchanges with white Baptist churches in the North End of the city. Most black folks lived either in the Central District or the South End of Seattle, and those who dared to buy a home in the red-lined real estate areas north of the University of Washington were often subjected to racist treatment, from the subtle disdain of their white neighbors to cross burnings on their yard.

But some white ministers attempted to prove that not all whites were prejudiced. Together with our ministers, they formed a religious group of people committed to doing what they could to bridge the racial divide. Our schools had "exchanges" with other high schools in which we might stay a night or two in the homes of white students and go to school with them; then they would come to stay with us and accompany us to our classes. By the same token, we had church exchanges, in which our Baptist Youth Fellowship (BYF) or our choir would visit a white church, and they would, in turn, worship with us.

My mother enjoyed preparing the Children's Choir for choral exchanges. We practiced for weeks the songs that we would sing in a mass interracial choir at some huge white cathedral.

"Once we went to a church in West Seattle that had beautiful grounds and was built to enhance the natural environment," my mother recalls. It was nice to see how other people lived, outside of our familiar neighborhoods. We hoped the whites were impressed with our lovely church, as well.

Each children's choir would sing three songs of their choice, then sing one together at the end of the concert. Our church participated for many years, in an effort to get the children to interact together, although we never saw the other kids outside of the rehearsals and the concerts.

To this day, I know the order of the first books of the New Testament because of the lyrics to one prayerful song we collaborated on that began, "Matthew, Mark, and Luke and John/Bless the bed that I lie on . . ." Another favorite was "The Gates Stand Open," with its marching cadence, and the melodious "Of the Father's Love Begotten." There was also a tune sung in rounds that I liked called "Sing, Sing, Sing, and Rejoice."

Now, looking back, it seems hard to believe that black and white parents and church congregations felt they were doing something positive for the civil rights movement by encouraging their children to sing together. But these were the same years, the early 1960s, when African-American children my age were bombed to death in the very Birmingham church that my mother's great-aunt and cousins were members of, and that Mom herself attended as a child when visiting them. So every small gesture took on enormous proportions. We felt we were doing our part to raise our voices in unison for the goal of racial harmony.

Rev. Dr. Samuel B. McKinney, who had baptized me when I was eight, was the pastor of Mount Zion from 1958 to 1998. A man of stature with his signature glasses and goatee, he was as tall as my father was short. He expressed the leanings of a Democrat; my father, of course, was a Republican. Yet, I saw them both as men of character and confidence, who commanded respect by their integrity and unconditional commitment to the community.

In January 2003, during the Martin Luther King, Jr., national holiday weekend, I called Rev. McKinney to chat about my father. I had made the appointment for the long-distance telephone conversation when I was home in Seattle a couple of weeks before for Christmas. Rev. McKinney has a deep and grand voice, perfect for oratory. Now, after using that commanding voice for years of memorable sermons, civil rights speeches, and political activism, in his retirement he enjoys participating in the annual Christmastime production of Langston Hughes's *Black Nativity* at one of Seattle's premier downtown venues, the Intiman Theatre. Before my mother took me to see the musical, I somehow had the impression that Rev. McKinney was playing the role of God. But the official program cites his role as "Narrator." In any case, I thought he was pretty accurately typecast.

Back home in New Jersey, I called and caught Rev. McKinney as he returned from a Seattle community celebration in honor of Martin Luther King, Jr. I explained that I wanted him to tell me what he remembered of my father. How did he meet him? What were his impressions? What influence had he had on the community as a politician? The good reverend patiently answered my questions for over two hours, telling me stories that I had never heard before. With him on the west coast and me "back east," as Seattleites call it, I turned on my laptop, plugged my headset into the cordless phone, and typed as he talked.

"Your father was instrumental in my coming here," he began. "I encountered him by phone in 1957. Since 1954, I had been the pastor of Olney Street Baptist Church in Providence, Rhode Island. On this particular night, I had preached a revival in a church in Cambridge, Massachusetts, about forty miles from Rhode Island. I had come home and gone out that evening to another church that was having a joint service with my church. When I returned, your father called and asked if I was interested in coming out to Seattle to become the pastor of Mount Zion. He told me about the church and that the seven-member pulpit committee, which was charged with finding a new pastor, was meeting. I guess I was tired and may not have sounded so interested. So he asked, 'Well, are you interested?' And I said, 'Oh, yes!'

"To get there for the interview meeting, I flew from Providence to New York, then I got on the largest airplane at that time, a DC-9—this was before jets. What is now a five-hour trip was a nine-hour flight back then. It was on a Friday evening, in late October. The plane landed over an hour early because of the headwinds. Your father and several others from the committee were supposed to meet me at the airport, but no one was there when I arrived. I called your home and your mother answered. She said they had already left for the airport.

"I held a certain mental image of your father. There had been a deacon in Providence that your father was enamored of because he was a good speaker and because he was a member of Kappa Alpha Psi fraternity, like him. So I was thinking he might look like this person. Your father was very proper on the phone, and I was impressed by the script of his typewriter used on the follow-up letter. I had an image of someone tall with flowing hair. I thought he would be sort of half white."

"An Adam Clayton Powell type," I interjected with my own image of what he was describing.

"Yes." He continued, "When he came up to me with the chairman of the deacons, Mr. Christopher Hatter, and Mrs. Hatter, and Mrs. Rilla Coleman, also on the committee, and said he was Charles M. Stokes, I was surprised he was short." Rev. McKinney and I chuckled together about this.

"He had a new Lincoln," Rev. McKinney continued, talking about my dad's prized palomino-colored automobile that I remembered fondly, "and the Hatters had a Pontiac. When I saw the cars, I said, 'You people out here in Seattle are living well!' And your father said, 'We're not going to treat *you* that well!' We laughed."

Daddy broke the ice, and McKinney obviously made a good impression on the pulpit committee of five men and two women. He was offered the job and he and his family moved from Providence out to Seattle. He began his forty-year ministry at Mount Zion in February of 1958.

"What was the role of the church in African-American politics?" I asked him. I thought I knew the answer, having spent my entire life sitting in church services where the minister used the "Announcements" segment of the program to let worshippers know that Election Day would be on Tuesday, and that they should vote. I thought it was the ritual of all ministers at all churches to take the Bible passage on, say, "love thy neighbor as thyself" and turn it into a message about the righteousness of the Equal Housing Law and our struggle to get it passed. But in our phone conversation, Rev. McKinney went back further than the role the church played in the civil rights movement. He took his answer back to the role of the church in the lives of our ancestors, whom he called "we."

"In slavery, when we gathered for Sunday services, there were two white people in attendance," he explained, referring to the overseers who attempted to prevent enslaved Americans from using the service to plot an escape or insurrection. "We talked in code language, such as singing "Steal Away to Jesus" to let others know an escape was imminent. The whites tried to interpret everything we said."

I knew about that, but I didn't know about what he said next.

"The patter-rollers went to sleep at six a.m. after patrolling to see if any slaves had gotten away," he said, using the slave vernacular for "patrollers." "Then others on the next shift went to monitor the morning worship services of the slaves. So many black churches in the southern coastal states had *pre*-worship prayer meetings, because that could be held between the shifts of the patter-rollers. And even after Emancipation, they kept that tradition."

During and after slavery, black churches provided a place for community gathering. "The churches were also schoolhouses," Rev. McKinney said, "where we tried to get an education, which was not easy because it was illegal to teach us to read and write."

Even in the 1960s, he added, "The church was a place where a lot of the action took place. In Seattle, the NAACP couldn't afford to rent places for meetings—they'd have gone bankrupt—so protest meetings convened at Mount Zion. On Saturdays and Sundays, we began our marches at the church that ended downtown.

"The black church has always been active in civil rights." As he spoke, through my earpiece I could hear the pride swell in his voice as clearly as if he was in the room. "Just about every slave rebellion—and if my reading of history is right, there were over three hundred—was led by preachers." And he began to name some of them: Gabriel Prosser, Denmark Vesey, Nat Turner. Their names were familiar to me from college classes in African-American Studies, but I had not realized they were all religious leaders.

"So if an African-American church is not active, if it's not leading or part of the struggle, it's not true to its founding and heritage," he stated.

Not everyone in every black church was in agreement on the length to which ministers should take politics. And then, too, there were church members who felt that preachers didn't do *enough* with their powerful platforms.

Rev. McKinney continued with an anecdote that concerned his predecessor at Mount Zion, Rev. Gil B. Lloyd, and my father's best friend, Atty. James McIver, that occurred in 1955.

"When Emmett Till was murdered," he began, "Attorney McIver wanted Reverend Lloyd to say something about it from the pulpit. But Lloyd wouldn't, so McIver placed a full-page ad in the newspaper denouncing the lynching." Rev. McKinney went on to say that McIver was so mad that his minister had not spoken out about this injustice that he left the church.

I thought about the death of the black teenager from Chicago, who while visiting relatives in Mississippi was kidnapped and murdered for allegedly whistling at a white woman. It was an emotional and explosive occurrence in the lives of African-Americans. His grisly death exposed to the world that our children were not exempt from the racist hate of white bigots, and that blacks could not always protect our children from them. Lynching was supposed to be over. The first year that there were no recorded lynchings in the United States of America since lynchings were kept track of was the year I was born—1952. And then just a few years later, Emmett Till's fourteen-year-old mutilated body was found drowned in a river. The national media attention seemed enough to ensure a semblance of justice when the suspects were put on trial. But the two men were acquitted.

I was too young to have remembered the conversations of outrage and sadness my parents must have had, or the picture in *Jet* magazine that showed the mutilated and bloated body of Emmett Till for all to see, positioned next to an insert of the "before" picture of his boyish, smiling, good-looking face. But I grew up learning that this unjust death of an African-American child was one of the cataclysmic events that galvanized activists in the civil rights movement.

I did fondly remember my father's friend "Mac" as a tall, light-skinned man with a gregarious personality who favored TV personality Ernie Kovacs, but I wasn't familiar with his politics. I was surprised to hear that he had quit the church in protest. I also remembered Rev. Lloyd, the minister before McKinney, who was nice to me, and fiery in the pulpit. A married father of a young daughter, he did not strike me as someone who would hold his tongue about the lynching of a child.

Rev. McKinney said that when he became the pastor of Mount Zion, "Your father said to me, 'There's a good man you need to get back.' " And he did reach out to Mac, who indeed returned to the church, assured that this new pastor would speak out against injustice.

"I was interested in freeing our people," McKinney said.

"What was my father's role at the church?" I asked.

"He was a faithful member, who sat under the balcony and held court," McKinney answered. Then he added after a pause for thought, "He also held his money close to him. I teased him that he could squeeze a penny 'til Lincoln hollered. He was one of the founding members of the board of the church credit union. It was only the second black credit union in town. The first was the NAACP's. Many people thought it would hurt the NAACP Credit Union, so the board had some opposition. He was also a member of the committee in charge of the building fund."

"The building fund"—that was the pervasive phrase at church during my childhood. It seemed as though they were raising money for that church *forever*. Although we worshipped in a grand sanctuary with a dramatic cathedral ceiling and colorful stained-glass windows, the church elders had another, more modern vision for the congregation. Seattle was a progressive place. The city exemplified the supersonic theme of the World's Fair that the city hosted. Stuffy, old-timey buildings and statues of dead white men were not part of its contemporary self-image. The leaders of Mount Zion wanted to meld the space-age with the ancient in a church of African-inspired architecture, which included an educational wing to house Sunday School classes, a preschool, and an expansive "fellowship hall" for church productions, Sunday suppers, and wedding receptions.

"We broke ground for the new educational wing in 1962, on the day the World's Fair opened," Rev. McKinney recalled. "We broke ground for the new sanctuary in 1974, the same day Mrs. King—Martin Luther King's mother—was shot and killed while playing the piano during church service in Atlanta. It was all completed in 1975."

Eventually, as I had done when I spoke with Rev. Davis, I mentioned Daddy's political history and asked what the predominantly Democratic congregation thought of this Republican representing them.

Rev. McKinney told me that in 1950s Seattle there were "three big black Republicans: Rev. Fountain Wright Penick, Prentice Frazier, and Charles Stokes. At that time, the attitude was that there should be some black Republicans and some black Democrats, and that we should stay in the middle so we could throw our weight to whichever one attended to our agenda.

"There was a history of black Republicans, and I understood it," he explained. "In Cleveland, where I grew up, there were lots of Republicans. In the south, the party was held together by black folks. If Nelson Rockefeller had won out over Richard Nixon, there might have been a lot of entrants into the GOP by black folks. A lot of us went to Rockefeller-supported schools. Spelman College was created by two white students from Wellesley. Things may have been different if Rockefeller had won. Trent Lott types came in office and things changed. Until that time, in the Republican Party there was a liberal element. It's a different party now.

"My father was once a registered Republican," he confided. "He said after Roosevelt came in, he voted Democratic."

Then he talked about his own political leanings. "I voted straight-ticket Republican once in 1956 as a protest vote because the presidential election was Mafia-driven to a large degree, and Adlai Stevenson didn't show us black people anything. That year, I was in Harlem when Adam Clayton Powell made a statement on 125th Street in front of the Hotel Theresa saying that he was voting for Eisenhower. The way Powell went, a lot of black folks went."

Rev. McKinney also recalled that Malcolm X was in the crowd that day, and that Adam Clayton Powell called him up to the platform to recognize him.

Although Powell took to the streets of Harlem to proclaim his political leanings rather than limiting himself to his Abyssinian Baptist Church congregation, in Seattle and elsewhere, each African-American minister dealt with the separation of church and state in his own way.

"I did not endorse people, because the Church could not," Rev. McKinney said. "But I could tell who I was voting for. And I had no problem telling the congregation when people weren't right. We also had issues other than people running for office. There were referendums to vote for." When he said this, I recalled the Washington state elections of my youth that centered on school levies that my mother wanted passed, so there would be more resources in her classroom.

And of course, black ministers, just like all private citizens, are free to speak their opinions to others in privacy. After church service, my father and his pastor often talked about—and debated—the issues of the day and how the points of view of certain national and local candidates and elected officials affected African-Americans.

"One Sunday, I said something about President Nixon's attitude toward black folks, and your father didn't like that," Rev. McKinney told me. "I said to him, 'You're kind of conservative.' He said, 'Don't call me that. Don't say that. The problem is, you're a Democrat *and* an Alpha."

I broke out laughing. I could imagine hearing my father say those exact words—and not just because he had supported Richard Nixon for president. It would have been just like him to defuse the subject of conflict—his Republican conservatism—by cracking on his minister's membership in a rival fraternity of my father's Kappas. But that didn't give him the last word.

"I told your father I was an Independent."

Evidently, there were other incidents involving my father's position on the political spectrum that caused him to be out of step with his more liberal black constituents, many of whom attended our church. Rev. McKinney informed me of one of them.

"There was a controversial campaign literature he gave out that didn't sit well with people," he told me.

"Really?" I responded. "Why?"

"It said, 'Drop the atomic bomb, but don't drop Stokes.' "

I was silent for a second. What did he mean? Was Dad trying to say, drop the atomic bomb *program,* but don't drop Stokes for re-election? When Rev. McKinney explained that Dad was stating that he was *for* America dropping the bomb, I couldn't believe it.

"What?!" I yelled into the phone.

Allowing my shock to sink in, he explained to me patiently, as I moaned, "Oh, no. Oh, no . . . no . . . no."

From what I could gather, when Dad was up for re-election during the Cold War, he attempted to sound patriotic by supporting the national dialogue on the use of the atomic bomb. I wondered if he had supported the actual use of the bomb on Hiroshima and Nagasaki that had ended World War II the decade before. I had never heard him say he had supported what I had grown up believing was an atrocity of humanity. All I ever heard him talk about was his belief in non-violence. So we should be nonviolent in the civil rights struggle, but drop the bomb in war? This didn't make sense to me.

But then again, I did know that he always supported the president of the United States, no matter who was elected, or from which political party. "The president may not always be right, but he is still the president," I heard Dad say on more than a few occasions. In political debates at the dinner table when I was a teenager, he often mentioned that the president knows best, because he has inside information from the CIA, the State Department, and the Pentagon that we don't have access to. So if the president was talking about dropping a bomb, then Rep. Stokes thought the president must know what he's talking about. But obviously, his Seattle Thirty-seventh District constituency didn't agree. They voted him out.

Rev. McKinney recalled how it happened. He said that my father's political rival, Sam Smith, who also worshipped at Mount Zion, was an appealing candidate to many of the black folks in town because he was not only a Democrat, but a more typical Negro: He was not an attorney, he was not the son of accomplished parents, he was not a sharp dresser, he was not from the midwest. Born the youngest of eight children, who became the father of six, Smith, a World War II army veteran who worked at Boeing before turning to politics full-time, was more "for real." People could relate to him.

"Sam Smith came to my house with his children and said, 'Would you vote for me?' He was running against your father," McKinney explained. "Sam had that down-home-poor-boy-from-Louisiana touch, and a lot of people in Seattle were from Louisiana. What hurt your father about that defeat was not that he lost to a Democrat, but that he lost to someone who was not as articulate. Your father was a patrician, so it was like 'the serf storming the castle.' It was a big defeat."

Being a Baptist was more important than being a politician. Each Sunday, the Stokes and Smith families worshipped together congenially at Mount Zion.

In the midst of the civil rights struggle, unity among black folks was called for by our leaders and heeded in many quarters. My father never called himself a leader. He relished in saying that "every chief needs a tribe." He could lead when called upon or when he took it upon himself, but he was also an excellent follower, a team player, a supporter of just causes.

That was the role he filled the one and only time Rev. Dr. Martin Luther King, Jr., visited Seattle, in 1961.

My mother had told me that Rev. McKinney had been a classmate of King's at Morehouse College in Atlanta, and that he had been responsible for getting King out to Seattle to speak.

"Is it true that you actually knew Martin Luther King?" I asked Rev. McKinney.

"Yes, I knew King and he knew me," he responded. "Morehouse wasn't that large. Plus, both our fathers were ministers, so I had met him before I went to Morehouse. We were in the same freshman class at Morehouse in 1944. He was fifteen years old because he bypassed his senior year in high school, according to the Georgia War Time Decree. Each year the draft was taking someone out of school. Uncle Sam called me when I was in Morehouse at seventeen. I went in the Army, then reentered Morehouse in 1947. King graduated in '48 and I graduated in '49."

"What kind of student was King?" I wondered aloud. "Did his classmates feel he was destined for greatness?"

"He didn't raise that much sand as a student," McKinney replied. "He entered many oratorical contests and didn't win one. He was a city student—he didn't live on campus—so in college he wasn't as well known as he became."

At that time in the mid-1940s, my own mother was in school in Atlanta at the neighboring Clark College. But because she was slightly older, and graduated in 1947, she said she didn't know King or McKinney. But McKinney said he thought he remembered her.

"I told your mother I hung out at the nearby Clark campus," he said, then added, "though not as much as at Spelman." We chuckled, because he knew that I knew that Clark was coed, but Spelman was an all-girls school. "I remember a well-dressed student saying she was from Seattle, Washington, and hadn't been in Seattle long. I think it was your mother."

"I wouldn't have been surprised," I replied, acknowledging those key words that would have identified her: well-dressed, not long in Seattle.

"Tell me about the time Martin Luther King visited Seattle," I asked him. I had no direct memory of this event myself, as I was just nine years old at the time, and I don't think that my parents took me along. I only recall attending a concert at Garfield High School four years later, in which his wife, Coretta Scott King, was the featured soloist.

Although the battle of the Montgomery Bus Boycott, which had brought King to national prominence, had been won several years before his visit to Seattle, the civil rights movement was still a hotbed of tension in 1961. The year before, four college students had staged a sit-in at a North Carolina Woolworth's store lunch counter, demanding to be served, and launching an antidiscrimination sit-in campaign throughout the south. Also in 1960, the Student Nonviolent Coordinating Committee (SNCC), a group of young activists that became a national force, was founded at Shaw University. In 1961, "Freedom Riders" took to interstate buses to call an end to segregation on buses and trains. Many of them were beaten, and buses were set on fire. That fall, King himself had announced an ambitious initiative of the organization he led, the Southern Christian Leadership Conference (SCLC), to register the majority of the south's five million potential black voters. It was in this climate that the esteemed reverend doctor was invited to Seattle to speak.

Although the public event was organized as part of an annual lecture series by the Brotherhood of Mount Zion Baptist Church, there was not a large enough space at the church to accommodate the thousands of people expected to attend. When the Brotherhood, of which my father was a member, ventured out to secure another Seattle venue, they were met with resistance.

"There was a controversy because the First Presbyterian Church, which was a white congregation, decided we couldn't use their church," Rev. McKinney told me. "We had chosen that church because all places that could have held it were not available, such as the Seattle Center, which was getting ready for the World's Fair. The Presbyterian church seated 3,000 and at first the pastor said we could use it. At that time, King was the most hated and feared man in America, and the committee there became nervous. So they said we hadn't followed procedures—procedures they had not told us about.

"Your father went with the eight of us to talk to them. I didn't want to go by myself. I asked him to go because he was an attorney and well known in the city," McKinney explained, reminding me that he had arrived in Seattle to lead Mount Zion just a few years before.

It happened that just previous to our phone conversation I had read about this incident in an online story archived from *The Seattle Times*. It had mentioned that King was just thirty-two at the time, so McKinney would have been the same age, but my father would have been considered almost an elder spokesman, at fifty-eight.

"His presence was a help. He was very much involved in the decisions the church made. There were a lot of people who were more comfortable about issues because they knew where Lawyer Stokes stood on them. His presence lent credibility."

But it wasn't enough to change the minds of the decision-makers at First Presbyterian. The white church leaders maintained that the Mount Zionites hadn't filled out the proper papers.

"I told them there wasn't any paperwork," Rev. McKinney recalled, still angry over forty years later. At the meeting, "An attorney from First Presbyterian said, 'I'm both judge and jury—you can't use it.'

"I said, 'Martin Luther King will come and will speak.'

"He asked, 'Where?'

"I said, 'None of your business.' And I said that we would tell the press about their denial. And we would tell the truth, the whole truth."

Sure enough, I read in the newspaper account that Rev. McKinney denounced the cancellation of their oral agreement as "prejudice of an extreme conservatism, religious or radical." Now, he called it "racist."

The event was held at Eagles Auditorium, a venue I mainly recalled as the place that held raucous James Brown concerts that featured go-go dancers during my teen years. Recently, my mother had told me that my father had also gone along with Rev. McKinney to greet Rev. King upon his arrival at the airport. And Rev. McKinney recalled that they all went out to dinner afterward.

Mom sent me a copy of the original program, saved from so many years ago. It lists Attorney Charles M. Stokes as having presented a citation to Rev. King after the delivery of the message. In view of the controversy, I was surprised to see that "greetings" were given by prominent white citizens, such as "The Honorable Gordon S. Clinton, Mayor of the City of Seattle," and by "The Honorable Albert D. Rosellini, Governor of the State of Washington."

It also seems that the passage of time softened the opinion of the leaders of First Presbyterian Church, according to McKinney. He told me that when he was retiring in 1998, he was cleaning up some papers in his office.

"I almost threw out an envelope, until I realized it wasn't open," he said. "When I opened it, I saw that it was a letter from the current pastor of the First Presbyterian Church, who said he apologized for the church's actions. He explained that it had been an issue that the church had been belaboring ever since, for thirty-seven years. I knew he could have told his congregation, 'It didn't happen under my watch, so get over it,' but he said he wanted the church to get on with the work of the kingdom. I met with him. And then, my wife and I invited him and his wife to be guests at my retirement celebration."

I had enjoyed my long-distance discussion with Rev. McKinney. Even though I had grown up with him as my pastor, seeing him just about every Sunday for most of my young life, I had never had the opportunity to have a personal conversation with him. Of course, I knew he would have had unique observations about my father, the man who had been instrumental in his coming to Seattle, who had shared with him an admiration for Martin Luther King and the causes he represented, and who had also held a mutual love of God and Mount Zion Baptist Church.

"Your father was a patrician," he said before we hung up. "There are a lot of folks who are middle class with middle-class tendencies. And there are a lot of folks who are ashamed of it and don't want to act middle class. Some people want to emulate rappers—instead of being like Charles Moorehead Stokes, they want to be like Big G." I laughed, because I knew he was making up that name.

"And I mean children of people whose parents are educated and middle class," he went on. "They think they're not 'authentic' in their blackness if they're not like rappers. But your father was unashamed of who he was. He felt that if it was worth doing at all, it was worth doing it well. He didn't suffer fools gladly—he didn't put up with foolishness for its own sake. Some people take pride in their ignorance. But you didn't have to be around him two minutes to know he was proud of his accomplishments and that he was *somebody*. This community is better and richer because of him."

As I thanked Rev. McKinney for his time and insights, he said one last thing that he wanted me to know personally. "So many people don't know who their fathers are, or are not proud of them. It's good you had a father to be proud of."

= 10 =

Respect

MY FATHER WAS ALWAYS *"GQ* down." Or, as he might say whenever I complimented him on his dress, "I stay *sharp!"* This was not stated in any boastful way, but rather as a simple fact of his life and personality that gave us all delight.

Of course, if you were to ask my mother about that, she would tell you that she had something to do with his elegant mode of dress. A fashion plate of wide repute herself, my mother kept her husband in ultrasuede or cashmere jackets, in Burberry raincoats, and suits from Littler's, a Seattle haberdashery.

Together, the Stokeses made a stylish couple, but it was not for the sake of vanity. In fact, it was a kind of political statement.

ABOVE: *All dressed up visiting Gran after church on Easter. In the background is Seattle's then-tallest building (pre–Space Needle), the Smith Tower.*

In the days of my childhood, for example, one was expected to get dressed up to go shopping downtown. If my mother wanted to take me shopping on a Saturday, that didn't mean rolling out of bed and throwing on some pedal pushers. I had to wear my "good clothes" and dress shoes. I didn't have to get quite as dressy as I did for church, few places required that level of frilliness, but shopping attire was right up there with school clothes. And in those days, girls wore dresses or skirts to school every day.

To get helpful service from the salespeople in the best department stores, anyone, regardless of race, was required to look the part of someone who demanded respect. But if you were black and wanted courteous and helpful service from salespeople—who were most often white women, because in the best stores, they didn't hire blacks in any generous number—you had a better chance if you were dressed in an affluent manner, as though you were already a frequent shopper of that upscale establishment.

Although we didn't live in the south, where Negroes could not shop at certain stores, or if they could, they were not allowed to try on the clothes, we were still aware of the subtle prejudices that could occur. No one ever spoke to me about this, but I began to gather that clothes could play an important role in how I was perceived by others, particularly by Caucasians. Dressing well was a way of forming a positive racial attitude upon first impression. You could never tell when you might encounter someone who would not naturally assume you were worthy of respect, so you felt compelled to provide some sign that you were not only worthy, but accustomed to it. Dressing with dignity was a way of sending a message to others that you expected to be treated with dignity.

But it wasn't all about getting served in a department store. It had to do with trying to change the assumptions and prejudice wherever you went. You might not have control over how someone felt about people with brown skin, but if you could adorn that skin with clothes that anyone of any race could wear, then wouldn't that have a neutralizing effect? Maybe clothes could be the great equalizer!

If I'm a teenager wearing a pink knit Jonathon Logan dress that I saw on a model on TV, aren't I as good as she is? If my mother wears the same Bill Blass outfit that Diana Vreeland raved about in *Vogue*, isn't she as chic as any *Vogue* reader? In the split second that someone sees your skin color, they also see your clothes and your style. And in that moment, a judgment is made that may affect your grades, your ability to get hired and earn a living, whether or not someone will vote for you. So dressing well was of enormous importance in my family and my community.

Black folks would get dressed for a protest march. Have you ever noticed how people are dressed in those black-and-white film clips of civil rights marchers? Martin Luther King, Jr., usually has on a suit and tie. Coretta Scott King is often seen in a cool, cotton dress with fitted waist, and sometimes with a chiffon scarf draped stylishly around her head and neck with dark sunglasses on her face. In my city, as in most of the country, marches often took place after church, so protesters were already clothed in their Sunday best. Even if the general public disagreed with their stance on open housing for all, or equal opportunity, at least it could be agreed that the protesters didn't look like "bums" or "scum." The choice of clothing was intended to give a picture of a decent, organized group of people respectfully demanding the rights unfairly denied them.

Aside from the political ramifications of dressing well, however, my parents just enjoyed fashion and admired those who presented themselves well.

"Just look at that little girl," my father said many times while driving me to junior high, pointing out various Asian-American children we might pass who were walking to school. "See her white blouse? Look at how crisp, clean, and pressed it is. That's how you should always strive to look. Take after the Asians. They stay clean." And I knew he wasn't just talking about hygiene, but was using the black vernacular for well dressed in a clean-cut kind of way.

As a political candidate, my father made a great effort to look his best at all times, and openly admired politicians who dressed well. Of course, President and Mrs. Kennedy were not only held up by the world press as a couple of style and taste, but were also admired by my parents.

On television, the Kennedys were often seen dressed in formalwear for some official state dinner or ball. I have reminiscent images of my parents also dressed to the nines. For black-tie occasions of the Republican Party, such as the annual governor's ball or national conventions, or for gala fund-raisers of their sorority, fraternity, or other organizations, my mother would shop for days for the perfect ball gown to top that last one she wore. On the evening of the event, from my perch in my child-size rocker in front of the television set in the living room, I could tell exactly what was happening upstairs from the fragrant mix of Old Spice and Chanel No. 5 that filled the air.

Mom and Daddy took their time bathing, shaving, and brushing their hair just right in the bathroom, and then dressing together in their bedroom. The evening did not begin when they made their entrance at the affair. It began with the sounds of my father shining his shoes just so, with my mother making sure the earrings she chose from her heather-green leather jewelry box were appropriate for the occasion. I might be called to zip up a dress or fasten a cufflink, but most of the time it was part of their ritual to do the honors for each other. My father would button the back of her dress, and then top it off with a kiss on the neck. My mother would adjust his cummerbund and give him a hug.

I recall one evening when André and I were in our pajamas watching "My Three Sons"—or maybe it was "Ozzie and Harriet"—on the television in the living room when my parents descended the stairs in the adjacent foyer from their second-floor bedroom. My mother's outfit was particularly spectacular: a green-and-gold brocade gown and matching floor-length coat with brown mink collar and cuffs. With the train of her coat trailing her and the rhinestones of her tiara sparkling around her upswept 'do, she looked like the Queen of Sheba, or at least the Queen of Seattle. My father was equally decked out in a gold cutaway coat with a brown mink bow tie to match the touch of fur on his wife's ensemble.

My eyes got wide with wonder. "Wow!" I managed. André whistled at our mother. I was sure there was no couple anywhere in the world more beautiful.

When I watched the presidents and the first ladies on TV, I thought they looked nice, but I'm sorry, they didn't hold a candle to my own parents. For most of my childhood, on many an occasion, I witnessed my parents descending the stairs, dressed elegantly. And unlike the images of sophisticated couples on television or in *Life* magazine, I could also smell their intoxicating fragrance and feel my mother's red-lipsticked peck on my nose and my father's mushy kiss on my cheek as they strolled out the door.

"See you later, alligators!" was Daddy's customary farewell. Giggling, I always replied the loudest, as if I'd never done it before: "After a while, crocodile!" To our playmates we would have added: "Tootle-loo, baboon!" But we did not say this to our parents.

"Be good!" Mom added, which was as much an instruction as it was a good-bye.

Over the years, as I admired them, my parents admired fashionable occupants of the White House with unabashed admiration.

"Look at how the president wears his shirts," my father would remark many years later when Ronald Reagan was president. "That man can wear a shirt! His collars always fit his neck just right. His ties are always perfectly knotted. His suits are impeccably tailored."

Ronald Reagan was not one of my favorite presidents, so I never wanted to give him any credit for anything, even for being well dressed. But my mother agreed with Daddy and also felt that Nancy Reagan was one of the best-dressed women in America.

"Oh, look at that suit Mrs. Reagan has on!" Mom would point out as the evening news broadcast some serious issue of world concern.

My mother's admiration of Nancy Reagan prompted me to take notice of similarities between them. My mother was just three years younger than Mrs. Reagan. The Reagans met in 1951, the year my parents married. Like the first lady, Mom was her Republican husband's biggest supporter and confidante. A petite woman, Josephine Stokes was about the same height and size as Nancy Reagan. Both had a penchant for the designs of Oscar de la Renta.

Mom related to Mrs. Reagan's desire to bring high fashion to the White House, and she took the first lady's side against critics who disapproved of her extravagant designer wardrobe. "I don't know why they keep criticizing her. Don't they want their first lady to look good?"

My mother didn't have any media critics on her case about her own constant clothes shopping and extensive wardrobe. I certainly didn't say a word, because her habits also extended to my own stuffed closet. But my father did express a complaint from time to time. Whenever he didn't know where my mother was, he would ask, "Where's your mother—*shopping?*" If she bought a new pair of shoes, he might ask her, "What do you need those for? You've already got more shoes in your closet than the law allows."

One thing he couldn't complain about was the bills, however. She paid for her wardrobe with her teacher's salary. "That is why I work," Mom said. "So I don't have to ask anyone for money for clothes, or anything that I might want for you kids."

But after years and years of Daddy's grumpiness about her fetish for fashion, he must have thought he was doing her a disservice. It came to a halt all of a sudden, after he admitted to me, "You know, your mother loves to buy clothes. But that woman does look good whenever she leaves the house!"

I just laughed. "Oh, Daddy, we all knew you were proud of her all along."

When it came to what I called their White House worship, I'm sure I got on their nerves with my irreverent remarks like, "I bet you guys voted for President Reagan just because you like the way he and Nancy dress." They just smiled, as though the comment was not worth answering.

Although my father did not have a White House valet to keep his collars as immaculate as those of a president, he took great care to make sure his own shirts stayed white, crisp, and pressed. It wasn't good enough to have my mother wash and iron his shirts. On his way to work, he took them to a Chinese cleaners near downtown and his office, and picked them up on his way home.

Sometimes I felt that my parents talked about the attire of the first couple more than they did their politics. But I think it was their way of discussing something that was not really debatable. Certainly, the presi-

dent of the United States and his wife were dressed in a manner befitting their station in life. That was obvious to anyone, Republican or
Democrat, radical or conservative. But whether or not the president
was leading the country in a manner that benefited black folks was not
so obvious—at least to me. Such were the matters of opinion on which
my parents and I differed as I began to grow older and to question
their Republican politics.

Ronald Reagan wasn't the only one to garner a compliment from my
father on his neckties. The bow-tied brothers of the Nation of Islam
drew his admiration as well. Now how is that for a political spectrum?
Daddy was an equal-opportunity observer of clean-cut dress.

One day, my father and I were driving by the Nation of Islam tem-
ple on Jackson Street in Seattle, when the service was letting out. We
both silently stared as people poured out of the building. The men,
young and old, were all clad in suits and the obligatory bow ties. The
women, in their white peplum dresses and matching head coverings,
looked as pious as any nun.

"Maybe you should join the Muslims," my father said, to my surprise.
I turned away from the scene to see if he was joking. "See those sisters in
those long white dresses with their heads covered?" he continued. "They
look so much more dignified than all these girls in these miniskirts."

Of course, I had on a mini, so I knew the comment was directed at
me. Just about every day, like a broken record, he asked me if I was
indeed going out of the house with my skirt hiked up like that. But did
he really think that joining the Nation was all about the clothes?

"And I like how the men wear those bow ties and suits," he was
going on.

I just laughed.

In the late 1960s, the Nation of Islam was a growing influence in
our community. Several of my high school classmates were dabbling
with the Nation, joining up and getting their X—meaning that they
were relinquishing their "slave name," the last name of some long-
forgotten white man on whose plantation their ancestors had been
enslaved.

My school friends and I would amusingly oblige those brothers who would come to the cafeteria and tell us, "Don't call me by my slave last name no more. From now on, I'm Michael X."

"Yeah, okay, we got your X," we would say. "But does your mama?"

That was the initial ribbing we would give them, but just as we admired another black Muslim, Cassius Clay, whom we followed in the media as he became Cassius X, and then Muhammad Ali, we gave the brothers our respect. X it was.

We heard through the grapevine that some of the more unruly converts were always on punishment for some infraction of the black Muslim rules of conduct. They couldn't date, be in a room alone with a member of the opposite sex, or even touch each other unless they were sanctioned by the mosque for permission to marry the person. We didn't see them at school ball games or dances either. Although I admired their religious devotion and abstinence from smoking and drinking, I thought my parents' restrictions were enough for me. I didn't think I would last long with other authority figures keeping me from the freedom and independence I so desperately sought.

But I did agree with my father's opinion on the style of the followers of the Honorable Elijah Muhammad. The women did look striking and feminine in their covered-up dress. And the bow-tied brothers were definitely "clean."

On our coffee table, visitors could always find the latest issue of *GQ,* lying right there next to *Time* and *Ebony*. My mother subscribed to *all* the women's high-fashion magazines, and I am convinced that she holds the world's record for the longest-running subscription to *Vogue*. It was on the coffee table since before my birth, and it's still delivered every month. *Harper's Bazaar* was always there as well. But it was her loyalty to *Town & Country* that made her the target of family teasing. At least *Vogue* and *Harper's Bazaar* photographed a colored model every once in a blue moon. But because *Town & Country* reported on high society, and obviously didn't include Negroes in that group, we ribbed Mom for sending her money each year to a publication that regarded her as invisible.

"I don't know why you read *Town & Country*, Jo," Daddy said to her. "They never have stories in there about any colored society folks!"

"Oh, yes, they do," Mom responded. "I once saw a story on Mrs. Johnson!" We knew she was referring to Eunice Johnson, the elegant society wife of the publisher of *Ebony* and *Jet* magazines, John H. Johnson of Chicago. Originally from Selma, like my mother, she was the founder of the Ebony Fashion Fair.

"Yeah, right—once," I chimed in, laughing. "Once is not enough. And she's not the only well-to-do black person in America."

"Your mother enjoys seeing how the other half lives," Daddy said, bringing the teasing to an end, as he usually did, by coming around to defend her.

"Black folks know how they live," I responded, with typical teenage angst. "That's in every magazine, every month. They need to see how *we* live. They know nothing about us." My comments were now met with silence, as my parents resumed whatever they had been doing before. As was the family custom, the conversation would come to an abrupt end as soon as one of us got the slightest bit emotional. That was the Stokes way.

"If you don't like it, change it," was also a Stokes adage, so as I grew into my own sense of fashion and got my mother to pay for my subscriptions to *Seventeen, Mademoiselle,* and French *Elle* (which I convinced her I had to have to help get good grades in French class), I noticed what I thought was a shift in the acceptance of black models in magazines. Seeing more of them in the pages of my favorite publications inspired me to dream about going off to college "back east," somewhere close to New York, the fashion capital of the world. And my mother's loyalty to her favorite magazines paid off. Eventually *Town & Country* embraced diversity.

Maybe my mother had been born too soon to become the fashion designer she had dreamed of as a young woman in Alabama, but with segregation breaking down in all areas of society, I felt that in no time the fashion world would acknowledge that "black is beautiful," and I would be free to be "fly."

In the meantime, my mother got involved in bringing the Ebony Fashion Fair to Seattle through her sorority, Delta Sigma Theta. A fashion show extravaganza that traveled the country with tall, beautiful black models, the Fashion Fair was quite an exciting event. In New York, only editors and retail-store buyers could go to the designer runway shows, but the Fashion Fair brought the runway to us. Throughout most of the year, it traveled from coast to coast. The schedule was posted in the monthly *Ebony* magazine and in its weekly sister publication, *Jet*.

Annually in *Ebony*, there was a spread that featured the photographs of the women responsible for organizing the event in each city. The year my mother's photo appeared in the magazine, it was a big deal in our house. She got telephone calls from close relatives and long-lost friends across the country. "Girl, I saw your picture in *Ebony!*"

That was about as close to famous as any of us had ever been. After all, my father's campaigns were major, but they were regional. This was national news!

I was an adolescent at the time, and was greatly impressed and excited when my mother took me backstage with her to meet the Fashion Fair models. About a dozen female models traveled with a couple of male models, a commentator, wardrobe mistresses, and, of course, Mrs. Johnson herself. I knew who they all were before they even arrived in town, because they were pictured in the Johnson publications, providing publicity for the shows. In *Ebony* I read about the brown-skinned beauty named Judy Pace, who was once a Fashion Fair model and became a Hollywood actress. In *Jet* I saw the swimsuit centerfold featuring Lola Falana, whose big, brown, sexy eyes captivated the male attendees of the Fashion Fair. Mainstream fashion reporting covered "the beautiful people," but overlooked these black beauties. Again, the prevalent segregation of our country made it so that black America could enjoy a nationwide phenomenon while the rest of the country paid it little attention.

The major fashion designers knew Mrs. Johnson, however. She traveled extensively, attending the runway shows in New York, Paris, and Milan, and cultivating relationships with all the most popular fashion houses. The fast-paced Fashion Fair show was usually held in an elegant setting, such as in one of the ballrooms of a major hotel. Dinner was served.

The glamorous Audrey Smaltz, who was commentator for many years, sat on a high stool on the stage and began the show with a flourish. "The designer of this fabulous ensemble is *Yves . . . Saint . . . Laurent*. And if you have to ask the price," she said, pausing for effect, "you cannot afford it." The crowd would go wild.

And just as they settled into that groove of thinking that all these clothes were too expensive for the average woman, she would start talking about another exquisite garment as the model slinked in and twirled around, flashing her cape or coat in exaggerated motion. "This fabulous outfit can be yours for the asking . . ." Again she would pause, and give a mischievous smile, "at your local Sears store." And the audience would lose it again.

The Fashion Fair was a highlight of our year, right up there with Johnny Mathis concerts and trips to Disneyland. The whole family attended, and included in our ticket prices were subscriptions to *Ebony* and *Jet*, which kept us informed about the couture of colored folks.

= 11 =

Let's Go, Let's Go, Let's Go

THE PENCILS ARE OVER FIFTY YEARS OLD, yet they still look new. They served as campaign paraphernalia, as a way to remind folks to vote for Stokes. Having ordered boxes and boxes of them, Daddy took them everywhere he went. He gave them out at church, on the street, downtown, everywhere in his Thirty-seventh District campaign area.

Now, they remain precious remnants of our family history. I found several of them recently in my art-supply box at my home in New Jersey. Mainly, they pop up in my mother's Seattle home, the one we moved into after the 1960 campaign. They're in her enormous china cabinet, often falling out when you open the one door behind which are found household supplies such as stationery, phone books, and

ABOVE: *Rep. Charles M. Stokes welcomes Republican Vice-President Richard M. Nixon to Seattle (with unidentified man in center);* Seattle Times, *November 1958.*

writing utensils, rather than the heirloom eating utensils and silver goblets. Those are behind the rest of the gold mesh doors. Many of these special pencils are white, mustard, or red. My favorites are the gold ones that look a bit too chic to be a cheap pencil. But when you give out campaign pencils, you have to make them stand out somehow.

The gold ones, I am sure, were Daddy's favorites too. If not, my mother—who loves gold, wears gold, decorates the house in gold, and drives a gold car—probably had something to do with it. I would have ordered all of them in gold, but Dad, in trying to appeal to the masses, would have opted for patriotic colors of white and red. I guess they didn't come in blue.

They were likely to be spotted at Daddy's office. Two or three could usually be found in our kitchen near the wall phone where we wrote down his messages from frantic clients and inquisitive voters. In the years when I was a snaggle-tooth, I found them to be very tasty for teething. If you look closely at a few of the beat-up and battered ones you might notice the tiny teeth marks. As the years went by and I went off to grade school, I found the pencils to be of little use because they had no erasers. Designed with grown-ups (that is, voters) in mind, for sure, these pencils were topped with wooden knobs for dialing rotary phones. They were popular among women constituents, who could keep their blood-red nail polish from chipping by using the knobs of the same color. In addition to serving as nostalgic and enduring symbols of my father's campaigns for elected office in the 1950s, the large number Daddy must have ordered ensured that the Stokes family would never have the need to buy pencils again.

The seven-inch-long pencils featured just about all of my father's campaign slogans crammed onto them. Rotating them around, you could read

Don't Take Chances—Make No Mistake
Be Sure, Re-Elect
Charles M. Stokes

Twirl it around some more: "State Representative, 37th District." The next line was the one I never could understand: "Stokay Is Okay." Why did he spell his name wrong? I guess his real nickname, Stokey, just didn't rhyme well enough with "Okay," but it was hard to believe that someone who was always correcting our spelling would misspell his own name on purpose. Around the same time Stokey was running for office, President Dwight D. Eisenhower, a fellow Republican whom he had supported, had campaigned with the slogan, "I Like Ike." Eisenhower had won the election, so Daddy said he thought that with a similar catchy phrase, he could too.

He wasn't sure at first if it would be appropriate. Would he be taken seriously with a slogan that rhymed? Would it sound too trite? "It didn't seem in keeping with the responsibility of the position," he told *The Seattle Times*. "I checked with several conservative persons first, and they thought it was all right to use. It did seem to catch on in the district."

The campaign pencils delivered as much information as a flyer, but weren't as quickly discarded. While one was talking on the phone or pondering a grocery list, a potential supporter could find more of his campaign message:

> *The Folks Are for Stokes*
> *Proven Ability*
> *Sterling Character*
> *Above-Average Legislator*
> *Best Fitted for the Office*

And just in case anyone happened to look for the union label, Dad also squeezed on a tiny logo that declared the pencil was "Union Made."

The long pencils were for his re-election campaigns for Washington state representative, which he won three times in the 1950s. The wins weren't easy, though. *The Seattle Times* reported that "Charles M. Stokes, the first Negro ever elected to the State Legislature, had a tough time finding out he won the 37th District seat in the House of Representatives in yesterday's election. 'I checked 12 precincts before I came home

about 1 o'clock this morning and then I was leading by only 15 votes,'
Stokes said this forenoon at his home. . . ." Maybe he gave out more
pencils the next time to ensure his win.

Shorter pocket- and purse-size pencils were purchased for his state
senate campaign. He lost that one.

By that time, his usual constituents still respected him—even though
he was a Republican. But it was no secret that they preferred to vote
for a Democrat. Dad's opponent, Sam Smith, was a man my father knew
well. He went to our church. Even I knew him and his large family of
boys and one girl. His twin sons were in my grade at school. Smith ran
against Dad—and Smith won.

Unseated but not defeated, Stokey decided to go for an even bigger
position—lieutenant governor. That would mean that he would be
second-in-command of the state. In Washington state, the governor
was almost as much of a big shot as the president. Governor Albert D.
Rosellini was always on TV, always in the newspapers. Even though the
governor was a Democrat, the lieutenant governor could be a Republican. They were elected separately, not on the same ticket, like the president and vice-president. Becoming lieutenant governor could be the
next step to being elected the actual governor of our state. Daddy for
governor? Hot dog!

Full of excitement that even my eight-year-old self could comprehend,
our family all pitched in to help Dad win the election. He spoke at our
church and visited other churches and synagogues. My job was to ride
around with him and keep him company while he scoped out places
to post a campaign sign on a lawn. In our brand-new, black 1960
Cadillac, the model with the fins that made it resemble a giant fish on
wheels, we drove around Seattle and the surrounding areas on weekend afternoons.

Mr. and Mrs. Coleman lived on Twenty-third Avenue, the main drag
of the Central District. Just about everyone would pass her house at
some point during the week, and many folks passed there every day
traveling to and from work. Their home was just two blocks from ours
and it was our family tradition to sit on the grass in front of their house

to watch the Mardi Gras parade, the one that went through the black community during the city's Seafair festivities in August. The Colemans went to our church, and had a daughter named Linda, who was my age. We could always count on them to put a big sign on their lawn encouraging passersby to "Vote for Stokes."

Sadly, Daddy did not win the Republican primary for lieutenant governor. Full of hope and enthusiasm in the weeks and days leading up to the election, Daddy was deflated at his loss. Like a balloon that had been punctured, he just lost wind. He returned to many of the people who had put signs in their yard, and graciously thanked them for their support. With me in the car again, he drove more slowly now, getting out every few blocks and sometimes several times in one block. Signs that he had hammered into the ground were now pulled up and thrown in our trunk with grass and dirt covering the wooden poles. Losing sure wasn't as much fun as winning. But I learned that one thing you made sure you never lost was your dignity.

In the early 1960s, it was customary to be asked by whites, "When did you first realize that you were a Negro?" The question assumed that there was a defining moment—a traumatic event in childhood that rocked you into the realization that you were different from the mainstream. No, not just different—inferior.

Having always known I was African-American, and always liking what I knew, that was never an issue for me. Seattle, Washington—that last frontier of the Wild West—was arguably more racially tolerant than most of the country. Though blacks composed less than ten percent of the population, I grew up surrounded by a loving family and a community in solidarity about its black pride.

Before I understood the double meaning of the question, I thought, *How dumb to ask what anyone can see in the mirror.* I always knew I was black, just like I knew I was a girl, that I was a daughter and a sister, that I was a Baptist. I was proud of being colored—or the more sophisticated moniker, Negro.

The black kids I knew weren't scared of white kids. In the midst of a racial schoolyard confrontation, I was likely to hear somebody chant:

"White paddy, white paddy, you don't shine. Call me a nigger and I'll beat your behind!"

But that same bravado was used intra-racially, as well. It was used between light-skinned Negroes and dark-skinned ones. It was used whenever someone perceived that someone else thought they were better.

So, if the question had been asked, "When did you realize that your black family was Republican?"—now that would have been another story. A defining moment actually did occur when I discovered that my parents' political affiliation set us apart from the Negro mainstream.

It happened the year my father ran for lieutenant governor. Because he had the overwhelming support of our predominantly black Central District, it hadn't occurred to me that there could be any dividing line between him and his constituents, and he never spoke of one.

Although my father had won several political campaigns with the support of whites, Asians, and blacks, he had done it with the overwhelming support of the blacks not because he shared a party affiliation, but because he knew most of the black folks in his district, and they knew him. Even though the black voters were largely Democratic, they had crossed over party lines to vote along racial lines, and put in office the person who was their political pioneer, the one our church members and neighbors called with pride "our Negro attorney." When there had been few, if any, black attorneys in town, he had defended them, or handled their car accidents, or written up their wills, or helped them get out of a pickle. He was part of their local black pride, and they claimed him as their own. They had put him in office with pleasure, until they found a Democrat who was one of their own.

In 1960, even as a second-grader I knew that politics loomed large, not only in our family, our community, and our state, but also in the country. Richard M. Nixon was running for president in a close race against John F. Kennedy. The two of them were always on our black-and-white television in the living room. My father and mother spoke favorably about their party's candidate at the dinner table. Earlier in the year, my father had even invited Vice-President Nixon to campaign in Seattle. Accepting the invitation to speak at a GOP Lincoln's birthday celebration, Richard Nixon stepped off the airplane and shook

Daddy's hand—a moment reported in *The Seattle Times* and placed for posterity in our family's photo archives.

I liked that Vice-President Nixon had daughters, one of whom, Julie, was just three years older than me. I watched her on television for cues on how I should behave as a candidate's daughter. What if some reporter was to shove a microphone in front of my face? What would I say?

I didn't talk about politics to my friends or classmates. At school, the only time we ever used the word "vote" was in our nonsensical jump rope rhymes.

> *Vote, vote, vote for Stephanie*
> *In comes Betty at the door*
> *Betty is the one who knows how to vote*
> *So we don't need Steph'nie any more.*

At age eight, I was more interested in whispering about the cute new boy in class, and guessing what was meant in the hit song "Let's Go, Let's Go, Let's Go" by the lyrics "a thrill upon the hill." As a matter of fact, it was mainly grown-ups who were obsessed with the very close race between Nixon and Kennedy. My mother made it clear that she did admire the fashionable dress and stylish manner of Jacqueline Kennedy, but not enough to vote for her husband.

As the presidential election drew near, my second-grade teacher got the bright idea to hold a mock election. Standing in front of our racially mixed, predominantly black class at Madrona Elementary, Mrs. Bracksburg, who was white, asked, "If you could vote, who would you vote for? Raise your hand if you would vote for Democrat John F. Kennedy."

Many hands shot up quickly and enthusiastically, I noticed.

"Now, raise your hand if you would vote for Republican Richard M. Nixon." My hand went up just as proudly as the others had. But immediately, I felt a stillness in the air. Glancing around my upraised arm to survey the room, I realized that mine was the only hand up. By the time recess came, I knew that meant trouble.

"Why'd you vote for Nixon? You think you're better than us, Miss Smartie Pants?" a particular Negro classmate who was known as a "bad girl" asked me, as her posse and other kids began to gather at our corner of the playground.

"I don't think I'm better than anyone. That's who my parents said they were voting for," I answered, admittedly nervous, but looking her in the eye.

"Is that so?"

"Yeah, that's so. So what?" I shrugged my shoulders to appear casual.

There was a pause as I realized she was deciding what to say next. Over her shoulder I could see my own group of friends coming my way.

"Why are you voting for Kennedy?" I blurted out in the silence, even though I knew the answer. Kennedy was the name she had heard at home.

After more verbal sparring that we called "ranking" on each other, the bell rang for us to return to class. But the hostility hovered for the rest of the day. Among the colored children of my elementary school, difference was not tolerated, even if ignorance was. The next day when Kennedy won, the kids felt they had too, and things returned to normal for me.

It wasn't my nature, nor was it allowed, to question the ways of adults. But I wondered about this Republican thing. Why hadn't anyone told me we were different? Why *were* we Republicans when most colored folks seemed to be Democrats, anyway?

As time passed, I pieced together the family tradition. As a boy in his native Kansas at the turn of the century, Daddy had lived among colored folks who were largely Republicans, still loyal to the "party of Lincoln." In the 1930s and 40s when many African-Americans made the switch to the Democratic Party in support of President Franklin Delano Roosevelt's New Deal, Dad considered changing parties too. But fresh out of law school and active as cochair of the Young Republican Federation, he felt committed to his party. When he moved to Seattle, the GOP showed commitment to him by backing his candidacy in half a dozen elections. And on the national level, he was given prominent roles as a delegate, an alternate, or a reading clerk at the presidential nominating conventions, which he never missed for over thirty years.

Although my parents weren't by any means the *only* black folks who were active Republicans in Seattle, being in a black Republican family was not the norm. We were minorities within the minority.

Emancipation had occurred forty years before my father was born and almost a hundred years before I was in second grade. But because a Republican president named Abraham Lincoln had freed the slaves, my father felt free to vote Republican.

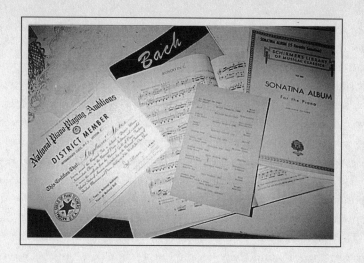

12

Beethoven's Rondo in C

A LARGE PART OF MY CHILDHOOD was spent playing the piano. I took lessons at the Cornish School of Allied Arts on Capitol Hill in Seattle, where I attended private, classical piano classes every Monday at 4:30 p.m. for twelve of my first eighteen years of life.

"Culturally deprived" was a media buzzword of the 1960s used to describe children who did not have the advantage, or so-called privilege, of spending their leisure time in museums, or at symphonies, or ballets. Of course, this term was usually applied to what was called "inner city" children, a code phrase for colored kids. We definitely were colored, and we did live in the "inner city," or central neighborhood, of Seattle. Our community was even called the Central District, or more familiarly, the CD. My mother was determined that her

ABOVE: *The piano books, competition certificates, and recital programs of my youth.*

three children would not be "culturally deprived" or otherwise stereotyped.

Mom had tried piano lessons with my older sister and brother when they started elementary school, enrolling them in private classes given by a respected lady of our community. Too young for the lessons myself, I always hung around when Vicki or André would practice a song at the beautiful upright piano in our dining room. A cherished possession, the piano was a gift to Vicki from her godfather, Mr. Prentice Frazier, a gregarious, pioneering black businessman and fellow Republican. Frazier, as Daddy called him, had been one of the first people with whom Daddy had made friends when he arrived in Seattle. The piano held a prominent place in the dining room of our old house in the CD, and then became an anchor piece in the interior design of the living room of the larger new house in the Mount Baker area of Seattle, where we moved in 1961.

Some of my earliest memories are of sitting on the end of the bench with my legs swinging and fingers banging the keys as my mother played church hymns, 1940s tunes, and one particular boogie-woogie I've never heard elsewhere. Eventually, my banging of the keys annoyed my sister enough to prompt her to teach me "Heart and Soul," and for years afterward, whenever the two of us sat down at the piano we would play our duet over and over and over.

Unfortunately, my siblings' piano lessons were not as much fun for them as they were for me. Their teacher's method of instruction included hitting her students' knuckles with a ruler whenever they made a mistake. This did not go over well with Vicki and André, who often came home complaining about it. Eventually, my mother decided it wasn't productive or necessary for the lessons to be so traumatic. She preferred for other adults to refrain from hitting us, and instead to tell her about major infractions, so that she could mete out the punishment herself. In her own profession as an elementary school teacher, her strategy for discipline was always verbally swift and firm, but never physically abusive. After a year or two, André and Vicki were allowed to discontinue their piano lessons. André took up the trumpet, and Vicki played accordion.

I had no such option. By the time I was in first grade and old enough to begin lessons, Mom decided to enroll me in a more structured course of study at the notably less abusive Cornish School of Allied Arts. Just as I was expected to advance daily through the public school system without ceasing until I finished the twelfth grade, I was led to believe that piano lessons were on a parallel, weekly extracurricular track from which only graduation at eighteen could provide release.

Cornish was the most elite arts school in town. The ivy-covered portico, in an L-shape around the front yard, sheltered me from the drizzle as I ran from the car to the entry of double glass doors. The building itself was ancient and spooky to me, with that stuffy smell of hallowed halls.

But having also started ballet lessons there at age four, I was aware that I was supposed to feel privileged to be enrolled there. The school was located in the old-moneyed Capitol Hill area, right next to the CD, but where none of "us" lived. There was only one other Negro girl taking piano lessons at Cornish at the time, the older sister of someone I knew from Jack & Jill. One of my mother's friends, Mrs. Gallerson, had her son, Clem Jr., enrolled in cello lessons there too, but he went on another day, so I never saw him there. Even at my young age, I felt the high expectations that came along with being one of the few colored folks at this classy, classical school. However, I never felt that anyone there was inherently smarter or more talented. I heard a lot of wrong notes while walking those halls or waiting for students before me to finish class, so I did not feel intimidated or out of place.

On Mondays, I came home from school, was greeted by my grandmother with a snack, then was made to practice for half an hour until my mother came home from her teaching job at four to drive me in the palomino-colored Lincoln the three miles or so to Cornish. For the first few years, she would wait for me in the lounge that doubled as the recital hall on Saturdays. By the time I was in third grade, though, Gran, who had come to our house each weekday to help with the cooking, cleaning, and child care while Mommie worked, had passed away. So Mom would drop me off, then rush home to start dinner, coming back sometimes as late as thirty minutes after my lesson. This seemed *forever* to me.

It became my habit to wait for her inside the school's large hallway on the steps leading up to the darkened third floor, closed because there were no ballet classes upstairs on Mondays. I had a spot where I could sit on the steps and look out the window over the entry without being seen by the departing student whose class followed mine. When my mother arrived, she would ask how class was, monitoring my progress and making sure I wasn't in trouble for not practicing enough. But I knew I could never ask her to be more punctual, much less complain about my wait. That just wasn't permitted. Children did not question the actions of adults, at least not in my house. I learned to pout (before she arrived) and live with it.

As I got older I began to understand that her many responsibilities as a wife, mother, teacher, community activist, and household manager gave her other things to do besides the delight of chauffeuring me around. Long before popular culture coined the phrase "working mother," Mom took on her busy weekday tasks with the immense energy we came to admire. This Monday routine of leaving work promptly at 3:30, picking me up, taking me to piano, stopping at the supermarket, going back home, starting dinner, picking André up from swim meets, coming back to Cornish, and returning us home to greet Daddy at seven with dinner ready was repeated with variation each day of the week. Yet I never heard her complain about it.

One by-product of her rushing around town was that she usually drove *fast*. Even when she wasn't in a hurry, she was accustomed to driving at a certain speed. I was amused that Mom was our family's Mario Andretti. But whenever Daddy was a passenger, it was his habit to remark, "Jo, you back out of the driveway too fast!" I guess he didn't want to add her to his client list. She was, however, a conscientious driver and could honestly respond, "I have *never* been in an accident!"

However, in January of 1968, she relieved herself of driving duties in a win-win situation for us both. On the very Saturday on which I turned sixteen, Mom accompanied me to obtain my driver's license. She's the only mother I knew who seemed genuinely delighted when her teenager was lawfully allowed to take the wheel. And she never took me to piano lessons again. It was cold turkey, just like that.

"You have piano fingers," people always said, whatever that meant. I took it as a compliment that they considered my fingers long and slim, the right size for tickling the ivories with ease. Even in first grade, though, I had the inherited strong fingernails of my maternal grandfather's clan, which naturally grew long and unbreakable. This became a problem for my first piano teacher.

An elderly woman, slight of build, and gracefully graying, my teacher was not mean, but I was still afraid of displeasing her. Her manner was all business, and she took playing the piano very seriously. She talked and moved slowly and deliberately, but became spry and alive when showing me how to play a passage. I was told that I was lucky to have gotten her because she was a legendary instructor who was in high demand and had been there so long she was like part of the woodwork.

Her own fingers were beginning to show the gnarls of early arthritis. She kept admonishing me to cut my fingernails low enough not to show above the tips if the hands were facing you. "Your nails are louder than the notes on the keys. It sounds like a nail symphony!"

Instead of using the metronome to keep time, she patted the piano using a circular hand movement, simultaneously calling out the beats in the measures with her voice. "Ta-fa-tay-fa. Ta-fa-tay-fa. Ta-fa-tay-fa." Her constant ta-fa-taying was monotonous enough, but to add to the annoyance, she made me say it too.

One day, however, she made me laugh and that private moment endeared her to me. She was trying to explain that one can express oneself on the piano in the same way that one can by talking.

"You can start by saying something low and quietly," she said, scooting me over on the bench to play whatever tune was giving me a problem. "Then, you can crescendo, gradually increasing the volume to speak loud and forcefully! Fortissimo!" She showed me by changing the melody accordingly.

Then she began to play something else sweetly. "Your fingers can linger on the keys like this, playing dolce."

Sensing my boredom, she startled me to attention when she went from lovely sonatina to lively march without missing a beat. "Or they can play quickly with staccato!" The sound was light and fast, and her fingers looked like they were flecking lint off the keys.

Class was soon over, but she continued to explain as I gathered my music books and headed for the door. "When you talk you can say one thing, then repeat it with a particular inflection, and listeners will get a totally different meaning. The same thing goes with playing the piano."

To keep my attention, she put her hand on the knob, preventing me from leaving, and lowered her voice. I leaned in to make her think I was listening, instead of what I was really doing—getting in position to make a beeline out of there.

"For example, it's one thing to say, 'Madame . . . foot got caught in the door.' And quite another to say . . ." she paused, and then raised her voice expressively. "My *damn* foot got caught in the door!"

We laughed together. That was the ice breaker that became our private joke. And, oh, yes, it also made me a better pianist.

As years passed, I was promoted next door to a younger teacher. My new instructor wore her brunette hair in a close, modern bob, and she preferred skirts and blouses over the more stylish shirtwaist dresses my mother liked. She was taller than my mother or I, which probably only meant she was average height because we were shrimps. A pleasant enough woman, she was kind to me and indulged my ambitions of playing music entirely too hard for me.

Measuring myself against what other kids played at recitals, and influenced by the radio, I wanted to play something that sounded "with it." My teacher introduced me to Johann Sebastian Bach, whose rhythmic music style immediately felt right up my alley. I've played every tune in the brown-and-navy music book that has accompanied me through life and subsequent pianos ever since.

For a recital, I once had to memorize Bach's "March," and it is still my favorite little jolly song. Whenever I sit down to play, that comes out. And then there was the "Minuet in G." The hit singing group the Toys had a hit in 1965 called "A Lover's Concerto" and we saw them perform on TV on "Shindig," "Hullabaloo," and of course, "American Bandstand." The kids in my neighborhood who didn't take piano didn't know that the melody for the R&B song was an adaptation of Bach's "Minuet." So, at age thirteen, I was able to amuse my playmates by hipping them to the "real" version.

The music of Ludwig van Beethoven was my teacher's favorite, and became both my joy and my challenge. The long, rapidly played passages of intricate fingering were difficult to learn and exhilarating to accomplish. Trills were my specialty, played ably with my right hand in the shrill treble clef even though I was left-handed. And I loved attacking the keys with both hands full of chords when I wanted to show off.

The music seemed like the perfect background accompaniment to the Shakespearean plays I was learning in eighth grade at Asa Mercer Junior High. After school, I would have to practice my Beethoven sonatas, and then go upstairs to my room to study for a test in English Lit. In which play, I would muse, did Puck say, "Oh, what fools these mortals be!" In my adolescent rebellion stage at the time, I thought the description applied perfectly to all the men who were doing such a bad job of running the world, allowing the wars and the race riots. I also knew several "backstabbing" girls I would have liked to ask, like Julius Caesar, "Et tu, Brute?"

At Cornish, however, I developed my own secret rivalries. I admit that my competitive spirit was aroused by a certain well-heeled, long-haired white girl who was around my age, but who had advanced far ahead in the Beethoven book.

At one Saturday morning recital, The Girl breezed up to the piano, sat down, put her hands in her lap first, then carefully on the keys, and played a particularly difficult piece with grace and flawless poise. By the end of her perfect performance I both admired and envied her. My own adequate performance was forgotten immediately by everyone, including me. I became fixated on playing that piece of work and one day sitting down to perform it in recital in front of *her.* It was my desire to slam-dunk her, like Lew Alcindor.

It didn't help that her father was some big-time lawyer with whom my father was acquainted, and evidently had high regard for. Daddy was always asking me, "How's Attorney So-and-So's daughter up there at Cornish?"

How should I know? I always wanted to say, but wouldn't dare. *I don't know her and don't like her.* "She's fine," I answered.

My goal to master Beethoven with more proficiency than The Girl could play it, motivated me like nothing else at Cornish had. At my Monday class, I turned to the page of my music book that featured that tune and asked my teacher if I could attempt to play it.

"No," she said dismissively. "You are not that advanced yet."

"Couldn't I at least try? I'd love to play like your other student at the recital," I purred.

"Well, just start with this first section," she said, giving in and marking where to stop with her extra-sharp pencil. "Play one hand at a time. Start slowly."

The piece was fast and furious. The appeal of it was its sweet beginning that ran smack into a surprise cadence of rich chords and ambidextrous finger work. I never could make myself play it slow, because I wanted to play it like The Girl, who played it *allegro*—lively, rapidly, and with authority. And therefore, I never could conquer it.

I have no idea why my mother made me stick with piano. I asked to quit, not because I didn't enjoy playing, but because it required more practice and commitment than a kid wants to give to anything that all her friends aren't doing too. But Mom never indulged me in long conversations about things she was resolute about.

"Mom, can I quit piano?"

"No."

"Why not?"

"Because I said so."

And that was that. Children in our house didn't argue with adults. It wasn't just disrespectful; it was out of the question. You might as well not even *think* about pushing your luck.

Perhaps, I surmised, she wanted to see if I could turn out to be a prodigy. I did learn to play church music from our hymn book, and next thing I knew Mom had me playing piano for the Junior Church Choir. Or maybe Mom secretly wanted to prove something—that if given an equal opportunity Negroes could play classical music as well as anyone else. It was a time when everything we did meant something or stood for something. You had to be a credit to the race.

You also had to stay "occupied," one of Mom's favorite words for keeping us busy during school breaks. To keep me "occupied" one summer, she tried to arrange for our music director at church to teach me more advanced gospel music than the hymns I played for the kids' choir. But in the meantime, she heard about organ lessons that were being offered at the humongous cathedral, St. Marks, near Cornish. The summer I was fifteen years old, I spent shuttling between organ lessons and Driver's Ed.

The Caucasian male instructor was also the organist during church services at St. Mark's. On an organ that seemed as old as it was grand, he taught me about the different keys, buttons, and pipes, and how to play the long, wooden-slat pedals with my feet—all skills I promptly lost after the summer was over. The best part of those lessons was that I couldn't practice at home. We certainly didn't have a pipe organ there and, thank goodness, it would have been too much of a hassle to arrange for me to practice at my own church.

Daddy was proud of my playing. Although my mother had had a piano when she was growing up and knew how to play and read music, my father did not, and liked to marvel that there was something I knew that he didn't.

"Steph can play the piano! What d'ya know about that?" he would say.

There was one tune in particular that I played over and over so many times, it became the song I was known for among the family. "The Spinning Song" is one of those fast, rhythmic pieces that most kids who take piano like to learn. It's a happy ditty that makes you sound as if you can play something well and impressively.

"Play that song you always play, Steph," Daddy would say, teasing. "That one that goes: Diddle, diddle, doo, *dah,* dot, dah! Diddle, diddle, doo, *dah,* dot, dah!" He'd do a little jig at the same time, and I'd break out laughing.

"You are so silly!" Then I'd play the thing.

I didn't turn out to be a female André Watts. When I realized that dropping out was out of the question, I asked if I could at least switch from classical piano to the jazz classes Cornish offered.

"When you get to the twelfth grade, you can take whichever piano class you want," Mom replied, "classical or jazz."

"Gee, thanks, Mom."

I had to wait until my last year of school. For years until then, I endured the monotony of the classical lessons and the isolation of taking them alone—not in a group setting with other students. Unlike band class when I played clarinet in junior high, or the choir class I took with a hundred kids at Franklin High, classical piano meant solo lessons and practice. The main thing that kept me going—besides my mother's unbending perseverance—was the reward of taking jazz piano.

In the fall of 1969, senior year finally arrived. True to her promise, my mother enrolled me in Cornish's Beginner's Jazz for Piano. It was humbling to be called a "beginner" after having just graduated from the most advanced classical course. But that didn't help me much in this genre.

I never knew of Cornish to have any Negro piano teachers. My jazz teacher could have been described as a beatnik. Young, long-haired, with a goatee, he had an easy manner that reminded me of Maynard G. Krebs on the "Dobie Gillis" TV show. I appreciated his friendliness and attentive method of teaching, but unfortunately, he couldn't make much progress with me.

After so many years of being accustomed to reading every note I played, I had a big problem with improvisation. It seemed to me that either you could play by ear, or play by music, but doing both at the same time wasn't working for me.

"All you have to do is get a walking bass line going," he said, showing me by playing "On Green Dolphin Street," a song I didn't particularly care for. "Then improvise the melody with the right hand."

I also had a problem with the fact that this white guy was trying to show me how to play black music. Then I had a problem with the fact that I had a problem. Was I prejudiced? It didn't occur to me that some white folks could have had a problem with little colored me learning European classical music. In my immature, self-absorbed, teenage way, I held a resentment that this person had learned to play jazz, and I, who was black, could not. I was sure I could dance better than he could. I was sure I knew the words to more R&B hits than he did. So why couldn't I grasp this genre of piano playing that was identified with my people? I wasn't trying to be a Count, a Duke, a Monk, or a Mary Lou. But I did make the mistake of thinking that one year of jazz would put me on the same level that twelve years of classical had accomplished. And so, I suffered through nine months of the class, which seemed much longer.

Toward the end of the school year, during choir class at Franklin when the teacher, Mr. Koehler, was out of the room, Deems Tsutakawa, a neighbor who had also been my classmate since the fourth grade, sat down at the shiny, black Steinway grand and jammed on "Song for My Father" like he was Horace Silver or somebody. A kicky tune with a bossa nova beat, it was just the kind of finger-snapping, danceable jazz I wanted to play.

"Deemie, you gotta show me how to play that, okay?" I asked as I walked up to the piano. Deems was Japanese, so a brother "minority" would be teaching me jazz, I rationalized.

"Sure, Steph," Deems said. And he did teach me, starting with the super-easy, repetitive, left-hand bass line.

I played that song to death! I played it so much, even I was sick of me playing it all the time. On Father's Day, it became my custom to play it for Daddy, while he read the Sunday *Seattle Times* after church.

"Here's a song for you, Dad," I'd say. "The name of it is 'Song for My Father.'"

"Oh, is it? Well, isn't that something!" he'd reply, as if he hadn't heard the tune a million times before.

At last, I had some jazz to play.

As for ol' Beethoven's composition, I worked on that piece for years and years—long after I had graduated from Cornish and stopped taking piano. There was nothing left for me to learn, I felt, but Beethoven. If I couldn't master that, why try anything else?

To my despair, I somehow misplaced the music book that contained it, somewhere between high school, college, adulthood, and moves back and forth between the west coast and the east coast. For years and years, I couldn't even recall the precise name of the piece. Was it a sonatina, a sonata, a rondo, or a bagatelle? Every so often it would haunt me, and I would go schlepping around to music stores, asking proprietors, "Are you familiar with a Beethoven composition that goes . . . ?" then I would start humming. They would shake their heads—though whether out of pity or nonrecognition, I never could discern.

One day quite recently, I was having lunch with my stepdaughter, Ahmondyllah, at an outdoor café in our New Jersey suburban town and noticed a music-book store nearby. I wandered in and browsed their racks. Picking up *Beethoven: His Greatest Piano Solos,* I stared at the dramatic painting of Ludwig's stern visage on the cover. I thought, boy, cover designs of piano books really had changed from the mustard-yellow covers of Schirmer's Library Classics featuring nondescript type treatments, the design of which was so standard that the teeny-tiny print on the bottom let you know it was copyrighted in 1939 and renewed without change in 1967. I realized that I had been more familiar with Beethoven's music than his face. But here it was on this brand-new piano book, staring at me in vibrant full color. Noticing the dark, curly hair, I recalled the rumors of German-born Ludwig van Beethoven having African, or Moorish, blood. In America with its "one drop" rule, this would have essentially categorized him as a Negro. Actually, in the late 1700s and early 1800s in which he lived, if such a claim had been even suspected, much less confirmed, he could have been sold into slavery if he had ever set foot in the New World. Even now, debate continues on the Internet over whether there was a cover-up about Beethoven's full heritage.

I flipped the pages of the volume, looking for the notes of the familiar first bars. Ahmondyllah sat down patiently. About halfway through the two hundred pages, I found what I was looking for— Rondo in C.

With the excitement of found treasure, I bought the book and took it home to my piano. But I was rustier than ever. Time and age had bested me. If I couldn't play it in my prime when I was practicing daily with the nimble fingers of a teenager, how could I have kidded myself into thinking I could master it now? I wondered if The Girl—who, of course, would now be a middle-aged woman—still played that piece. I noticed that although my memory had always selected the more aggressive passage of heavy chords that she performed with gusto, the composition began with instructions to play dolce, sweetly.

All of a sudden, for the first time in over thirty years, I had no desire to attack the piece myself. Instead, I thought how wonderful it would be if only I could sit back and hear the magnificent performance of a certain confident pianist as she commenced Beethoven's Rondo in C dolce one more time.

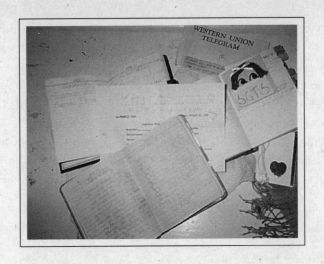

= 13 =

The Impossible Dream

THEY ARE THREE of my most cherished possessions. Two of them are preserved in the well-kept gift-boxes in which they arrived over forty years ago. Their good condition belies the fact that they are almost as old as I am. First, they were hidden in my desk drawer out of the sight of the curious eyes of my parents in Seattle. Now, a generation later and a continent away, they are stored in my attic, in the big, black trunk I took to college, far out of the reach of the quick little hands of my step-grandchildren. These treasures are my diaries.

After I joined the church at age eight, I was obliged to take a class on what baptism and being a Baptist meant. One of the pamphlets for children required that we write down our lessons in a diary that we

ABOVE: *Dear Diary—my childhood journals documented both the monumental and the trivial.*

could refer to later. This was how I came to possess a very sophisticated, hunter-green, bound volume that had a lock with a key now long gone. In the days before Barbie diaries and other girlie-looking pink journals that extended the brands of popular toys, my diary had the impressive appearance of something Sojourner Truth might have used. Its own stateliness encouraged my young mind to take it seriously.

Opening the still-clean and precious book, I see, in newly learned penmanship, words written with a blue-ink fountain pen, probably sneaked out of my father's cherished collection of Mont Blancs:

> *This Diary Belongs to*
> *Stephanie Jo Stokes*
> *March 1960–1962*

The first entry reflects the class lesson I copied from the book.

> *March 21, 1960*
> *Dear Diary,*
> *The beauty of a tree makes me think of God.*
> *Dear Lord:*
> *I love this world. You made this world for men. For all of us to enjoy. I love this world.*
> *Amen.*

Still following my religious studies, I wrote this a few days later, obviously without benefit of my teacher's correction of the punctuation.

> *Dear Diary,*
> *Prayer*
> *Dear God I do love Jesus help me to love him enough really to live as he taught.*
> *Amen.*

But two days later, my studies must have been completed, and I realized that I could use my diary as a friend that I could trust to keep all my secrets. Not having a tradition of confession, like the Episcopalian church across the street, I confided in my journal.

> *Dear Diary,*
> *I made a girl mad.*

And then there was this other time.

> *Dear Diary,*
> *Today I had a nice day until Mom hit me on my rear (hard) for arguing*
> *at school with a boy.*

Well, so much for Christian education! With no elaboration in the journal and no personal recollection, I can't say what all that was about. My memory has conveniently blanked out the days when I was a "bad girl."

However, an entry written on April 3, 1960, characterizes the more common kinds of writings I would share with that diary and others for years to come.

> *Dear Diary,*
> *Mark relly relly said he relly likes me.*

A kind of "lonely hearts" vehicle for a child experiencing puppy love, my diary became a confidant, a psychotherapist, a nonjudgmental place to put my feelings, misspellings and all. Knowing I couldn't talk to my parents or siblings about "boys" for fear of being called "boy crazy," "fast," or otherwise ridiculed, I found refuge in my diaries.

Four years later for my twelfth birthday, at a party held in an indoor amusement park that allowed us to go on rides in spite of the winter drizzle, my neighbor and classmate Debra Burns gave me a five-year diary. This journal was to become not only a fun record of my adolescent love life but also an invaluable documentation of my view of the country's political and civil rights events of the decade.

Obtained in January 1964, the diary was dutifully kept until I turned eighteen, near the end of the 1960s. The first entry, however, docu-mented a national event that had occurred two months earlier, but that still reverberated amid the sorrow of the entire nation: the assassina-tion of President Kennedy.

1963
On Nov. 22 at 1:30 p.m. Pres. Kennedy was shot by Lee Oswald. Two days later he [arrow pointing to Oswald's name] *was shot by Jack Ruby. (I saw it on television.)*

I was in my seat at John Muir Elementary School on that fateful Friday when our teacher's assistant from the nearby high school entered our sixth-grade classroom less ebullient than usual. We knew something was wrong when he didn't make us laugh as he walked in. Instead, he whispered something into Mrs. Fancher's ear, then the two of them stepped out into the hall and closed the door behind them. Thirty eleven-year-olds were left to look around at one another in confusion. When the teacher and the aide returned, Mrs. Fancher spoke to the class.

"We have just been to the principal's office, and as our assistant told me, President Kennedy has been shot. Everyone should pack up your things, put on your coats, and go home now." She sounded calm, but we knew this was highly unusual and downright scary.

In those pre-bussing days, most children lived in the area near the school, but kids in my neighborhood probably lived the farthest away because, although we were in John Muir's district, our homes were located near the dividing line, over a mile away. This was a *long* walk for a child. We had to walk up the entire length of a great, big hill on Thirty-first Avenue South that was at least ten blocks long itself. I looked around for the other kids in my neighborhood, and wished I lived as close as my buddy Leslie, whose house was just around the corner and whose mother, unlike mine, did not work. At the time, my mother was informing her own young students of the assassination, at her job as a second-grade teacher at another public school several miles away. Daddy was at the office—or was he in court? I had no idea, and no way of calling him. So, I looked for the kids with whom I always walked home from school, and got to stepping.

On the long walk home, some of the kids started telling tales.

"I heard that the president got killed—and that could mean World War III with Russia!" said my neighbor, the "bad boy" who was always stirring up trouble. We usually paid him no mind, but today we listened in fear. Realizing he had our attention, he got bolder. "You know, they'll probably bomb the United States before we even get home. And if they do, they'll probably drop it right here on Seattle because we're the closest part of the country to Russia!"

Actually, Alaska, one of the two new states, was closest, but this was no time to be technical. Washington state was closest on the mainland, so that was enough for me to stay scared for days. We had had the Cold War, air raids, bomb shelters, bald-headed Soviet leader Nikita Khrushchev shaking his finger at us, and now this. The television news reported that they didn't know when school would resume. That weekend, all day, every day, the television news ran repeat footage of the motorcade's ride through the streets of Dallas—the blurry home movie of him being shot, Mrs. Kennedy trying to get the heck out of the back of the convertible limousine, and the shocked and crying Americans on the lawn in the aftermath. I searched the TV set for Negro faces in the crowd, and found them—their faces in anguish, mirroring those of our parents, our neighbors, our church members.

Black folks were saddened, Daddy and Mommy included. They walked around the house talking in hushed tones and shaking their heads in disbelief. In the homes of many Negroes were pictures of Kennedy, on the walls right up there with Jesus Christ and Abraham Lincoln. During his short time in office he had further ingratiated himself to the black community with words like this, spoken shortly before his death.

So, let us not be blind to our differences, but let us also direct attention to our common interests and to the means by which the differences can be resolved. And if we cannot now end our differences, at least we can help

make the world safe for diversity. For in the final analysis, our most
basic link is that we all inhabit this small planet. We all breathe the
same air. We all cherish our children's future. And we are all mortal.

Over that weekend and the Monday off from school for the funeral, I
was allowed out of the house only to run directly to Renee Miller's two
blocks away. In the home that Renee (pronounced *Ree-nee*, whose real
name was Maureen) shared with her good-looking, youthful parents,
Waymond and Audrey, and her three lively siblings, sandy-haired
Butchie (my boyfriend of the moment), pretty Stephanie, and baby
Lori Ann, I found refuge. The Millers always allowed me to come into
their house through the unlocked side door. I never had to call first or
even knock. Mr. Miller started the family habit of referring to me affectionately as "Stokes" to differentiate between me and their daughter
Stephie, who was two years younger than I. Mrs. Miller—whose pretty
face, ironically, looked like that of a light-skinned black Jacqueline
Kennedy—often referred to me affectionately as just another one of
"the kids."

On Sunday morning of November 24, after spending the night at
the Millers', my eyes were transfixed on the constant television coverage of the aftermath of the assassination. As all other programming
had been preempted for the first time ever by this unusual coverage of
our nation in mourning, even I, at my young age, knew that this was
historic. I was watching, following the coverage, when the slight-
bodied, alleged killer, Lee Harvey Oswald, was brought out of jail to be
transferred to another prison facility. I don't recall who else was in the
second-floor playroom with me, but I do remember precisely what I
saw. A man in a tall Texas hat walked up, and—*pow!*—just like that, he
shot him.

"Oh my gosh! Oh my gosh!" I yelled to everyone in the Miller house.
"Somebody shot that man that killed Kennedy, right there on TV!" It
seemed unbelievable, at first. But I quickly realized that this wasn't some
shoot-'em-up, and these weren't actors in a movie. It wasn't even the
often-replayed, blurry Kennedy tape that was hard to make out at the
moment of death. No, this thing had happened as clear as day. The

detachment of television didn't lessen the shock of having witnessed the murder. I felt that with my very own eyes, I had seen Jack Ruby kill Lee Harvey Oswald.

I wrote in my diary: *What is the world coming to?*

On the day of the funeral, the preeminent sounds from the television were of the four drummers from the United States Army Band. Keeping a muffled cadence on drums that replicated those in the American Revolution, they droned on for what seemed like hours and hours.

> *Dat-dat-daaaa (da-da-da)/*
> *Dat-dat-daaaa (da-da-da)/*
> *Dat-dat-daaaa (da-da-da)/*
> *Dat-dat-da-dat!*

I can still hear it, etched in my memory forever.

In the years to come, my diaries would reveal a continuing appreciation for the political events of the day. On February 11, when I was twelve, I wrote:

> *Dear Diary, VOTE DAY. The school levy passed. Braman & Cherberg are nominees for mayor. (We voted for Irving Clark, Jr.)*

Of course, *I* had voted for no one! But the school levy was of utmost importance in my house, because it usually affected either my mother's paycheck or the resources she would have with which to teach her class. It happened that J. D. Braman, a Republican, won the mayoral race the next month. But who was Irving Clark, Jr.? I have no idea.

Also in February was George Washington's Birthday, a holiday we took off from school on the twenty-second, no matter on what day of the week it fell. In 1964 (before there was such a thing as President's Day) my diary shows that I spent the night with my friend Frances, an exceedingly smart child who lived a bike ride away. But most of the time I noted that I "stayed home all day, went nowhere, talked to no one, did nothing." Bored, I wrote this entry one year:

> *Washington's Birthday*
> *(Big deal! I never knew him)*
> *He probably had slaves and hated blacks anyway.*

On March 14, 1964, the Kennedy assassination still reverberated:

> *Dear Diary,*
> *Our school was supposed to be on "Quizdown" [a local TV show], but they showed the Jack Ruby trial instead. We won anyway, though.*

A month later, on April 15, I knew history was being made at the Academy Awards.

> *Dear Diary,*
> *Tonight on the Academy Awards, the first Negro was selected for Actor of the Year (Sidney Poitier).*

I had filled all the space allotted in my diary for that entry. But what I didn't have space to elaborate on was how proud my parents were of Sidney Poitier. I had seen *Lilies of the Field* and thought it was a silly story about a colored guy and a bunch of white nuns. I liked it better when Sidney was being defiant, as when he said to that white man in one movie, "They call me *Mr.* Tibbs!" Not *boy*, not the n-word, but a name of respect. That was Oscar-quality acting to me.

The day after the Oscar program aired, my mother and I went over to my aunt Katie's house. I knew the events of the evening before must have been historic when I saw my mother and her older sister get all choked up. As we drank hot cocoa and munched on homemade biscuits in the kitchen, Aunt Katie made it plain. "Girl, I am telling you—it's about time a Negro got an Oscar. I am so proud of that Sidney Poitier!"

My father was proud of colored folks who held national political offices, regardless of their party affiliation. It was a rainy night in December of 1966 when he and Mom made me tag along to hear freshman Democratic Congressman John Conyers speak. I was prepped in advance as to why it was important for me to witness the appearance in our city of the man who was only the twenty-eighth Negro, and one of the few since Reconstruction, to serve in the House of Representatives.

"This is a very prominent person about whom you should know, Stephanie," Daddy informed me. "One of these days, you'll say, 'United States Congressman John Conyers came to Seattle, and I saw him with my own two eyes.'"

"History isn't just in your textbooks," Mom chimed in. "You'll be able to go to school tomorrow and tell your teachers that you heard a member of Congress speak."

At age fourteen, I can't say that was one of my top priorities, but I knew my parents well enough to understand when they were trying to expose me to important people, so I just listened.

The First African Methodist Episcopal Church was the second largest black church to our own Mount Zion. The sanctuary was turned into a lecture hall, full of people who were members at the two churches and other residents of the Central District. I noticed white reporters from the newspapers standing along the wall, taking notes. Maybe this was a big deal, after all.

But it was a school night and I'd had a long day. There were only a few other young people there, and my parents did not allow phony bathroom breaks. So I just sat there in the red-velvet cushioned pew between Dad and Mom and stared drowsily at Mr. Conyers's handsome face and jet-black wavy hair, and half listened to his calm, easy voice for the duration of the evening.

Afterward, my parents led me up to the podium to meet him. Full of charm and charisma, the representative from Detroit shook my hand and obliged me with his autograph as he and Daddy traded small talk about politics.

In my diary is taped a small piece of the bright yellow paper used for the evening's program. Cut in a trapezoidal shape, the crisp paper displays Conyers's neat, backhanded signature in the thick and thin letters of a black fountain pen. A green blur between the *c* and the *y* marks the spot where a raindrop splattered the perfection of my prize on the way to the car after the event.

> *Dear Diary,*
> *The person behind that rain-spotted autograph is 1 of the 1st Negro*
> *Congressmen. He came from Michigan. Gave a speech at First A.M.E.*
> *He sure is "fine" to be 37 years old. Boring speech though.*

Of course, my parents thought otherwise.

Having an attorney for a father meant learning at an early age to answer the telephone in a mannerly and professional way. My father didn't believe in baby talk, and when it came to his clients, he didn't play. How we spoke to callers was important to him.

"Enunciate!" he would tell us. "Speak up."

Potential clients could call at any time of the day or night. If someone had just been put in jail on a Saturday night, they might make that one call to their lawyer by dialing our number. Or a car accident might occur after office hours, and a person might need to call our house. We had strict instructions on how to take phone messages, in case Dad wasn't home.

"Hello?"

"Hello, is Attorney Stokes there?"

"No, I'm sorry, he isn't. May I take a message?" I was told to say. Not *can* I take a message.

"Of course, you *can*," Daddy would chastise us. "You can because you can write, but it's better etiquette to ask if you *may* take the message."

How one presented oneself was important. First impressions on the phone—even from children—could influence a client, we were told.

When I was fourteen, my father must have decided that I had mastered the skill of answering the telephone enough to work in his office that summer.

Dear Diary,
Today I got my first full-time job working for my dad as secretary while
his takes a vacation. I get paid $3 a day. Maybe when I can type I'll get
a raise.

I hadn't even started the job, and was already maneuvering for a raise.

I always liked going to my father's office. Because he worked down-town in the vicinity of the department stores, my mother usually took me by there and we'd leave with money for shopping. Or we'd make him close up the office to go out for dinner with us. On Saturdays, I sometimes went to work with him for a few hours, as he met with clients who couldn't get away from their jobs to make appointments during the workweek.

In one office building, I recall, on the block near where Amazon.com is located now, there was an elevator that had no walls, only bars like a cage. You could see every floor and if someone had buzzed for the ele-vator, you could see them standing there as the elevator approached, and the elevator operator would stop for the person. The wrought-iron bars of the door opened like an accordion and closed with a loud clankety-clang.

When you stepped off the elevator, Dad's door was on the left and had a frosted window on the top half on which his name appeared in fancy gold leaf script:

Charles M. Stokes
Attorney at Law

I can't recall any of the names of the secretaries he had over the years, but my memories are of courteous and prim colored ladies in shirt-waist dresses, like the kind reporter Lois Lane wore on the "Superman" TV show. The secretary sat in the reception area at a sizable desk made of light-colored wood that had a typewriter attachment on one side. She had a Dictaphone machine that I was sternly told not to touch when I was younger, and never could figure out how to work as I got older. It looked a lot like the precursor to the telephone answering machine, or a fax, with its phone cradled on the side. When visitors arrived, the secretary would rise and walk to Daddy's office in the rear of the suite to inform him. I usually just barged on in, unless he was meeting with a client.

Dad sat behind a massive mahogany desk with a glass top that he kept clean with daily spurts of Windex. Volumes of thick, green law books surrounded him on the bookshelves that rose from floor to ceiling. Two sturdy, red leather chairs were pulled up to the desk, always in preparation for conference. Neat and tidy, Dad never let things get out of place; that would spoil the image.

I thought Daddy had a cool job just because he had a cool office. Even when he moved to other buildings, the furnishings remained the same, so the comfort factor was always there.

In the summer of 1966, I put away my pedal pushers and tennis shoes, donned my Sunday-go-to-meeting clothes, and went to work at Daddy's office. The first day, I wore my Easter outfit—a beige-and-brown tweed jacket and skirt with a yellow silk top. I had started wearing nylons at thirteen, but it was my mother's firm rule that I still couldn't wear high heels until I turned sixteen. So my slingbacks were what was called "squash heels," one-inch high.

Sitting at the secretary's desk, I was instructed to greet those who came to call, and to come knock on Daddy's door to inform him, as his secretary did. At the time, he shared an office suite with two other lawyers, Attorney Lockett and Attorney Johnson. Both of them were also family friends, so I knew them. They were nice to me and treated me as though I was actually old enough to be a secretary. I took myself seriously, and begged them all to give me things to type, to take the edge off the boredom and to position myself for a raise. But no such luck. I came to find out that there was no way they were going to trust the private papers of their clients and the official forms they had to file in various courts of law to a fourteen-year-old.

Still, I enjoyed answering the phones, filing briefs, and opening the mail for the attorneys. I was glad to get up and stretch my legs when I had to announce that someone with an appointment had arrived. To get a jump on the typing class I would have that year in ninth grade, I pecked out letters to my sister, Vicki, in Los Angeles, or to Aunt Bootsie in Selma. When the lawyers were out to lunch, in court, or otherwise out of the office, and I was left alone to hold down the fort, letters would be carefully drafted and neatly typed to a VIP—my boyfriend.

But for the most part, it was a great way to get paid for being able to have time for my favorite pastime, reading. At lunchtime, I would have a burger, fries, and a chocolate shake at the luncheonette on the ground floor, then buy a *Seventeen* or *Mademoiselle*. Several times a week I checked out books from the nearby Seattle Public Library, and was pleased when my efforts and competitive spirit paid off. Having read the most books of my age group, I was awarded first prize in the Summer Reading Program. I recall devouring, in my teen years, Willa Cather's books and also Sammy Davis, Jr.'s autobiography, *Yes, I Can.* I did not read one book by or about a colored girl, because there were none that I knew of. But I did relate to Anne Frank, the teenage girl who had received a diary for her thirteenth birthday, just before she and her family were forced into hiding in Nazi-occupied Amsterdam. In my own journal, I wrote:

> *Dear Diary,*
> *I finished reading "Diary of a Young Girl" by Anne Frank. Her diary is almost as good as mine. (Ha! Ha! Ha!)*
> *It was so sad that she died at the same age I am!*

Teen vanity aside, it strikes me now as I gaze at the worn paperback that became a treasured possession, that children relate to other children their age, regardless of race. And they always give more weight to life than to death.

In books, I learned about the world beyond Seattle and people who made a difference in it. Working in my father's office, I learned about being an attorney. One day, while I was working in the office, Daddy took me to see the legal profession in action.

> *Dear Diary,*
> *During my lunch break Daddy took me to eat then we watched a trial at Judge Charles Z. Smith's court. (He's Negro.) Then Daddy took me to see the jail. Here's a souvenir.*

Taped to the page is a pink piece of paper that is folded in half. Gingerly opening the page, I see it says:

KING COUNTY SHERIFF'S DEPARTMENT
APPLICATION TO VISIT PRISONER

It was an official form with lines to fill out with your name, the name of the prisoner, your telephone numbers at home and business, your relationship to the prisoner, and reason for visit. Then there was a double line with instructions, "Do Not Write Below This Line" and space for signatures on lines next to "Visit Approved By" and "Not Approved By." I don't recall going to see any prisoners that day, but it seemed to me that Daddy was always saying he was "going down to the jail." I did not envy him.

But he never complained about his work. Mom says that he always chided her for bringing home papers to grade and for venting her frustration about the bratty little kids in her classroom.

"Leave your work at work," he would say. And that's just what he did. He didn't talk about his cases, and he rarely opened his briefcase in the house. It was his habit to be home for dinner every night by seven o'clock. That was the time everyone in our family was expected to return from wherever they were, so that we could have dinner together at the kitchen table.

Dad knew how to turn off his work life to give full attention at home to his children, and to make dates to go out on the town with Mom. After my trip to the jail, my diary states, I had the fun of spending another night over at the Millers' house. We had a few babysitters when I was a child, but by the time I reached adolescence, I pretty much took for granted the fact that I had my choice of caring relatives, extended family, and close neighbors at whose homes I was always welcome. In return, our house was open to young friends and family whose parents needed a night out. Just about every weekend, someone was spending the night somewhere. If I had a dollar for every time I stayed overnight with friends, and added to that another dollar for each of the many times kids stayed at my house—sharing my double bed, zipped up in sleeping bags on the floor, or sneaking into the guest room—I'd be rich.

On this evening, Dad and Mom, dressed to the nines, dropped me off and traded greetings with Mr. and Mrs. Miller. Then they sped off in the Caddie. Eartha Kitt was in town, Jack!

Unfortunately, the joys of family, friends, and finger-popping were tempered by monumental events of profound sadness and hopeless-ness. More untimely, headline-making assassinations would be docu-mented in my diary. For some unknown reason, I have no memory at all of the events surrounding Rev. Martin Luther King, Jr.'s murder. But on that day, I was compelled to confide in my journal my feelings:

> *April 4, 1968*
> *Today the second assassination in my lifetime was committed. REV.*
> *MARTIN LUTHER KING, JR., WAS KILLED. He was a Negro leader*
> *for civil rights & a Nobel Peace Prize Winner. Daddy & Mommy once*
> *had dinner with him & his wife, Coretta. Survivors include: his wife,*
> *his 4 children, & a nation!*

Notice that I felt it necessary to identify who King was, just in case no one should remember in years to come. I am sure that I had no idea that Martin Luther King would be as celebrated as he is now. At the time, there were plenty of civil rights leaders on television, in the news-papers, and sometimes visiting our city. There was Roy Wilkins of the NAACP. There was Whitney Young of the Urban League. And more important to me, there were young men closer to my age, such as Huey Newton of the Black Panthers and Stokely Carmichael of the Stu-dent Nonviolent Coordinating Committee (SNCC).

I never considered what their places might be in history, because I was too busy living for the moment. History was what I studied in high school. The events of the day were deep and confusing. Each day brought such unbelievable, life-changing, and often life-threatening news that it was all one could do to navigate the uncertainty of the time. Without nostalgic thoughts of the past (like whites had of days that were "gone with the wind") or projections of a hopeful future (that kept alive the faith of our enslaved ancestors), the motivations of my generation of Afro-Americans, as we began to call ourselves, were exemplified in chants of "Freedom Now!"

> *What do we want?*
> *Freedom!*
> *When do we want it?*
> *Now!*

The evening of the King assassination, riots broke out across the country. Looting and civil disturbance occurred in Seattle, as well. But I was already familiar with rioting. The summer of 1967, I had written:

> *Dear Diary,*
> *There's quite a revolt in the U.S.A. now. All over the states there are riots involving Negroes & Whites. People are being killed, houses burned down. People homeless, hungry.*
> *Jimmy* [my boyfriend from Jack & Jill, who lived in Oregon] *said in Portland a boy he knows wuz rioting and put in jail with $3000 bail. No riots here, but the kids are restless & are causing disturbances.*

As a memorial to Rev. King, the Seattle Public Schools were dismissed the day after the assassination at 11 a.m., I noted in my diary. And then Spring Break began.

But there was no rest from the unrest—or the assassinations. Just two months after King's murder, on June 5, 1968, I wrote:

> *Dear Diary,*
> *Another assassination in our nation's history! The brother of the late Pres. John Kennedy, Robert F. Kennedy, was shot by Sirhan Sirhan when he was thanking supporters in a speech for his victory in the California presidential primary. Isn't that shameful?*

I was just sixteen, but I liked Robert Kennedy, and had hoped he'd become the next president. By this time, my father had become a judge, and had begun declaring himself "nonpartisan." But most black folks—my parents included—took note that this Kennedy was often accompanied by blacks, such as former football player Roosevelt Grier, who was by Kennedy's side when he was killed.

RFK didn't just pose with a token black person here and there. He addressed us directly in speeches, and in so doing, he gave us the impression that he actually *cared* about race relations and the well-being of African-Americans. As they would say in the Central District, he wasn't just paying lip service.

On the day that Martin Luther King was assassinated, Senator Kennedy was in Indianapolis, Indiana. His remarks upon hearing of King's death were examples of the kinds of comments that gave him favor among many African-Americans:

> *I have bad news for you, for all of our fellow citizens, and people who love peace all over the world, and that is that Martin Luther King was shot and killed tonight.*
>
> *Martin Luther King dedicated his life to love and to justice for his fellow human beings, and he died because of that effort.*
>
> *In this difficult day, in this difficult time for the United States, it is perhaps well to ask what kind of a nation we are and what direction we want to move in. For those of you who are black—considering the evidence there evidently is that there were white people who were responsible—you can be filled with bitterness, with hatred, and a desire for revenge. We can move in that direction as a country, in great polarization—black people amongst black, white people amongst white, filled with hatred toward one another.*
>
> *Or we can make an effort, as Martin Luther King did, to understand and to comprehend, and to replace that violence, that stain of bloodshed that has spread across our land, with an effort to understand with compassion and love.*
>
> *For those of you who are black and are tempted to be filled with hatred and distrust at the injustice of such an act, against all white people, I*

can only say that I feel in my own heart the same kind of feeling. I had a member of my family killed, but he was killed by a white man. But we have to make an effort in the United States, we have to make an effort to understand, to go beyond these rather difficult times. . . .

What we need in the United States is not division; what we need in the United States is not hatred; what we need in the United States is not violence or lawlessness but love and wisdom, and compassion toward one another, and a feeling of justice toward those who still suffer within our country, whether they be white or they be black.

So I shall ask you tonight to return home, to say a prayer for the family of Martin Luther King, that's true, but more importantly to say a prayer for our own country, which all of us love—a prayer for understanding and that compassion of which I spoke.

We can do well in this country. We will have difficult times; we've had difficult times in the past; we will have difficult times in the future. It is not the end of violence; it is not the end of lawlessness; it is not the end of disorder.

But the vast majority of white people and the vast majority of black people in this country want to live together, want to improve the quality of our life, and want justice for all human beings who abide in our land. . . .

His was not the most militant or strident voice I would hear in those days, but how prophetic that Bobby Kennedy would say that it was not the end of violence, lawlessness, and disorder, when his own demise so soon thereafter would encompass them all.

Robert Kennedy had been running for office when he was killed. In my house, the activities of the Kennedy brothers, and Rev. King were linked by one honorable thing: political activism. John F. Kennedy had been campaigning in Dallas; Robert F. Kennedy had been doing the same in California. Martin Luther King had been in Memphis speaking about the "difficult days ahead" in the sanitation workers' strike and in the civil rights movement.

These influences, and my own father's political activism, were not lost on me. My family's indoctrination and the news around me made me keenly aware of the importance of using political office to make a difference. In that same year of sadness, for instance, Shirley Chisholm's achievement as the first African-American woman elected to Congress was cause for great joy. Leadership seemed synonymous with running for office. I decided to try it out in my own teenage way.

In eighth grade, I ran for Girls Club president. This was a very prestigious office to hold at Asa Mercer Junior High School, and it was quite competitive. It was tradition for the outgoing ninth-grade girls to help campaign for the next year's officers. Patsy Sullivan, the outgoing president, offered to be my campaign manager.

This delighted my father! He was happy to see not only that I was interested in politics but also that my campaign manager was the daughter of a colleague of his in Seattle legal circles. When it came time to make the campaign "buttons" out of colored paper, felt-tip pens, crayons, and glue, Daddy volunteered to give us the money for the materials. This was no insignificant offer—he usually had to be begged to get off some money.

"Want to assemble the buttons here at the house?" he asked, not wanting to miss the action. "You can do it at the dining room table."

"Really? Not in the kitchen?" I asked, astonished. Our dining table was customarily reserved for formal occasions. I had no idea that campaigning for president of all the girls at my school would fit the bill. As it turned out, we did need the greater expanse of the dining table to cut the hundreds of pale green, three-inch paper squares. There was no going to a printer for expensive metal pins, like the grown-ups wore. We made every single little pin ourselves.

> *Dear Diary,*
> *I'm running for Girls Club President at school against Claudia Winston and Robin Luke (who used to be my classmate at Madrona Elementary). Patsy Sullivan is my campaign manager. It sure is a lot of work! I hope I WIN! Here is an example of my campaign buttons.*

There, I glued to the top of the diary page one of the buttons. It features a girl's face. By not coloring in the face on the pale green paper,

we made her not of one race, but of the human race. We made hair
out of dark brown yarn, then tied and glued a tiny white grosgrain ribbon at the top. On the bottom half of the square is a flap on which we
wrote SGTS. When you open the flap it intentionally misspells my
name to read:

Steff's Got The Stuff
(for G.C. Pres.)

Other diary entries tell of the candidate who was eliminated from running, and had to drop out of the race. It was definitely a political campaign drama!

I was black; Patsy was white; my opponent, Robin, was Chinese.
This mix of races was not unusual at the schools I attended. In the
South End of Seattle, school integration didn't mean just black
and white. In Washington state at the time, there were about equal
numbers of Asians and blacks. I went to school with Filipinos,
Jews, WASPs, blacks, Chinese, and Japanese, and shared friendships
outside of school with classmates of different races. My mother
always said, "Anyone is welcome in this house if you are welcome in
theirs."

I learned from my mother that one could often tell the difference
between Chinese and Japanese by their last names. Chinese surnames
commonly had one syllable, such as Lee, Chin, or Wong. Names with
more syllables—Mikimoto, Kataoka, or Sakaguchi—were more likely
to be of Japanese origin.

Being friendly with everyone helped my campaign for elected
office. I sought the votes of all the girls at school, regardless of race.
And I earnestly wanted to represent them all.

Almost a month after I declared my candidacy, I wrote in my
diary:

*Well, guess what? I WON the election for Girls Club President of Asa
Mercer Junior High School. Tomorrow I have to make an acceptance
speech. Daddy's giving me a reward of $50.*

This campaigning for office and winning was exciting and fun. Having my father's blessing, enthusiasm, and support was the icing on the chocolate cake. Besides the position of Student Council president (which no girl had ever won yet), Girls Club and Boys Club presidents were big deals at my school. The presidents represented half the student body of hundreds of seventh-, eighth-, and ninth-graders. We took our elections seriously too. We voted by using the same machines that the adults who came to vote at our school on Election Days used. Becoming the first black to win Girls Club president made me want to be a *winner.*

The next year, after being in office a few months, I confided:

Dear Diary,
Being Girls Club President is cool. Everyone at school knows me—even those I don't know. I don't wanna get conceited tho. I'm trying to get real good grades.

Bolstered by my junior-high election, and my successful year in office, when I entered Franklin High School, I declared my candidacy for sophomore class president. This was the big time.

Franklin had a couple thousand students. Although Garfield High School had the highest proportion of black kids, Franklin came in second and that made it Garfield's biggest rival. In my observation, Franklin seemed to be one-third black, one-third Asian, and one-third Jewish and other whites. The perfect racial mix.

By this time, my father had not run for office since he had lost as lieutenant governor seven years before. Concentrating on his private law practice, he'd had some high-profile cases that had gotten him attention on TV and in the Seattle newspapers. But my candidacies got him all revved up.

"Why don't you say this when you give a speech? Four score and seven years ago . . ." he'd begin. I'd roll my eyes, and we'd crack up together.

All the suggestions he gave me sounded like corny remnants from the Dark Ages. I didn't feel that I could use any of the advice of this unofficial campaign manager. The interests of our two constituencies were divided by a generation gap. But I appreciated his enthusiasm, and particularly, his campaign funding.

> *Dear Diary,*
> *The primary elections were at school today. I got in the finals!!! Against*
> *Mark Abolofia. I hope I win.*

The time between the primary and the general election during our school year was quite compressed—one week. There was no time for button-making, just speech-making and assemblies. Half the sophomores had come from Sharples Junior High, so I wasn't as well acquainted with them as I was with my classmates who had come from Mercer. I tried my best to introduce myself to kids I didn't know, with the help of one friend from church who had gone to Sharples. Many of my Mercer classmates lent their support and showed me what it meant to have a campaign committee.

After all the campaigning had ended, the votes were in, and the tally posted, I gathered my books, closed my second-floor locker, and walked home from school as usual. Sitting cross-legged on my bed on the evening of the big day, I recorded the election results—where else?—in my journal.

> *Dear Diary,*
> *We had the final election at school.* **I LOST.** *Ain't that a shame? I don't*
> *feel too bad, though. You win a few & lose a few.*
> *And anyway, Mark will make a good president. I was hurt at first,*
> *but the blow made me grow up a bit, I guess. Now I know how to lose.*
> *I blew up at Daddy because I thought he expected too much of me. He*
> *wrote me this note. Gave me $5.*

A folded white piece of paper with the title "Sophomore Final Election Results" was placed without glue or tape in the book between the pages for October 17 and October 18. Typewritten are the winners:

President . . . . .Mark Abolofia
Vice-president . . . . .Peggy Mizrahi
Secretary . . . . .Debbie Terry
Treasurer . . . . .Linda Gabutero
Chairman of Chairmen . . . . .Uncounted—Will be posted after school

The name "Stephanie Stokes" is nowhere to be found. But handwritten in blue fountain pen across the top is a personal note to the also-ran:

> *Not failure, but low aim is a crime.*
> *You aimed high—tried—and are much the better for it.*
> *I'm proud of you.*
> *—Daddy*

$$\equiv 14 \equiv$$

Say It Loud—
I'm Black and I'm Proud

Three, six, nine
The goose drank wine
The monkey chewed tobacco on a streetcar line
The line broke
The monkey got choked
And they all went to Heaven in an integrated boat!

THE CONCEPT OF "INTEGRATION" was ingrained in our heads from an early age. We learned about it in our playground rhymes, ministers

ABOVE: *So happy to be nappy—me at sixteen in my first Afro.*

preached about it in sermons, we saw on our television sets that people died fighting for it.

There were several vocabulary words that had an enormous impact on my life, but that I was not taught in school: "Segregation." "Discrimination." "Desegregation." "Integration."

I had to find out what they meant by listening to the context in which they were used. I gathered that "segregation" meant the exclusion of Negroes from public accommodations and legal rights (such as voting) that whites were free to enjoy. It also resulted in our humiliation and degradation when we tried to exercise these rights.

"Discrimination" was the implementation of prejudice—meaning we were prejudiced and denied our rights based solely on the color of our brown skin.

"Desegregation" meant the abolishment of the segregated facilities, restaurants, and accommodations, usually by way of the president signing some bill.

"Integration," according to a 1962 speech by Martin Luther King, Jr., cited in the book *Testament of Hope: The Essential Writings and Speeches of Martin Luther King, Jr.* by James M. Washington, is the "positive acceptance of desegregation and the welcomed participation of Negroes into the total range of human activities. Integration is the genuine intergroup, interpersonal doing. Integration is the ultimate goal of our national community."

We knew that our parents were passionate about voting rights in the south and housing rights in the north. Among us children, however, most of the time the civil rights movement felt like an unseen Goliath that grown-ups took on. We did understand that they were doing it for our generation to be able to enjoy rights they had not had— important rights, such as going to an amusement park.

In Seattle, there was an amusement park right downtown on the expansive grounds that had occupied the World's Fair. We were free to frequent the Seattle Center amusement park and get on as many rides as we wanted to, whenever we wanted to—and I wanted to quite often. So the first understanding I had of segregation, and how important the goal of integration was, hit home when I heard King say in a speech that his six-year-old daughter had asked him to take her to Funtown, an amusement park that was advertised on television in the south. I was appalled to realize that a man of the national stature of Martin Luther King had to tell his daughter that she could not go to Funtown, not because they couldn't afford it, not because they were too busy to take her, but because the amusement park did not allow blacks admission. "But we are working to change that," King said he stammered to Yolanda.

Later, he would relay a tale about one of the times he was jailed during a protest march. When he called home, his wife told him that she had explained his whereabouts to the children, and that Yolanda had said, "That's okay. Tell him to stay in jail until I can go to Funtown."

Many whites thought King's generation was pushing too hard. Author William Faulkner, a Mississippian, wrote in *Life* magazine that the NAACP should "stop now for a moment." According to *Testament of Hope,* King eloquently responded, "It is hardly a moral act to encourage others patiently to accept injustice," exploitation, and indignity, "which he himself does not endure."

But my generation had more of an edge, more pent-up anger. As our group of post–World War II babies approached late teens and early adulthood in the mid to late 1960s, we began to get impatient with the progress our parents were making. We didn't indulge patronizing liberals. Either you were with us or against us. We didn't have that much love and patience for "the enemy." To those who opposed us, to those who stood in front of schoolhouse doors to prohibit Negroes' admission, to those who called the dogs on us to quell a protest march even if children were in attendance, we were more vocal in saying, "Later for those racist honkies!" And the words "later for" were more subdued than the expletive that some used.

The innocent juvenile nursery rhymes were replaced by the more serious chords of "We Shall Overcome," a song that expressed our parents' sense of mission. But by the time I was fifteen, young black men and women stopped singing "This Little Light of Mine" and "Kumbaya" and started chanting "Umgawa! Black power!" Little did we know that "Umgawa!"—a jungle call made popular by Tarzan movies—was fictitious language. But that was beside the point of our earnest attempt to grasp anything African. If America didn't love us, surely the Motherland did. Yet, we wanted our homeland to live up to its promise. And we had hope that it would if we only demanded that it do so.

At rallies and marches, the rallying cry rang with the call and response of

> *What do we want?*
> *Freedom!*
> *When do we want it?*
> *Now!*

This rebellion and change of temperament coincided with my own teen years of confusion and identity-seeking. My parents' politics seemed suddenly passé. I listened to the music, to the speeches, to the prose and poetry of my generation and began to form my own opinions, which were less conciliatory than those of my parents. It became a challenge for them to allow me to develop as an independent person without feeling that my new philosophies might bring harm to me somehow.

The biggest influence on my "consciousness," as the kids called it, was the Seattle visit of Stokely Carmichael, the fiery head of SNCC, who coined the term "black power." On April 19, 1967, he was scheduled to give a speech at the predominantly black high school, Garfield. Even as a fifteen-year-old ninth-grader, I had heard about his controversial appearance weeks in advance. It was all the buzz at school, at social events, among the kids at church. Either you were going to be there, or "be square." I was determined to be there.

"No, you cannot go to any Stokely Carmichael rally," my mother stated flatly.

I started to feel a whine coming on. *"Mom! Why not? Please?"*

"What if there is a riot afterward," she said as a statement, not a question.

"What if there *isn't* a riot afterward?" I shot back. "Stokely does not tell people to riot. That's a lie that the Establishment wants you to think about him."

"There is a strong likelihood that there could be violence there, so I don't think it's a good idea for you to go," she said with finality, and went back to her cooking.

I knew there was no arguing. It was rare for my mother to change her opinion based on your argument and then acquiesce by saying, "Oh, okay, I see your point. Sure, you can go." My only recourse was to seek a second opinion. I had to persuade Daddy.

At the dinner table, I brought up the subject, speaking directly to him as though it was the first time I was bringing it up. "Dad, I would like to go hear Stokely Carmichael speak at Garfield."

Mom gave me that didn't-I-already-tell-you-no look.

"Who would you be going with?" Dad asked.

I hadn't thought of that. They might have let me go with André, but he had already gone off to college at Wesleyan in Connecticut. Vicki was living in Los Angeles. My cousin Gloria was at Fisk University in Tennessee. So anyone in the family who was young enough to relate to Stokely, but older than I, was away. I thought about my girlfriends, but they were having similar problems getting permission from their parents.

"I don't know. I'll get someone," I answered feebly.

"I told Stephanie that it could get violent there," my mother interjected to let Dad know she had already rejected my request.

He thought about it for a minute as though he was deliberating in court. After eating one of my mother's delicious salmon croquettes in silence, he sliced a piece of hot corn bread in half. As the butter melted in the crevices, he handed down the verdict solemnly. "I'll take you."

"Thank you!" I said, but with subdued joy in front of Mom.

This was a major decision on appeal for me. Not because I prevailed over my mother's disapproval (I knew she would defer to my father's judgment), but because my father held more conservative views about the civil rights movement than the ones I was beginning to form. I didn't think he was afraid of violence, but I didn't know what he thought of Stokely. However, as an attorney and later a judge, he was always up for hearing a good argument. He often went to the courtrooms of his colleagues just to hear them give closing statements at trials. He was proud that André had been on the debate team in high school. He also knew that this speech was going to be a media event. Everyone in Seattle was talking about it. The newspapers were publishing the background disputes among the public over Stokely's visit. Many thought it might flame racial hatred of blacks against whites. Although Daddy never discussed his reasons for going with me, other than to chaperone, I think he just wanted to hear for himself who was influencing me and what Stokely might say about the racial issues our country was facing.

To me and my friends, Stokely Carmichael was the most handsome, charismatic spokesperson for our generation. I admired Martin Luther King, Jr., but he was my mother's age, for Pete's sake. Malcolm X was also of my mom's generation—born just six months after her—and because he had been killed two years before (in 1965, when I was just thirteen), I didn't really become familiar with his militant philosophy until I was in my late teens, when I picked up his autobiography.

I admired Stokely because he went to Howard University, the Harvard of the black community. Hadn't my parents taught me to admire college-educated intellectuals? He was an activist with the SNCC. Because I planned to be a college student in three more years, I was studying how black-conscious college students acted, what it meant to be an activist, a militant, a revolutionary—all these labels I had heard. I was just trying to sort it all out.

Whenever I heard Stokely speak on TV, I agreed with what he said about black people becoming self-determining. And with my teenage hormones raging, I liked him just because he was fine!

At the time, there were few actors or singers who were black and young enough to be our celebrity idols. Sidney Poitier was of my mother's generation. So was Sammy Davis, Jr. We had the Temps and Smokey Robinson, and other singers we admired, but the men who reflected our image of *manhood* were the revolutionaries. These were our heroes. We had no idea that so many of them would be killed or jailed or otherwise compromised by the targeting of them by J. Edgar Hoover's FBI.

My parents were longtime members of the National Association for the Advancement of Colored People. My friends and I, on the other hand, would say we *used* to be colored, but now we were black and proud. I followed the activities of the local Black Panther Party—mainly because I knew so many of the brothers in it who went to school with me or at Garfield—the way my parents followed the NAACP. I never joined the Panthers because they were largely too thuggish and male-dominated for me. But I supported what they were trying to accomplish through their free breakfast program for schoolchildren, and their manifesto of demands for justice and equality.

April 19, 1967, arrived, and as he had promised, Daddy came home early from work. He said we would need to get to Garfield early to get a good seat. It would be crowded, and also difficult to find a parking space.

On one hand, I was slightly embarrassed that I had to go with my dad. When we arrived, I saw all races of students, mostly college age. I didn't want anyone to think that I was a big baby who had to come accompanied by her daddy. But actually, there were so many unfamiliar faces that I didn't see as many people that I knew as I had anticipated. It wasn't the usual community crowd of the Central District. Students from the nearby colleges, Seattle University and the University of Washington, had turned out in big numbers.

Garfield High's auditorium featured theater-style seating that accommodated public events quite often. Tonight, however, there were so many people there, including TV crews and newspaper reporters, that by the time we arrived, the auditorium was already full.

People were spilling out of the huge double-door entrance to the school, down the wide concrete steps, and over the walkway toward the gymnasium. We heard someone say that the overflow crowd would have to sit in the gym and hear the speech by a piped-in public-address system. There would be no closed-circuit screens showing Stokely's image. I was disappointed that I wouldn't be able to fix my gaze on his fine face, but I settled for hearing his clear and confident voice, and knowing he was possibly as close as I would ever get to him. It wasn't every day that we saw exciting national figures in Seattle.

I was surprised to see that the gym was already full of people too. I saw hippies and college students, some high school kids I knew, and quite a few adults. There were black people, white folks, and some Asian-Americans. Most of them were under twenty-five. Daddy gestured to me that our seat in the bleachers would be near the door. The better to make a quick dash if things got ugly, I assumed.

Then I heard the speech that made a great impression on my young mind. It definitely changed some basic ingrained notions about myself as a black person in predominantly white America.

He started by saying, "Good evening. It is good to be here. You know what happens is, in the newspapers they call us racists and anti-white and say we hate white folk and all other irrelevant nonsense. And they do that because they use white people as their measuring stick. But I want you to notice that in all their beautiful, liberal press media there isn't one black man!"

I could hear the crowd howl over the PA system. Looking around, some whites were nodding without changing expression, and a few male blacks were yelling, "Right on!" There were no black anchors on the news, there were no black reporters. In my childhood, I didn't know one black journalist. He was right—they were primarily white males. Women of any race were scarce.

Stokely went on to state that he wanted to talk about some "basic assumptions" from which SNCC operated: the theory of self-condemnation, denying one's freedom as opposed to giving one free-dom, the need for black people to define themselves and have those definitions recognized by our oppressors—white society. Then he said that he was going to talk about violence. I looked straight ahead, not at Daddy, because I didn't want him to look back with disapproval.

Stokely continued in his rapid, staccato style: "We want to talk about violence because it's going to be important. I don't know why everybody's so scared about it—they going to draft you all and send you to Vietnam. I guess you going to go over there and make love to the Vietnamese!"

That broke everybody up. The intensity eased.

He talked about freedom, saying that nobody *gives* us our freedom.

They can only *deny* us freedom. Blacks are all born free and then enslaved by America's institutions of racism. So it is our job to stop America from being racist, to stop it from not giving us our freedom, to civilize white America, because they are the ones who are uncivilized. Then he gave an example.

"I'm black. I'm a human being," he said slowly, with the audience's full attention. "I know that comes with certain dignities that all human beings have. One is to be able to enter a public place. But now there are some dumb honkies who don't know that. So every time I try to enter a store, the honky gets in my way, shoots at me, bombs my church, kills my children, or beats me up. 'Cause he doesn't know that I'm a human being. So the white folks in Washington, D.C., got to write a civil rights bill to tell this honky, when I come, get out my way . . . get out my way . . . get out my way. "

Stokely talked like a young person, "making it plain," as we called it, to other young people. He was not an elegant speaker in the mode of Dr. King, who impressed whites and blacks with his Ph.D. and an eloquent vocabulary to match. Stokely's attraction was that he was dangerously honest. He spoke about things we usually said only to one another—never to white people, and surely not in public.

He mentioned that our generation was accustomed to watching all the news about integration on TV. We saw our leaders talk about integration and we knew they were speaking on our behalf. "When they said, 'We want integration,' we knew they meant good schools, good houses, good jobs, and a good way of life," he said. "But there was always some dumb honky who would jump up and say, 'You want to marry my daughter, don't you?' " Stokely said in a mocking drawl.

Then to more howls and laughter, he imitated black leaders, who responded, "Uh . . . uh . . . we don't want to sleep in your bedroom, we just want to live next door."

He continued by saying something that definitely distinguished him from the traditional black leaders: "At SNCC we tell them right out: The white woman is not the queen of the world. She's not! She's not the Virgin Mary. She can be made like anyone else. Let's move on to something important."

Oh, my gosh! I had never heard anyone say anything like that about white people, much less with them present. Talking as though the crowd was all black, or not caring that it wasn't, he moved on to blacks' collective low self-esteem brought on by our diminished place in society.

"The most insidious thing they could have done to us is to make us believe as a people that we are ugly," he stated. "The criteria for beauty in this society is set by white folk—in the books you read, in the television programs you see, the movies, magazines, and the newspapers. . . . They've mesmerized our women's minds so that they process their hair every Friday night. And the rest of them get their fifty dollars and buy wigs. We have to, as a people, gather strength to stand up on our feet and say, 'Our noses *are* broad, our lips *are* thick, our hair *is* nappy—we are black and *beautiful!* Black and beautiful! Stop being ashamed of who you are!"

He was talking to me. I felt this part of his message was specifically for my benefit. I had studied fashion magazines, looking for beauty images to emulate, but there were few, if any, brown-skinned African-American models within their pages. This made me feel that I was not beautiful, and that no one with brown skin could be considered beautiful. Maybe I was a cute kid, but *beauty* was unattainable for a black woman. I had grown up hoping my nose wouldn't get any wider. I had curled my top lip under when taking pictures so that my photographic image would be closer to the beauty standard. It had never occurred to me that that those standards could be flawed. I thought black people were fun, were smart, were resourceful, and that perhaps we had been cut a bad deal. I never wanted to be anything other than black. No, I take that back; sometimes I thought it might be nice to be Filipino, because they were brown, yet had straight hair too. But now I had to rethink all the "basic assumptions," as Stokely put it, that I had learned as a colored child. I had never put the two words "black" and "beautiful" in the same sentence. That was a new concept for me, one I grasped with a passion.

I wondered how Stokely had come to have such conviction against the entrenched norms of the dominant and prevalent white American society, and blacks' acceptance of it. And how could he stand there and articulate our deepest feelings with so much courage and confidence? I didn't know the answers, but I knew he was, as the brothers would say, "my man!"

The next year, another larger-than-life public figure would come to town and reaffirm the ideas Stokely was espousing. Muhammad Ali paid a visit to the University of Washington. Banned from boxing from 1967 to 1970 when he was stripped of his heavyweight title for refusing induction into the United States Armed Forces because of his religious beliefs, Ali had become a popular speaker on the college circuit.

I don't know what he said in his speech; I wasn't there. But word of an offhand remark he made to a certain young sister got around, and made the biggest impact of all.

There was a girl named Sandra Hailey, who went to my church and had a beautiful smile and a pleasant personality. The deep brown color of her skin was complemented by a smooth, flawless complexion. But in those days, "blue black" skin color, like that of Nat King Cole, was totally unappreciated, and it was more accepted on a male than on a female. If blond hair and blue eyes were the beauty standard, then where did that leave those whose features were the exact opposite?

When I was a child, it was common for black kids to "rank" on one another about skin color. At an early age, you learned the rhyme

> *If you're light,*
> *You're all right.*
> *If you're brown,*
> *Stick around.*
> *But if you're black—*
> *get back!*

I was brown, or in the middle of the skin-tone spectrum, so I caught it from the light-skinned kids. But for every time I had to fight back after being called "jungle baby," I knew there was someone darker who had to endure taunts of *"jet-black* jungle baby" and worse.

Color consciousness and self-hate were still rampant when Muhammad Ali came to town. I had even ordered blue contact lenses, hoping they would lighten my dark brown eyes to hazel.

My church friend managed to get up to Seattle's mammoth college campus and claim a perch in a building by which Ali would be walking. As he passed, Sandra and her friends waved out the window. "Ali! Ali!" they chanted to get his attention.

He looked up and saw her. Then he stopped the entourage, and from the middle of the crowd, Muhammad Ali pointed up to the black girl in the window.

"You," he shouted. "Sister, you are *black and beautiful!*"

We had heard the phrase "black is beautiful" before, but never in the context of anyone we had known! This man that we admired so much believed that our dark-skinned friend was beautiful! Surely, he knew what he was talking about.

The story went around the community like wildfire. You would have thought Jesus had walked through the multitudes and turned the darkest among us into the most beautiful of all. We realized that the veil of slavery, oppression, segregation, and degradation had hidden God's artwork from us. Now, with the veil lifted, our eyes were opened. We began to regard this young sister with awe and to admit that she had never been anything but a pretty girl. In acknowledging her beauty, for the first time we also saw our own.

= 15 =

We're a Winner

Fᴏʀ ᴍᴇ, 1968 was both a good year and a dangerous time.

It started out groovy enough. On January thirteenth, I turned sixteen. The day began with one of my mother's good friends calling.

"Hi, there, Stephanie. Happy Birthday!"

"Thank you," I responded.

"So you're sixteen today, huh?"

"Yep, that's right," I responded, trying to act like I wasn't smiling. Sixteen was hunky-dory with me.

"Are you sweet sixteen and never been kissed?" she asked.

"Oh, yeah, right!" I muttered, probably unconvincingly. "I think I hear Mom now. Let me get her for you."

ᴀʙᴏᴠᴇ: *My sister, Vicki (second from left, rear),*
and her daughters, Tina and Lisa, visiting from Los Angeles.

If she thought I was going to tell her my business, she was mistaken. I wasn't about to reveal to her that I was quite experienced in the kissing department, thank you. Kissing was romantic. It was what I saw in every movie at the Orpheum or the Coliseum, and it was what I did at every movie. But anything beyond that was "nasty." Plus, I was too afraid of my parents' wrath to let any boys do anything more than smooching. And to be honest, since their parents would have killed them, too, none of the ones I went steady with ever tried. So I didn't feel pressured. My girlfriends and I talked about boys but never about sex, which led me to assume that it was something that none of us did. In my diary there are references to being a "stone-proof virgin." I admit to being surprised when several girls I knew got pregnant that year.

On my sixteenth birthday, which fell on a Saturday, my mother took me to Renton, the neighboring town, to get my driver's license. André came along too. In my diary, I still have the yellow carbon paper that served as my temporary license, preserved along with the results of the driving test. I've always thought I was a good driver, but the results show that I got an 84 on the written test and 72 on the driving test. Parallel parking and parking on an incline were trouble spots for me. I would have to continue to practice parking on hills, because Seattle is full of them. The city is built on seven hills that are as steep as mountains. The hills of San Francisco are only slightly worse, in my opinion. In Seattle, it's not unusual to drive up a very steep hill and then have to stop at a light, while your car seems to be heading toward heaven.

My temporary driver's license had my vital statistics.

SEX: F
COLOR EYES: BRN
WEIGHT: 115
HEIGHT: 5 FT. 5 IN.
VISION: 20/40 w/ CORRECTIVE LENSES

I looked for the category of RACE, but thankfully, it was not there.

Later that month, a tall, dark, and slim brother with an Afro caught my eye at a choir dedication at church. I knew who he was. His grand-mother Mrs. Shields was my sister's godmother. Mrs. Shields and her husband had owned the apartment house on Twenty-third Avenue that was my father's second home in Seattle.

Jon lived a block from that apartment building in a house that was a couple of doors down from my childhood beautician, Mrs. Dawson. As we were in the same grade, and he had a sister close in age, I often went by to play with them when my mother was getting her hair done. But that had been a long time ago, like seven whole years before. Even though we went to the same church, for some reason, I hadn't paid much attention to him since.

At the choir dedication, I was playing the piano for the Children's Choir. Jon was singing in the Chapel Choir, the one that the teenagers sang in. It was hip to be in the Chapel Choir at Mount Zion. Most people's mothers made them go anyway, for something positive to do. So it became cool because "everybody" was in it. It was hard for me to hang with the Chapel Choir because my duties with the Junior Church Choir conflicted with the times that the teen choir sang in "big church." But with all the choirs singing at this Sunday evening concert, I was able to sit back after the little kids sang and watch the teenagers do their thing. The choir director, Rev. Byrdwell, had selected Jon to sing a solo.

"Lord, I need your power each hour of the day . . ." he began in his baritone. The earnestness of his voice and the chocolate color of his smooth skin had me entranced. My journal entry for that day stated that when he sang that song, "Come into My Heart," I thought, *His voice sends me, and he does too.*

At school the next day, I saw his older sister, Beth. A junior, she was a year ahead of me. I liked her because she always had a pleasant word for me and was quick to laugh. Jon went to our rival high school, Garfield.

"Beth, why didn't you tell me your brother got fine?" I began when I ran into her in the halls of Franklin. "I saw him at church last night. He's cute."

"You think so?" she asked, amused. "I'm going to tell him you said that."

"Okay, you do that," I said, happy that she had fallen into my plan so easily. "And here, give him my phone number too."

He called. Using my new driver's license, I drove to my girlfriend Geri's house the next Sunday and picked her up to go skating. The two of us dropped by Jon's house, where we hooked up with him and his friend, Timothy. But being afraid that a quarter tank of gas might not get us to the north end of Seattle to the rink and back, we opted to head to my house instead.

"You brought those boys over here on purpose," Daddy said accusingly. He was sure that I had said I was going skating as a way to get his approval to drive his Thunderbird to pick up the guys. "You knew you could have gotten to the rink on a quarter tank."

"No, I didn't!" I whined honestly. As a new driver, I really didn't know how far the car could go when the gas gauge was low, and I didn't have enough money to fill the tank. And actually, I would have preferred not to be under my parents' watch with my potential new boyfriend. But taking male friends to our rec room in the basement must have made them suspicious that I was only going there to make out.

We played Monopoly. I wasn't uninhibited enough to kiss and hug in front of Geri and Timmy anyway. And Jon and I had just gotten to know each other. Even with teenagers, there was a certain courting period; a couple of months of passionate phone calls and letters passed with Beth as the mail carrier. It was March before he asked me to "go with him."

Of course, I said yes. And that relationship lasted through our remaining high school years, through two junior proms and two senior proms. Our parents were all friends and approved of our choice of each other, but they kept us on a tight watch that served as more birth control than we thought we needed.

We were bonded by the fact that neither of us wanted to jeopardize our future. Our hearts stayed close when we went off to colleges that were separated by a continent, and we stayed true for two more years of seeing each other only at Christmas and during summer vacations. Frequent letters and occasional costly phone calls kept us connected, just as other couples held it together when the boyfriend went off to Vietnam. Fortunately, the draft didn't catch up with Jon, a brother with a passion for basketball who aspired to be a psychologist. My "first love" and I supported each other despite parental overseers, political rebellion, and sexual temptation, all of which we resisted together.

I was going with Jon when Rev. Martin Luther King, Jr., was assassinated, and a couple of months later when Sen. Robert F. Kennedy was killed. I felt fortunate to have Jon to confide in during these ominous times.

Yet, they were tempered by the joys that only being sixteen can bring. I was allowed to date, and that meant going to lots of house parties.

Of course, if you weren't invited, crashing a party was always an option. After football or basketball games at my high school, kids would drive to the Dag's hamburger joint on Rainier Avenue and sit around in their cars in the parking lot. I saw a lot of things go down at Dag's. There were fights, arguments, guys getting busted by girlfriends for being with other girls, and even a shooting over a four-dollar debt once.

But the most useful thing about hanging at Dag's, besides getting my usual order of a burger, fries, and a shake, was that I could find out where the parties were.

"What's happenin'?" we'd ask anyone and everyone. Meaning, who is having a party and where is it?

In Seattle, most families lived in homes. Poorer families just had smaller homes than richer families. Even folks who lived in the projects had dwellings that resembled townhouses. There were no tenements to speak of in Seattle. We didn't even know exactly what that was. At the time, public housing was housing with dignity. When I was young, my own maternal grandmother, who was a homemaker and "club woman," meaning she was active in many church and civic organizations, had lived in Yesler Terrace after her separation from her husband. We kids loved going to her apartment, which was high on a hill with a great view of Chinatown. At the end of her building's parking lot was a large playground for the residents of the housing project only, so we thought this was an "exclusive" playground. It had huge, parklike swings and other impressive recreational equipment, as well as a softball field. There was also a community center, which we called our clubhouse. From our own house about two miles away, we had to walk about seven blocks to the park near Garfield High School in order to get on swings at a playground, but these kids had one in their own backyard.

Gran's ground-floor, one-bedroom apartment had a patio and a small garden, which she kept beautifully. Because she was in the corner unit, she also kept the grounds around the side of her building looking lovely. Gran's adult neighbors were friendly, fostering a sense of community, and their kids knew us and made us feel welcome when we came to visit, which was often. I don't recall any sense of stigma attached to living in the projects. It was considered much like unemployment insurance is now—a helpful government-assistance program.

As a teenager, I went to parties in the Holly Park projects, and in the homes of Jack & Jill members. My mother had been one of the charter members of the group of women who founded the Seattle chapter of Jack & Jill of America, Incorporated. Established by twenty black mothers in Philadelphia in 1938, it was created to offer social, cultural, and educational opportunities for the children of African-American families whose fathers were largely professionals, such as doctors, lawyers, and dentists. Currently, there are over two hundred chapters throughout the United States, and even two chapters in Nigeria.

My brother and I had mixed feelings about being in Jack & Jill, mainly because our mother *made* us participate in the monthly age-group activities and frequent chapter-wide events. But also, it had a reputation for being "bourgie" because it was an exclusive organization, with an invitation-only admission policy. It was considered by many nonmembers to be a snobby gathering of the black bourgeoisie. The organization came under the increasing criticism of kids I knew who were not included, but who were becoming more and more influential in other, more politically charged groups. Those included "young-bloods" I knew in Seattle's Black Panther Party, which was started in 1968, and those in my high school's Black Student Union.

On the other hand, all these people wanted to be seen at Jack & Jill parties, and weren't above crashing them to get in. A party at the home of a Jack & Jill teenager was likely to be held in the well-appointed basement of a spacious home with the blessing of the parents, who provided all the food and drinks, and who were upstairs chaperoning.

My own mother was generous in allowing us to give parties. I assume she felt that at least she would know where we were if the parties were in our own basement. Plus, she and my father liked to dance themselves, and they agreed that the teen years were a time for social events and enjoyment. On that we had consensus.

One thing I learned from a young age is that people like to party. And even though they may talk about you behind your back at school one day, if you're giving a party the next, they want to be invited.

In 1968, a party that I gave for a friend's birthday was to become the fodder of family tales for years to come. My brother had given good parties, and was now off in college, so it was my turn to continue the family reputation for "blue lights in the basement."

"You're going to have to send out invitations, Steph," my mother said.

"For what?" I responded. "I'll just tell everybody at school."

"If you tell *everybody*, you'll have to turn people away. Everybody won't be able to fit in our basement. Plus, etiquette dictates that people should have invitations."

I sent out the invitations.

But in my own passive-aggressive way, I let the word get out at my school, Franklin, and then it got around Garfield and Cleveland high schools too. I was pleased that everybody was talking about the "hap'nin' " of the weekend—the party at my house.

On the Saturday night of the party, things started out pretty cool. I had on a maroon minidress with a boat-neck collar that I had had to beg my mother for because she thought it was inappropriate for some-one my age to show her collarbone. But it was the bell sleeves with lace trim that gained her nod of approval. My brown suede over-the-knee boots completed the outfit. With my Sassoon haircut (one side long to the chin, one side short to the ear), false eyelashes, and caramel-flavored lipstick, I was looking pretty "splab."

Kids started coming, and I directed them down the stairs to the basement. Our recreation room was decorated with deep gold wallpaper that had a jazz motif. A closet in our den was renovated to make my father's bar. The door was cut in half horizontally in the middle so that it opened at both the top and bottom for the "bartender" to be able to serve. Daddy had made the liquor cabinet off-limits by installing a conspicuous combination lock. In addition to my father's Kansas University Jayhawk mascots, Kappa Alpha Psi mementos, and party decorations, the bar area displayed various risqué pieces of paraphernalia he had collected over the years that had to be put away. My favorite artifact, however, was the aging copper-colored metal sign he had confiscated in the south from a railroad car back in the bad old days of segregation. Hanging over the bar by a short rope, one side of the sign read in fancy lettering

FOR WHITES ONLY

The other side stated

FOR COLORED ONLY

"I took that sign because I hoped that one day it would become obsolete," he once explained. I was always grateful that he hadn't been caught. At one time in the south, any risk you took—even for the sake of posterity—could result in a lynching. But like my father, I looked at the sign as symbolizing how far we had come, rather than the negative, racist actions it had previously perpetrated. There was something about the 10-by-12-inch relic that I felt captured an era of our country that my generation was about to squash forever. So I have always considered the sign a treasure that I would inherit someday, so I could show it to my grandchildren and tell them, "Can you believe that in this country, white people and black people rode on trains in segregated cars?"

And they would say, "What's 'segregation,' Grandma?"

Well, my parties weren't exactly segregated, but there were definitely more black kids there than any other race. The music had to be jammin', the dancing had to be slammin', and whoever was down with that could come. The partying had an unspoken purpose: They helped us counter the fear and anger we had about the society around us. The news may have shown young black people at lunch counters getting hit over the head with bottles by segregationists, but at our parties, kids sitting at a basement bar cheered on the winners of dance showdowns and argued over who could do the 'Gator the best. Police dogs may have been turned on our contemporaries down south, but hitting the dance floor to Rufus Thomas's "Walking the Dog" allowed us to put aside our rage for a few evening hours. Socializing was no solution to our anger, but it was better than drinking or drugging, which were not tolerated at my parties.

Several hit records of 1968 reflected the growing black pride across the country, and made us feel militant even when we were partying. "We're a Winner" by the Impressions was a crowd pleaser, and "Say It Loud (I'm Black and I'm Proud)" by James Brown turned it out every time.

Allow me to digress a moment to say a few words about James Brown: In the time of sophisticated Motown hits, and when refined music men such as Duke, Count, and Nat King Cole were still kicking, James Brown, a country boy from Georgia, was just not as highly regarded by us city slickers. Whenever he came out with a new tune, we resisted it. "He just sings the same line over and over," we moaned. Where was the poetic storytelling, as in the Temptations' "My Girl" or the Miracles' "Ooh, Baby, Baby"?

Even my father made an observation about J.B.'s monotonous tunes. One early morning while driving me to school for six a.m. cheerleader tryouts, he tolerated my customary blasting of radio station KJR. James was wailing, "Open up the door/I'll get it myself."

Those are pretty much the extent of the lyrics of that song, repeated over and over and over. But the bass line was jammin' and so was I in the passenger seat—my head was bobbing and my shoulders were rolling. Daddy drove the mile to school in stony silence. Then, when we got to my customary drop-off point across the street from the entrance to Franklin High, he pointed to the car radio and said to me, "In this song, I think someone wants somebody else to open a door for them. You open your own door. Now get on outta here!"

I knew he intended it as both a joke and a life lesson.

At parties, when someone played a new James Brown tune, we would stand around profiling and trying not to dance. "This song is so lame," we said when we first heard "Cold Sweat." But as the horns played the first bars, our toes would start tapping, and then heads would start bobbing, and shoulders would get to swaying. By the time J.B. was hollering, "Give the drummer some!" we'd be in a cold sweat on the dance floor ourselves. It was so hard to be a James Brown snob.

We even tried to shun his seeming lack of black activism and consciousness, symbolized by his conked hair. But then he came out with "Say It Loud (I'm Black and I'm Proud)" and sported an Afro, and all was forgiven as we conceded that he was, indeed, the Godfather of Soul.

I had no illusions about being considered a beauty, but there was one area in which I had total confidence. The one thing I knew I could do better than most of the cutest girls was dance. As a result, I was rarely a wallflower waiting for a boy to ask me to dance. Cute girls got asked first, but if they couldn't dance that would be the end of it. I might have been asked second, but at least I knew I'd be on the floor after that until the end of the party.

At the party at my house that year, I had my boyfriend Jon, so having a dance partner was not a concern. But what began to alarm my parents was the number of kids who rang the bell. Soon the rec room, where the dancing was going on under dim lights (or no lights if the person watching out for my parents was alert), was jam-packed with more than sixty teenagers. Then folks had to crowd into the den. Eventually, someone opened the door to the patio, and the party over-flowed into the nippy, foggy evening.

Finally, Daddy said that no one else could come in.

"Someone in the neighborhood might call the police if it gets too rowdy in here," he said. Daddy's thing was always law and order, even at partytime.

We kids definitely didn't want that, but I didn't know how to tell anyone they couldn't come in. I didn't want people to say that I was bourgie—the ultimate insult—because I had turned them away. I knew that folks would take it personally, and I was at an age when pop-ularity was important.

"You can't come in here," my father practically barked at the rough-necks he didn't recognize. He took over the door and let in only kids whom he knew, like the ones who had spent the night, were neighbors, were in Jack & Jill, or whom he otherwise recognized.

As I anticipated, one drunk fool took it personally and decided to strike back. The DEAD END sign that had been planted at the top of our driveway by the city years ago suddenly appeared on our front porch. Who had known it could even be uprooted? A big boulder from our yard had been placed at the bottom of the steps. Someone said that they almost slipped on all the nails that were spilled over the long incline leading down to our house. We could hear shouting and loud voices from the street that we could not see from our secluded doorway. Someone was not happy that he could not get into the party.

After dealing with the juvenile delinquents, my father, a non-smoker who had been wearing a wine-colored satin and velvet smoking jacket, went back to join my mother and finish his newspaper in another part of the house. In the basement, I turned off the blue lights and made "Stay in My Corner" by the Dells drop from the record-changer to the turntable. Couples clutched each other and wordlessly melded into a slow drag.

That summer, there was a regional convention of the high school mem-bers of Jack & Jill held at the University of California at Los Angeles—

UCLA, Jack! My friend Renee and I packed our fake hair, our false lashes, our new culottes, and our windowpane stockings, and flew half-fare on standby from Seattle to L.A.

Kids ranging in age from high school sophomore through just-graduated, college-bound teen gathered each year. Represented were Jack & Jill chapters from Seattle, Portland, Oakland, San Francisco, Los Angeles, and other west coast cities. The first year I attended, my own brother had served as regional teen president of the conference at Stanford University in Palo Alto, California. I was so proud that André had run and gotten elected to this prestigious position. Daddy, Mom, and Vicki, too, were happy that André had followed family tradition and won an election. Watching all the girls poo-poo over him was a riot. André, who would be off to Wesleyan University in Connecticut that fall, was practicing his "preppy" look by wearing loafers with no socks. His style statement was captured in a group photo of the hundred or so of us on the school's football bleachers with him seated in the center of the front row. We discussed the fact that our mother would have considered it a fashion faux pas for him not to wear socks, but hey, she wasn't there.

Parents from the host chapter in L.A. chaperoned us. We had seminars and discussion groups on relevant issues, such as how to stage a peaceful protest, and how to choose a college.

"You should go to Howard University in Washington, D.C.," Bonita, a girl I met from Oakland, told me. "I'm going there, and if you go, too, we'll be west coast homegirls."

Bunny, as she was called, and her friend Linda (nicknamed Twiggy because she was tall, like the British model, and did fashion shows for Joseph Magnin department store), were some of the coolest girls I had ever met. Renee and I followed them around throughout our four days at the conference, hanging on their every word. Two years older than I, and one year ahead of Renee, they were confident, stylish, and smart. We hoped we'd seem just as groovy by association. Bunny's suggestion made me feel like I'd been given some important insider information as to which college was "acey-ducey"—the best. I kept her suggestion in mind.

Since the conference had been in Los Angeles, after it was over I went to visit Vicki, who was now married with a family of her own in L.A. Renee went to spend the week with her uncle, music producer Quincy Jones. Vicki and her husband, Clifford, went to work, and my nieces, Tina and Lisa, were at their grandmother's, so I was pretty much home alone with not much to do during the day. Fortunately, Renee came to spend the night, then the next day Quincy, his daughter, Jolie, and his wife, Ulla, a Swedish model who had appeared recently in *Harper's Bazaar*, were nice enough to come get us and take us to his job.

Well, Quincy's job was different from anybody else's I knew of in Seattle. Quincy was producing theme music for television shows then, and he took us all to Universal Studios, where he was working on the music for the upcoming TV show "Ironside," starring Raymond Burr.

"Raymond Burr, the actor who played Perry Mason, is going to be the star of this show," Quincy told us. I couldn't wait to tell Daddy that. "Perry Mason" had been his favorite show, because it featured an attorney who always won his cases.

"This is where we lay down the tracks for the theme song of the show," he informed us, walking us through a cavernous space with black walls and lots of spotlights overhead. It looked a lot like the band room at my school, except more sophisticated.

I thought that it was incredibly nice of him to take us around Universal, and to let us star-struck kids hang out with him all day. With Ulla at the wheel, we went by their friend Sidney Poitier's house, but no one was home. We stopped by Bill Cosby's house, too, but no luck there either. Finally, we drove up to the Joneses' own magnificent house, and Jolie showed us all around. The view from their backyard in the Hollywood hills was fantastic. I had been in big houses in Seattle, but never one with such massive grounds. There was the obligatory swimming pool, and a tennis court, and lots of fun areas outside and in the house for Jolie and her younger brother and sister. It seemed more like a park than a yard.

Jolie was visiting for the summer. She lived in New York with her mother, Quincy's first wife. She was a model like her stepmother, and she had already appeared in *Seventeen, Ingenue,* and *American Girl* magazine.

"I want to be a model," Renee said.

"Me too," I chimed in, although I didn't kid myself about being anywhere as cute as the two of them. But if the model bookers were looking for gumption, maybe I'd have a chance.

"Well, to really make it big, you've got to go to New York," Jolie advised us. Although we were two years older than she was, we listened to her because she was obviously more successful in that endeavor already. In fact, Jolie was about to make it very big as one of the first black models to appear regularly in magazines. For years after that, I followed her career, tearing out the pages of all the magazines that carried her pretty face. She and Renee had the same beige complexion and adorable pug nose. There was a magazine hair care ad that ran for years featuring Jolie lying across the double-page spread, with blunt-cut brown tresses falling to one side of her face that stared with confident, hazel eyes. It was just that color of eyes that so many black women wished they had back then.

But Jolie had it like that, and she definitely had star power. I was so proud of her when she made it to the cover of *Mademoiselle.* She was one of the first black girls to do so.

As a teenager in the 1960s and early 70s, I felt it was necessary to choose an area of civil rights activism. Mine was in monitoring the integration of the fashion magazines. Hey, someone had to do it. We still had progress to make there too! More and more young black women were showing up as models in the national women's magazines, and that was a source of pride for those of us who were fashion-conscious.

As I mentioned earlier, my father's area of activism was in fair housing. In the legislature, he fought to get laws passed that would allow blacks to live anywhere they pleased. Education was my mother's passion, and although she didn't think we needed to be bussed to white schools in order to get an equal education, as a teacher she advocated for the predominantly black schools to get equal resources, equal funding, and fair treatment.

"I went to black schools in Selma, and I got a good education," she would say. "It doesn't matter who sits next to you in class. What matters is if the students are motivated and apply themselves to their work. Self-discipline matters."

Theoretically, if blacks went to their own schools, and whites to theirs, their dual educational systems were considered "separate but equal." But many of the black schools had substandard buildings, torn-up books, and antiquated equipment. So many believed that if blacks and whites could go to school together, the standard for the white schools would prevail. The concept of integration had a lot of complexity to it.

At sixteen, I thought my integration plan would be pretty simple. The fashion magazines just needed to stop having a token black model every once in a while, and accept the truth behind the phrase that was gaining popularity, "black is beautiful." In my life, I saw black people every day, so I couldn't understand why I didn't see them in every issue of *Seventeen* and other magazines I loved. But the inclusion of black models was still so rare that just like when we looked at TV and saw a black person on and called the family to see, when I saw a black girl in a magazine, I would call all my friends.

"Did you see Jolie Jones in *Mademoiselle* this month? Girl, I've got the magazine! Come on over and check it out!"

In August of 1968, *Glamour* magazine had a black girl on the cover— the first women's magazine to do so. She was a pretty, deep-brown-complexioned girl who had won *Glamour*'s college contest. That was a nice gesture, but it was the November cover of *Ladies' Home Journal* that featured Naomi Sims that became the buzz among black women around the country. Naomi was not only dark brown—and that was important because it meant a mainstream acceptance of the "black is beautiful" movement—but she was a popular model. The *Glamour* cover girl had been an anonymous student, so although she was a "first," she did not have the appeal that Naomi did. Naomi's cover signaled an acknowledgment of black beauty, elegance, and sophistication. Surely, she was headed for the cover of *Vogue* next, we thought. Little did we know that it would take six more years—almost half a lifetime for a teenager—for a black girl, Beverly Johnson, to make *Vogue* history.

But in 1968, Naomi Sims made news in all the black newspapers and magazines. Everyone I knew ran out to buy *Ladies' Home Journal*. It was a first, and that marked progress and showed that things were changing. Sims went from a model to a supermodel.

Jolie seemed to be making a mark for herself in New York City, the same place where Naomi Sims lived. Ever since I had been a youngster, I had wanted to grow up and live in Los Angeles, like my sister. But in 1968, I began to realize that just as Los Angeles was the capital of the movie business, New York was the hub of the fashion world. And it was that kind of glitter, style, and fame that attracted me.

My first impression of New York, so far across the country from home, was from the time Daddy and Mom had driven Vicki and me there in a five-day journey one summer for a Links convention. I had thought that the city was too crowded and ridiculously noisy. But now, my mind began to change, as I realized that New York's excitement and exuberance just might hold something for me. With a popular song on my mind, as usual, I began to daydream about living one day where the neon lights are bright—on Broadway.

In Los Angeles, we had seen brothers in Watts with four-inch-high "naps." There had been a boy who had moved from California to Seattle and had come to a Franklin High basketball game with his hair like that. It had been the talk of the school for days.

"They call it an Afro," he told everyone. "It's natural hair. Don't you Negroes in Seattle know about it yet? You people are *too* square."

We had laughed at him, but he had called us Negroes *and* square, and as kids used to say back then, "them's fightin' words." He got in a lot of fights over his hair and his mouth. We admitted among ourselves that we were intrigued by his hairstyle, though. It was close cut on the sides, and high on the top. I did think it looked better than a conk. That was a men's pompadour style of straightened hair, also called a "process." And it definitely was an involved process to achieve. James Brown had a process. Entertainers such as Jackie Wilson and Nat King Cole had them. Sammy Davis, Jr., was well known for his.

But most of the men of my father's circle didn't conk their hair, although they did put loads of pomade on it and brushed it a hundred strokes before sleeping in a stocking cap. This regimen was to ensure the formation of waves in one's hair upon arising. Daddy slept in a stocking cap made from one of my mother's discarded cinnamon-colored nylons every night.

Shortly, we began to see girls in Afros too. Having a "natural" meant that you could wear your hair in its natural texture, without the burning hot straightening combs or the harsh lye of chemical "perms." We didn't understand why *perm* to whites meant curling the hair, as in a Tony Perm, when to us it meant straightening our tight curls. But we did understand that it was permanent, at least until new growth showed.

For as long as I can remember, my mother and I had a standing hair appointment at the beauty salon every other Tuesday. I have no memories of my mother washing my hair. I was probably an infant the last time she did it. In the 1950s it was customary for those black women who could afford it to have their hair done at a salon. It was widely believed that one needed the services of a professional to successfully tame those naps and kinks. I mean, you wouldn't try to fix plumbing in your kitchen yourself, would you? No, you would call a professional plumber. By the same token, when that "kitchen" of naps at your nape needed to get fixed, you'd better use a professional. You needed someone experienced with pressing the hair straight with a hot comb, and skilled in heating the comb and the curling iron, and preventing people from getting burned.

Although many women had a talent for doing it themselves at home, saving time and money, my mother was not so inclined. Although she took pride in combing, brushing, and styling my hair each day, she never washed or pressed my hair at home, and I never learned to do it myself either. We used the services of black professionals. We went to the doctor. We went to the dentist. We went to the hairdresser.

In 1968, perms were becoming more popular. Rather than risking the heat of the hot comb scorching your scalp, or worse, that the steady hand of the beautician might miss and hit your ear or your shoulder, leaving a burn mark for life, the gloppy Crisco-looking perm product could be administered to your head and washed out—if the hairdresser knew exactly how long to let it set. If not, the lye in it could do a job stinging and burning your scalp. I had seen grown women squirming and pleading to get that stuff washed out. But that was a risk one took for beauty.

I wanted a perm, and I made a big stink about it. Perms, or relaxers, as they were also called, made your hair much straighter than hot combs. And you could swim and get your hair wet in the rain (a big plus for a Seattleite!) without the hair "going back," that is, reverting to its natural state. Hot-combing was only as effective as you were in staying away from water. But a perm could take it. With a perm, I told my mother, I could slick it down and get the close-cut Twiggy look that had also been made popular by Mia Farrow on TV's "Peyton Place." Mom conferred with the hairdresser, who said that she didn't recommend a perm for children or teenagers. It might be too harsh and take my hair out.

I kept begging, but they kept saying no. I was trying to get modeling jobs, so I wanted to have the same style as the successful models. There were few black role models for this, so to have the hairstyle I saw on white models, I pulled out my fall, which gave me the long straight hair that was denied me because the pressing and curling kept my hair fragile and thin. But I also liked wearing my hair super-short, as was the style of the most fashion-forward young women. One day, I'd have it in a curly short style, and the next I would wear a fall or even a wig.

That summer, my mother allowed me to enroll in Kathleen Peck's Modeling and Finishing School, a chic academy downtown that I never knew another black person to have attended. It was rumored that they didn't take very many of "us" so I was especially pleased to get accepted. I took to saying that I had helped integrate Kathleen Peck. Who knows if I actually was the first, but when you are sixteen, accuracy is not a priority. It's the *feeling* about what you are doing that's important. One thing was for sure. A professional photo of our class shows that I was the only black girl in it.

There, I learned many of the social graces of the day. Who would know that there was a proper way to walk up stairs in public? Going up and down the steps to the entrance of the school's second-floor offices, we practiced keeping our backs straight (for poise and grace) and our legs together (so no one behind us could look up our dresses), as we rolled our knees around each other in a way that made our hips swivel.

We learned the ladylike way to get in and out of a car too: Put your behind in first, then keeping your knees together, swing both legs together into the car.

There was one course that became as important to me in my future career as a women's magazine editor as a class in torts would be to an attorney: how to tweeze the perfect brow. The secret involved putting a pencil on the side of your nose to mark where the brow should start, then moving it to the outside of the eye for where it should end. We were instructed to tweeze upward in the way the hair grows, not down or out. And never again would I utter the word "pluck," which was to be reserved for what was done to chickens, when referring to my eyebrows.

I was taught what color clothes to wear—and not to wear—for my skin color. Out with brown, which was too close to my own color. One wouldn't want to disappear, now, would one? Banish red (too loud). Forget my favorite color, purple (a dictate I obeyed like a trained puppy for over ten years).

Although I never smoked, I learned how to do so in style: Always roll a burning cigarette on the rim of an ashtray instead of flicking the ashes with your index finger as a man would.

Mom encouraged—and paid for—my enrollment at Peck because she wanted me to learn the etiquette, polish, and social graces they taught. I wanted to go because of the photographic modeling and runway instruction. A teenager was more likely to get modeling jobs if she could say she was a Peck Girl. After graduation, I was accepted into their modeling agency, and was called to go-sees at I. Magnin and Nordstrom-Best department stores. When I was chosen to appear in Nordstrom's "back to school" fashion shows for a promotion with *Glamour* magazine, I was ecstatic!

My hair was cut in the latest fashion-magazine style, but still no perm. When school started in the fall, I saw that more black girls were experimenting with wearing their hair natural. *Jet* magazine gave us a peek at brave black women who dared to do it, such as singer Nina Simone and actress Cicely Tyson. I began to wonder what I would look like if I went "au naturel." One attraction of the style was that to obtain it meant *not* doing something, rather than doing something to the hair. It meant not having to pay every time you needed a shampoo, because you could just wash it yourself and not have to follow the washing with the straightening process. It would be an unimaginably wonderful reprieve from my lifelong biweekly torture. And best of all, the style itself symbolized a growing pride in accepting who I was.

I had gone to Los Angeles that summer on my annual visit to my sister's and had seen black-pride posters in Watts. The artwork featured men and women with Afros. A black hair care company began to sell Afro Sheen, a spray specifically created to give shine and make your natural glisten like a halo. Brothers were often seen with combs that resembled my mother's exquisite silver cake slicer. As a matter of fact, many people actually did use cake cutters to pick out their hair. Eventually, plastic picks or forks became popular items at drugstores, and mothers found their cake cutters missing less often.

On September tenth, I announced to my parents that I would be getting an Afro. Daddy took it well. I always figured that at sixty-five he had seen so many changes in his life—three or four wars, the Roaring Twenties, the Depression, and now the civil rights movement—that nothing fazed him. But my mother, who was younger and took pride in staying within the mainstream parameters of accepted standards of sophistication, bristled. She wasn't having it.

"No, you cannot do that to your hair," she said unequivocally.

"Getting a natural isn't *doing* anything to my hair," I argued. "Taking a burning comb to my scalp is doing something terrible to my hair."

"Never mind that. You will not be going to school with your hair looking like that. What would people say?"

"People I know would say it looks nice," I responded, knowing I was getting in deep water. I had been raised to know that if my mother or father said no, that was supposed to be the end of the conversation.

"Not any people I know," Mom said. "Not your teachers, or anyone else with any self-pride." She believed in black pride and "black is beautiful." But she thought it was beautiful enough as it was, not as this younger generation was defining it, to mean something new and invented.

"Mom, women with self-pride wear their hair natural in Africa every day," I countered. "That's why it's called an Afro. We are Afro-Americans."

"Children in Africa may wear it natural and cut close to the head, but women don't wear big Afros. That's something Afro-Americans made up," Mom said, digging out an old issue of *Ebony* with a picture story that showed an African president and his wife being hosted by the U.S. president and first lady at the White House. The Africans were dressed as sharp as the Americans, in western formal attire. The African first lady wore a tiara with her hair coiffed in a style similar to that of the American first lady. "See?" Mom said, pointing to the page. "They wear their hair like we do—pressed."

Case closed. The queen had commanded, "No Afros in this house." But her rebellious subjects (including my brother, who was away at college growing his hair out) risked her wrath by not obeying.

The next day, my mother flew to Chicago or Philly or somewhere back east to a Jack & Jill Foundation board meeting. I went to the barber.

My girlfriend Geri was my partner in the crime. After school, I went over to her house, and she helped me wash my hair so that it would revert to its normal, bushy state. Then she loaned me one of her headscarves and accompanied me to a nearby barber shop, just a couple of blocks away from my mother's hairdresser, Vogue Coiffure, on Twenty-third Avenue.

Sitting in a barber chair was a familiar feeling for me, because my father had owned a shop in which barbers rented space, and he often took me with him when he got a haircut and collected money. After the shop was closed for the day, the barbers would let me sit in the huge, red leather chairs, and twirl them around as if I was on a playground ride.

This time, though, I was the one getting the cut. I nervously tried to keep my face turned away from the large corner windows on that main drag of the 'hood, hoping none of my mother's friends would drive by and see me. Women's hair salons weren't doing natural hair yet. There was more money in the press-and-curl business, and even more to be gained by doing perms and touch-ups. Cutting nappy hair was a man's job.

When the barber finished and handed me the mirror, I did think I looked a bit mannish. But not enough to regret my decision. I thought I'd get used to it. I never liked that just-done look after leaving the beauty shop either, so I decided to give it a few days. By the time my mother returned, she would see it looking all black-and-beautiful, and change her opinion of natural hair.

I went home and waited for Daddy to arrive from work. He immediately noticed my hair and remarked, *"Au naturel!* I can dig it." We cracked up, and then in my job as substitute cook in my mother's absence, I pulled out the electric can opener, zapped open three tins—corned beef hash, string beans, and pork-and-beans—and heated the contents for our dinner.

A few days later, my mother returned. She took one look at my hair, and hated it.

"You just had to go and do it, didn't you?" she asked in a tone that made it more of a statement than a question, and that made it clear she was livid. Then she stopped speaking to me.

It was her opinion that whatever we did reflected on her as a mother. She felt that her friends might think she was not in control if we did things to which she did not consent. In addition, this hairstyle represented a dangerous radical notion that could attract trouble. What if the police judged us by our hair and, assuming we looked like criminals, arrested us for no reason? What if I didn't get accepted into a good college because I looked like a militant? Photos had to be sent with college applications, you know. Her resistance to what was technically "just a hairstyle" was her way of protecting us from racial prejudice.

Plus, I believe that she truly felt that straightened hair just looked better. Having grown up in the segregated south, and at a time when colored people went to tremendous efforts to counter white media images of pickaninnies and sambos, she had been raised with strict rules about hair. For example, for generations of women on her mother's side of the family there was the three-braid rule, which dictated that a child was never to wear more than three braids on her head. As a child, I usually wore my hair parted down the center (my mother would start the comb at my nose, then up my forehead and down to the neck) with one braid on each side; occasionally I got to have a third one to the side in the front, as well, with a ribbon at the top. Any more than that was frowned upon as inelegant and unsophisticated. These lifelong issues of self-esteem were ingrained in her, and in a large proportion of black women. That, along with an aversion to change, made my mother reluctant to embrace natural hair.

But I was sixteen, and ready for all the changes the world had to offer, especially something that made my hair feel strong and healthy, not wimpy, and straggly. They didn't call it a natural for nothing.

On September 19, my father was appointed a judgeship. *The Seattle Times* reported that "Charles M. Stokes, an attorney for 36 years, today became the first Negro in the state to become a Justice Court judge." Succeeding a judge who passed away after forty-eight years on the bench, Daddy was appointed by the Board of King County Commissioners and was told by a fellow judge, Evans D. Manolides, that he would be a great asset to the court and the community.

"I know that you are a man of the law and that your many years of dedicated service to the law, both as a practicing attorney and a member of our state legislature, eminently qualify you for the position," Judge Manolides said in a ceremony.

Daddy responded by thanking the commissioners and all who sent messages of congratulations.

"Naturally, I am elated at my appointment," he told the attendees. "My ardent wish is that my performance will live up to the confidence shown in me. If a judge is efficient, factual, and fair, he should get along all right. That is what I intend to do. I may never reach the stars, but I should have stardust on my fingers."

My mother took off from work to attend the ceremony. The newspaper also reported that in the audience was Superior Court Judge

Charles Z. Smith, the first Negro in the state appointed to the Superior Court bench, to whose court my father had taken me the summer I worked in his office. I was not in attendance.

On one hand, Daddy's judgeship was just another of his many achievements that my parents were proud of, but low-key about. There was not even one reference to it in my diary. On the other hand, it was a momentous occasion, and in years to come, I would wonder if there had been a decision not to invite me. Had I been left out because my parents didn't believe in taking me out of school for anything short of near-death illness? Or was it because of my Afro?

I did not ask and was not told the answer to those questions until I began writing this memoir. My mother said it had nothing to do with my Afro. "The swearing-in was performed on short notice," she explained, surprised at my assumption. "I found out about it myself that morning after I had already gone to work. I had to ask my principal if I could be excused to attend." Since it had made the newspapers and was catalogued for documentation in the important clippings of Seattle's department-store-sized main public library, I had imagined a grand ceremony celebrating King County's first black district court judge. I held this erroneous assumption about the swearing-in and my exclusion—not with an attitude, but just as what I thought was fact— for over thirty years.

But this I know: Mom did prevail in having me get rid of my natural hairstyle. She quickly convinced her hairdresser that the perm I had originally begged for wouldn't be so bad after all, and that it couldn't turn out worse than the radical, nappy hairstyle I was wearing against her will. By the end of the month when I was photographed for my class portrait, I had a super-straight, slicked-down Twiggy 'do.

Caught up in my own teenage drama, with everything being about me, me, me, I did not fully appreciate my father's achievement in being appointed the first black Washingtonian to the Justice Court bench. I always knew it was a good thing, but in later years, as an adult, I wondered how the decision had been made to nominate him and give him the job. Had there been opposition within the all-white county commission that had appointed him? Who had been the white man bold enough to even suggest a black person?

My mother wisely advised that I speak with John D. Spellman, the former county executive who had decided my father would be the right man for the job. Spellman had also later served as the Republican governor of Washington state from 1981 to 1985. In 2003, I found a listing in cyberspace for him at a Seattle law firm, and contacted him. I was relieved to receive a return voicemail saying he would be happy to speak about my father, whom he "knew well and greatly respected."

On a summer day during which my suburban New Jersey town was having rainy Pacific northwest–like weather, while Seattle was a beautiful, sunny eighty degrees, we chatted by phone. I learned that Spellman and Daddy had known each other since the early 1950s, when they were both "people lawyers" in private practice with offices a few blocks from each other downtown.

"In those days there were many right-wing Republicans in our state," he explained. "It changed nationally with the Goldwater period, when you also had members of the John Birch Society in the party. But your father was the exception. He could get elected," Spellman said, about my father's initial political forays in the 1950s to the Washington state House of Representatives.

"He was a prosperous lawyer and a good speaker with credibility in his community. He was good in his profession . . . no bad marks against him . . . good looking," he added, and we both laughed. "All those things.

"The Democrats had a conspiracy," he continued. "In the primary, they would put all kinds of black guys and one white person—so the white guy won. On the other hand, the Republicans actually thought your father was the better man." And so they supported him alone, and he won.

Spellman went on to confirm that years later, in 1968, "As a county commissioner, I nominated your father for district court judge. I had to convince the other commissioners—old-timers who wanted their own favorite candidate, who was a nice man, but didn't have the judicial temperament or experience your father did. You had to have a majority of the votes out of the three commissioners. So I was able to dominate them and get them all to vote for Stokes."

I still wanted to understand how he came to the decision to take that risk. "I was a reformer," he explained. "In those days, the Republicans were reformers—people who were for good, innovative, honest government. No cronyism, favoritism, or the spoil system. We put in the first civil-service system, and merit systems for employees." We laughed about those being the good old days for Republicans before Watergate.

"But wasn't race an issue?" I persisted.

"Seattle wasn't the south, but it had all the prejudices that the country had," he said patiently. "For example, it had lots of offensive names of restaurants . . ." Then he paused and added carefully, "I don't want to offend you . . ."

"Oh, thank you for your concern, but, please, go ahead," I answered. Now my interest was definitely piqued.

"Well, they had names such as Coon Chicken Inn." We chuckled incredulously together.

He went on. "But Seattle was also ahead of much of the country. We were the example during the tense time of unrest. We didn't quite have riots, but unrest over the construction trade. My administration negotiated with them to have minority apprentices that became a nationwide plan."

I remembered that time of unrest, but didn't know how it had been resolved. I asked about my father's performance as a judge.

"As an attorney myself, I've talked to a lot of lawyers, and they said he was always respected. He was always pleasant. If you lost a case, he didn't make you feel bad. He soothed people, even when they lost. He knew the law. I never knew anyone to complain about his judgments, and people didn't automatically go to overturn his cases on appeal. Some judges never should have been on the bench—they had never been lawyers—but your father was part of the new breed of educated, experienced judges. He got the respect of both blacks and whites."

"What do you think his legacy was?" I asked.

"Being a first is always a legacy, unless you're bad at it. He did it well, brought honor to the office, and people have held him up as a role model because of that."

I thanked Mr. Spellman for his courage in appointing my father to his judgeship, and for his role in the little piece of history-making of which our family was so proud. Across the country, many black judges, male and female, have been appointed since 1968, and I felt that those whites who took the first steps to create equal opportunities for such nominations and elections and make them commonplace should be acknowledged.

He replied graciously, and surprisingly forthrightly. "I always thought it was important to appoint women and various minority people because there was an imbalance of old white men. They did not represent anything but a stacked deck. The opposition was those who thought they were getting squeezed out; they resented most a minority or woman replacing them. It was hard to do. The difference now is that we *don't* do the unpopular things to face the problems. But it didn't take much courage—it was the right thing."

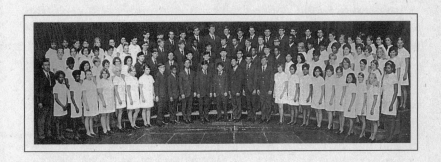

= 16 =

Lift Every Voice and Sing

"I PLEDGE ALLEGIANCE to the flag of the United States of America, and to the Republic for which it stands, one nation, under God, indivisible, with liberty and justice for *white people.*"

That's pretty much what the black students at my high school recited when we were required to attend school-wide assemblies. These gatherings—for pep rallies or student council election speeches, or invited speakers—were usually held in the school gymnasium, where we also enjoyed Friday night basketball games against other Seattle high schools. No matter the occasion, the black students would enter the gym, turn to the bleachers on the right, and then head up to the center of the top rows.

ABOVE: *My high school choir, the Bel Cantos, made an album and traveled throughout the British Isles in 1969.*

I was no exception. I sat in the black section proudly. However, there were sections within the black section. I sat in the front of the area, which made my seat in the center of all the rows. That way, I was seen as part of the black section and could hear the comments and remarks made by the rowdiest folks in the top rows, yet I could also talk with my other classmates, who were largely Jewish, Filipino, and Japanese (and not always sedate either), in the rows below.

But when it came to saying the Pledge of Allegiance in the late 1960s, every student had to decide how they felt about the words they were reciting. Did they believe it? Some of the African-American students muttered, "liberty and justice for *white people*," under their breath. But quite a few black students wouldn't stand, wouldn't put their hand over their heart, or say a word of the Pledge at all.

"The Pledge of Allegiance is *bull!*" someone shouted emotionally at a Black Student Union (BSU) meeting one day. "And until this country delivers some of that liberty and justice for *all* motorscooters, I . . . ain't . . . saying . . . it." Because we were on school premises and were being monitored by a faculty member, he used the word "motor-scooters" to stand in for a more profane four-syllable, compound word that began with the letter *m*.

I understood his sentiment. King had just been killed in '68, and riots were becoming commonplace. Fred Hampton, a former high school activist and charismatic Black Panther in Chicago, was killed in an early-morning police ambush while he slept. He was twenty—the same age as some of the students at my school who had dropped out and returned or been "left back" a couple of times. Hampton was the same age as the brothers and sisters we partied with at the University of Washington. We felt the turmoil of the nationwide struggle personally and emotionally.

When we were required to recite the Pledge, I always stood up. All the teachers and administrators knew who was standing and who wasn't, but they didn't waste their time trying to get everyone to stand. I felt I should show respect for the country. As my father would say about deferring to the decisions made by the president, "I might not agree with him, but he *is* the president." In the same vein, I may not have agreed with the second-class citizenship of my people, but I did respect the power and promise of the country to change it. Yet, I was impatient and angry with the Establishment's reluctance to treat African-Americans equally and justly. Sometimes, I would just stand at attention and cover my heart without mouthing the words. Other times, I would say the Pledge, but stop short after ". . . under God." If there was one thing I agreed with in the Pledge, it was that the United States was *under* God. It might have had power over us black folks, but it was still under God's power. And in those tumultuous and wrenching days, I prayed that God would help us, and heal our country.

There were several activist organizations at school. The most high-profile was the BSU, which inspired the founding of a sister club, the Asian Student Union. I wanted to be "down" with the BSU, although it was run by some male students who many of my friends and I felt were dubious leaders. But the biggest problem I had with BSU involvement is that I had a scheduling conflict. The BSU met on Tuesdays, and I had been chosen to represent the school on the all-city modern dance team, which rehearsed at the same time on Tuesdays and Thursdays at Roosevelt High, quite a ways from my school. Franklin was in the south end of town; Roosevelt was on the north end. There had been a major competition to make this team, and girls at school considered it on the same level at which male jocks held all-city varsity.

My father acquiesced to my begging and let me drive his sporty new Thunderbird to school on those days. Driving, I told Daddy, would allow me more time at BSU meetings. If I took the bus to Roosevelt, I would have to leave school right away. If I drove, I could go to the meetings and stay for maybe half an hour. "It's important for me to go to BSU," I argued, "because if I should run for school office, I'll need their endorsement or I'm a dead duck." He related to this strategy for getting the black vote, of course, and he graciously took the bus to court on the days I had the car.

The support of the BSU really was no joke, however. At one point, when two black students were to be selected to represent the school at a human rights conference, the principal decided that I should be the female representative. I knew I had to go to the BSU meeting that week, because I had heard that the president was going to raise the subject of whether the BSU should have been consulted on who should represent the school. Sure enough, at the Tuesday meeting, he did just that.

"Who would we have chosen to represent black students at Franklin?" he asked the gathering of maybe fifty or sixty kids, sitting at the study tables in the center of the stacks. "Would we have chosen the two students that the principal picked?"

He asked the question as though I wasn't even in the room. I was sitting by the door, because I had to make my getaway for dance class. I began to get nervous, because if I left I would be seen as not caring as much about the BSU as I did my predominantly white dance class. It wasn't an *African* dance class, after all. But time was getting tight, and I had to stop at Garfield High to pick up two dance classmates whom I knew from church. If we were late, the white dance teacher, who didn't seem to want us black students in her class anyway, wouldn't allow us to take class. If we missed too many classes, we wouldn't be able to perform in the all-city recital, which would shame me and embarrass my school.

At first, I was relieved that the BSU president started talking not about me but about the male student who had been chosen for the conference. "He dates white girls," he stated. "Is this who we want representing black people?" At least I knew they couldn't hold *that* against me. Everyone knew my boyfriend was not only African-American, but attended a school considered "blacker" than ours, Garfield.

My watch was ticking closer and closer to the time that I needed to leave. I began to get nervous, because I figured if I were to leave, they'd probably start talking about me behind my back. The president, who made a sport out of "hitting on me" when no one was around, knew I usually sneaked out, and now he seemed to be purposefully ignoring me and holding me up. I sat and stewed a minute, staring at him in his black leather jacket and Panther beret, although hats were not allowed in school. I put my own brown leather double-breasted jacket on over my purple knit turtleneck minidress, and pulled my chocolate suede boots up over my knee, while plotting my escape.

Finally, I decided I wanted the group to give me their approval, so then I could leave. I raised my hand.

"Yes?" he said, pointing to me. All heads turned my way. I took a deep breath.

"As you know," I began, and stood up, "I am the other student that was chosen by the principal to participate in the human rights conference on race. It would be my honor and privilege to represent Franklin. But if anyone has a problem with that, I need to know right now." I didn't mention it was because I had to leave.

"Does anyone have a problem with Stephanie Stokes being the female rep?" he asked with a sly smile.

I held my breath.

He looked around the room, but no one said anything. I noticed that some were just shrugging their shoulders as if I was a nonissue. The discussion of the male rep had become heated, so I was essentially holding up the juicy gossip about his dating habits (blatantly referred to as "talking black and sleeping white"), and other arguments of whether he was "black enough" for them. With a wave of the hand, I was dismissed. So, on I went to fight my next battle of the day—proving that my Martha Graham modern dance technique was as good as, or better than, the white girls'.

On July 23, 1969, my high school choir, the Bel Cantos, culminated two years of candy-selling and concert-giving by taking off to tour the British Isles. My parents and my boyfriend drove up to Vancouver, Canada, to see me off on the plane to London. I was so excited, I hardly slept the night before. I was on my way to Europe!

I had auditioned for the competitive one-hundred-voice group in my first year at the school by singing Gershwin's "Summertime" and accompanying myself on the piano. I didn't make it. "You play the piano very well," Mr. Koehler, the choir director, told me as a tactful way of saying I wasn't as proficient in singing as I was in playing. I had tried to impress him with a soulful "Porgy and Bess" imitation, but I failed miserably.

I had to wait an entire year to try out again. This time I took the hint from studying how other kids got in. Most just sat on a stool and sang folk songs. I couldn't play guitar, but I practiced singing "Puff the Magic Dragon" for weeks. In my room by myself or at the piano when I was home alone after school, I made sure my voice was strong and more firmly within my alto range than it was before. I rehearsed sounding perky, jumping a bit whenever I got to the word "Puff." At the audition, I took all the black out of my voice and imagined I was singing with Peter, Paul, and Mary. Wearing a lot of suede fringe, sitting on a stool, and going at it a cappella, I gave it my best shot. When I noticed that Mr. Koehler was looking right at me this time, rather than with his head down feigning writing, I knew I had made it.

I enjoyed the Bel Cantos. We sang 151 performances in one year to raise money and to practice for our European tour. I had a grueling schedule that demanded that I be at school every morning at 7:30 for the elite Honors Choir, which I also auditioned for and barely made, as well as choir class during the day. The culmination of our Pacific northwest appearances was a concert at the Seattle Opera House, where we cut a record that became one of my dearest keepsakes.

The choir was a racially diverse representation of our student body, and, I thought, our country. Traveling throughout England, Scotland, Ireland, and Wales by plane, bus, and train, I imagined that we were ambassadors for the United States. It had been arranged for us to live with host families abroad. So when our big buses rolled up in quiet, quaint European neighborhoods, residents spilled out of their homes to greet us.

Upon landing in London, I noted in my diary that there were many, many more black people on the streets than I had expected to see. But in Scotland, it was a different story. Soon, the third of us who were African-American noticed that when the people came outside as we got off our buses, they all looked mainly at us. "Why are they just staring like that?" some of the black girls asked. One of our chaperones explained, "They don't see black people every day here. Don't take it personally."

I was assigned a family who lived in an attached townhouse-style home that was modest, cozy, and clean. I wrote in my diary that night:

Dear Diary,
After a 10-hour train ride from London, we arrived in Glasgow, Scot-
land, at 10:30 a.m. I am staying with a family named Holmes, who
have a daughter named Emma, 15, who has a boyfriend named Phil,
17, who likes Elvis Presley.

I was a covert Elvis fan. So we instantly had something in common.

The Holmes family were nice to me, and I bonded with them more than any other family I met on the trip. That was probably because Emma and I spent most of our several days together giggling. We were at an age when everything was game for ridicule, but we were even laughing at ourselves because we could hardly understand each other. She thought my Pacific northwest accent—seasoned with copious references to "you guys"—was hard to decipher. And at first, I thought the Scots spoke something other than English. Yet, I found it so charming when Mr. Holmes said to me, "Steph'nie, weel be wakin' ye up at eight-therrrrrty." I loved the way he rolled his *r*'s! For the rest of our trip, I cracked up all the kids on my bus by rolling my *r*'s "to the bone."

During the day we toured the countryside and historic tourist attractions. In the evenings we sang for our supper.

We started every concert with our national anthem. As I mentioned, at school I was reluctant to recite the Pledge of Allegiance, but I have to admit that I *loved* the music of "The Star-Spangled Banner." The Bel Cantos sang the mess out of that song! We had a killer arrangement that featured the rich, male voices, and started our performances in a quite impressive way. As a pacifist, I had a problem with the words— for example, singing nostalgically about bombs bursting in air. But as a musician, I appreciated the lyrical quality of the words. The women would sing "the rockets' red glare," then the fellas would do a staccato echo in a harmony that was *bad.* Meaning it was good, of course. The guys could have rivaled any military chorus. Our feelings for our country were so conflicted because of the racial disturbances at home and the war in Vietnam, but when we represented our country abroad, we sang our national anthem with pride and gusto!

Mr. Koehler and our assistant director, Mr. Clarence Bishop, also taught us the national songs of other countries, so just like at the Olympics when they play the songs of the countries of the athletes, we sang ours and then theirs. "God Save the Queen" was next, then we also sang "Scots Wha Hae." In addition, our repertoire included tunes in French, Spanish rounds, and the melodic Israeli "HaTiqvah." When we first learned that song, of course the Jewish kids already knew it, but it took the rest of us some time to get it right. After we did, and I found out the title translated to "The Hope," I never tired of hearing those first bars: *"Kol'od balevav, p'nimah . . ."*

Prayer in school may not have been allowed, but there seemed to be no problem with the deeply religious songs we learned, such as "Exultate Lusti In Domino" and "Reconciliation." And in a nod to inclusiveness, Mr. Koehler had us sing "Elijah Rock," which I had always thought was a Negro spiritual, but I eventually learned that it was a more contemporary song written by Jester Hairston, a songwriter-turned-actor who in later years was part of the cast of the sitcom "Amen." This time, I already knew the song while the others who were not black had to learn it. The guys in the choir got a chance to use their bass voices for the deep, rhythmic cadence of the song, "Elijah rock . . . shout! Shout!"

The part of our concerts I enjoyed the most was when we pared down to the twenty-voice Honors Choir. Wearing long gowns instead of the short (but not mini), white, short-sleeved dresses for the girls and dark slacks and white shirts with ties for the guys that were our choir uniforms, we belted out show tunes that must have been on the hit parade of Mr. Koehler's youth, such as "Lullaby of Broadway," "The Nearness of You," and "It's a Good Day."

I thought we should sing some of the latest jams like Sly and the Family Stone's "Everyday People" or give the audience something to think about with "Choice of Colors" by the Impressions. The closest we got to singing R&B was Fifth Dimension's "Up, Up, and Away." One day during rehearsal for the song, we just couldn't enunciate well enough for Mr. Koehler. Over and over he had us sing the line "Suspended under a twilight canopy."

"Canopy . . . canopy," he kept saying to us in frustration. Mr. Koehler was a handsome man. He was tall, with wavy brunet hair and an intense blue-eyed gaze that contributed to his charisma and gave him a commanding presence.

"The word is *canopy.*" He paused for effect. "You make it sound like *can of pee!*" We immediately got his point—and busted up laughing. From then on, no matter where we were in the world, when we sang that line, our choir director would give us a smile that signified our inside joke.

Of all the places we visited, Dublin stuck with me the most. There, I saw a black mannequin in a store window for the first time. It was dark brown with a huge Afro. Even in Seattle, I had never seen a mannequin that remotely resembled a black person. Here, where there were few black Irish, I saw several.

My choir roommate was Loretta Williams, whom I also knew outside of school because our families were friends and her sister, Barbara, was my brother's girlfriend. Although she was taller than most of the girls, Loretta had skipped two grades, so she was the youngest choir member at age fifteen. Loretta and I were assigned to a family named Tetlow in Belfast. They had a beautiful, spacious colonial home on the water, Loch Belfast. We stayed up half the night talking with their two daughters about race relations in the States and the Catholic-Protestant conflict in Ireland.

"I don't understand why your country is fighting over skin color," one said. "That is so stupid." They had seen the rioting back in the urban cities of America on the TV news.

"I don't know why people in America hate other people for no other reason than they are black."

We were grateful for their empathy, so we tried to explain white supremacy, which was totally illogical, so they were even more confused. Embarrassed for the state of our nation in the eyes of the world, we got on the defensive.

"Well, we don't understand why white people here are fighting other *white people,*" I said. "How can you even tell them apart to know who is Catholic and who is Protestant?"

"Yeah, at least in the States you know who is black and who is white," Loretta said.

"We can just tell," they answered.

We all just shook our heads in silence. These conflicts in our world made no sense to us. We changed the subject and found common ground by discussing where we would go shopping for the best bargains in miniskirts the next day. Several days later, after we moved on to Galway and Killarney, we found out that intense fighting had broken out in Belfast. We hoped our new friends were safe, but we had no way of finding out.

On July 20 we sang at the Sunday service of the beautiful, historic St. Mary's Lutheran Church in Swansea, Wales. We were staying at the Swansea College of Education, and we had free time during the day, but I was getting homesick. After one too many days of cold cuts, including a tongue sandwich (which I ate unknowingly and became the butt of many jokes by the group), I longed for a tamale with melted cheese and the tater tots we called Mexi fries from Taco Time, my favorite fast-food joint back home.

In addition, we felt as though we were missing out on a national TV event. As we performed that evening, our concert was interrupted by an announcement by our Welsh hosts. "We have heard that the Americans have landed on the moon," the man told the audience, as we stood onstage.

Applause and pandemonium broke out as people began to chatter. We were under strict orders not to speak while onstage, and to always look nowhere else but at Mr. Koehler. No wandering eyes or whispering mouths. But now, we let down our discipline and began talking among ourselves on the four levels of our choir stand.

"Yeah, right," someone black said, under his breath. "You can't tell me no white man has gone to the moon!"

"They need to use that money to give all black folks a college education," somebody else said.

The white kids were joyous. The Asians were subdued. I didn't know what to think. I did have the feeling that I was missing out on the excitement back home, however. Everyone would have been watching it on television, like a national event. I wondered what Daddy had to say about it.

Our choir director accepted the handshakes of several people who rushed the stage to congratulate us, as though we were the Americans who landed on the moon. Then he quickly turned to us and gave us a stern look that meant we should come to attention. He whispered so that only we could hear, "We will now sing 'America, The Beautiful.'" We usually sang that anthem to end our concerts in a dramatic way, and in full harmony.

The next evening in a rare moment of solitude, I tried to sort out my national pride and my political consciousness.

Dear Diary,
We successfully LANDED ON THE MOON! It was televised and
publicized all over the world. The lunarnauts were Neil Armstrong and
Edwin Aldrin and Michael Collins (Black). We left for Havant,
England, today (pronounced Haven't). I am staying with a family
named Grant. They have a cool daughter named Cherry, 20. She
turned me on to some jazz and the new Beatles sound on her stereo. They
have a modern house. I have a room to myself!

Now, where I got the wrong idea that Michael Collins was black, I have no idea. It must have come from the fact that the only folks I knew with the name Collins were African-American. Steve Collins was my neighbor and Franklin classmate. Or maybe I just wanted the history maker who orbited while the other two did the moonwalk to be black so that I could feel justified in my excitement. I can't recall if I saw a picture, but I think it was really wishful thinking.

On our trip, the 108 of us students and twelve chaperones were given the opportunity to tour all sorts of educational and historical sites that we teenagers didn't fully appreciate. We had heard about "kissing the Blarney Stone" for good luck (or more precisely, to be given the gift of persuasive eloquence), but when we stood on the roof of Blarney Castle in Ireland and saw what we would have to go through to do it, many of us said, "I don't think so!" Those who were determined had to lie on the ground on their backs and bend downward in a tricky position, holding on to bars or having someone else hold on to

them while they attempted to land a smooch on a rock that was difficult to see.

In England, we wandered around Stonehenge wondering what the
big deal was about a bunch of boulders standing in the middle of
nowhere. I spent most of my time at Stonehenge giving attention to an
ice-cream sandwich I bought at the concession stand. But of course, in
the years since, whenever anyone mentioned Stonehenge, I could
boast, "Hey, I was there once! I have seen Stonehenge with my own two
eyes!"

On the last day of our journey, we finally returned to the destina-
tion we were most excited about, London. At Buckingham Palace, I
ran out of Polaroid film while photographing the changing of the
guard. So I scampered off to find a camera store. When I returned to
the group, I discovered I had just missed Queen Elizabeth waving from
the back of her Rolls-Royce. Everyone in the choir saw her but me. My
African-American female choirmates and I put the film to good use,
though, taking pictures of all the fine black studs we met on Carnaby
Street. We hoped to run into new London resident Jimi Hendrix, a
Seattle homeboy of whom we were so proud, but no such luck.

After almost a month in the British Isles, we took the long flight
back across the Atlantic and over the entirety of North America, and
returned home to Seattle with a lifetime of memories.

That fall I began my senior year. The SATs were held in October at
Seattle University. My guidance counselor and my parents helped me
figure out what college I would attend. Would it be the all-girls' Spelman College in Atlanta, where black girls learned to become proper
black women and maybe snag a Morehouse man from the neighboring
all-male college?

Another women's college, predominantly white Barnard in New York
City, recruited me by inviting my mother and me to a Sunday afternoon tea at a hotel downtown. It felt a bit stodgy to me, but I applied
anyway. Going to New York did appeal to me, since I still had hopes of
becoming a model. I had done well in Seattle, and could take my experience to make it big in the Big Apple. Or maybe my constant child-

hood sketching and high school art classes would pay off and I could become a fashion illustrator.

Also back east was Howard University in Washington, D.C., where I could dig being a part of an entire campus of "young, gifted, and black" students. I was instructed to send in an application to an Ivy League school, so I took a shot at Princeton in New Jersey. And I was told I should have a school at home to fall back on, which became Seattle U.

Josephine Funderburg, an administrator at my school who was also a family friend and a member of our church, tried to persuade me to attend Scripps College, because the highly rated Claremont, California, girls' school was opening its door to more black students. There was a lot of pressure in those days to make a difference for the good of the race. We were expected to make our decisions based not only on our own personal preferences but also on what they might represent to the black community. But I wasn't convinced that I wanted to spend my college years away from home as a token black student. I felt isolated enough as one of a handful of African-American students in my high school honors classes. But I ended up applying to Scripps anyway, because Mrs. Funderburg and my other teachers were so excited about me doing so.

My parents shared the values of a genteel life powered by the hard work and achievements that education could bring. They also believed in serving their communities, both the black community and the American community.

Sometimes the ways in which my father gave service to the country gave us kids pause. During the time I was applying to colleges, the young men in my life were hoping and praying not to get drafted and have to go to Vietnam. In December of 1969, the Selective Service got the bright idea to hold a lottery to determine the order of call for induction in 1970, the much-anticipated year of my graduation. My boyfriend was skittish that the upcoming lottery might mean he wouldn't get a college deferment. My brother was afraid he would get called to serve just as he was applying for law school. All the fellas I knew were nervous about it. Most of my friends, black or white, had a lot of anger about eighteen-year-olds being considered old enough to fight and die in a war, yet not old enough to vote.

In the middle of all this angst and controversy, my father took a seat on the local draft board.

It wasn't as if he came home and said with glee, "Hey, guess what? I'm helping to select who gets drafted." I don't recall that he announced it to us at all. But I do remember when the threatening phone calls began.

They came in the middle of the night. As soon as I got deep into a stone-cold sleep, the phone would ring. I was accustomed to picking up the phone late at night to intercept the call in case it was my boyfriend, but although I knew he would never call that late, I answered it out of habit. Simultaneously, someone usually picked up on the phone downstairs.

"Judge Stokes, stop sending young men off to die," the voice would say, all slow and cold. Then as we said, "Who is this?" or "Stop calling here!" he would add all kinds of threats and racial slurs. It sounded like a white male, probably around my or my brother's age. He began to call a few times a week; then, before long, I noticed the calls came every night. The caller would throw out a threat and hang up, or not say anything at all and stay on the line until we disconnected. Sometimes, I would pick up and hang up without even bringing the phone to my ear. My father never mentioned it to me, and I did not talk about it to either him or my mother. Sometimes I would forget about it by morning, hoping it was just a nightmare. Other times, it just felt like a part of the scary times we lived in.

One night when my parents went out for the evening and I was home alone, I drifted off to sleep, only to be jolted awake by the ringing of the phone. Half asleep and hoping it was my boyfriend, I said, "Hello?"

"You tell him he better stop killing our boys—" he began.

I was wide awake in an instant, and I had had it. "You coward-ass, stupid-ass, punk m-f—," I spoke firmly into the receiver, using the street language I had acquired when defending myself at school and in the neighborhood. "Don't you *ever* call here again. If you do, I'm going to get the police to tell us from our phone tap just who you are, and make sure *your* butt gets drafted *right* away!"

Click. The caller hung up on me. But as my adrenaline was still rushing, I didn't put down the receiver right away. Then I noticed that I hadn't heard the phone go completely dead. In a split second, I realized that someone was on the other line. My parents had evidently come home, and in my drowsiness with the TV going, I had not heard them. I hung up *fast*.

I had a feeling it was Daddy on the line, because Mom would have chided me on the phone as soon as the caller hung up. In our house, their master bedroom was on the main floor; my bedroom and my siblings' rooms were on the second floor. I waited for him to climb the steps and bang on my bedroom door. But no knock came. The next day, I was sure either Daddy or Mom would confront me to mete out punishment. Nothing happened.

Fortunately, the caller never bothered us again.

When André came home from college, he did have a conversation with my father and let him know that he didn't think highly of having a dad who served on the draft board. But Daddy was adamant in his feelings that black people needed to be involved in such controversial things, to make sure that if the country was going to draft people, that people of color and poor folks wouldn't be drafted in disproportionate numbers. He also felt that since he had been asked to serve, it was his civic duty, like jury duty. He considered it as important as his participation on the boards of the Red Cross, or the Urban League, or the Christian Friends for Racial Equality. He didn't want to see anyone die in a war any more than we did, but if men had to be drafted, he wanted to ensure equality even in that patriotic, though increasingly unpopular, endeavor.

My mother was in support of him. In World War II, her first husband had been a Tuskegee Airman, and her cousin had served in the Navy. Cousin Frank had turned his stint into a career that the family was proud of. So she didn't see military service as something to shirk.

But Daddy must have kept our feelings about his draft-board service in mind. I'm sure he didn't want to see André get drafted any more than we did. And he knew that we admired and related to Muhammad Ali for refusing induction into the United States Army with his famous line, "No Viet Cong ever called me a nigger!" Even though it had cost Ali three years away from boxing at the height of his career, at least he had stood up for his beliefs. Surely at some point, Daddy had to reflect on the fact that he and Mom, Republicans, had raised radical children. He might not have agreed with us, but to his credit he did accept the airing of our opinions. Many years later, he would remark in a self-deprecating way that during that time his son was always admonishing him, *"Please,* don't tell anyone you're a member of the draft board!"

Our dad was conservative to us, but within the Republican Party he was considered a social liberal. And unfortunately, the GOP was moving even further to the right than he had ever imagined it would.

In 1964, he had been a "Rocky Republican," supporting New York governor Nelson Rockefeller in his bid for the presidential nomination against Arizona senator Barry Goldwater. That nominating session had divided the party into those who were in support of the passage of the Civil Rights Act (the Rocky Republicans) and those who were openly against it (the Goldwater Southern Strategists). Goldwater won the nomination and carried five southern states—Mississippi, Alabama, Louisiana, South Carolina, and Georgia—in his landslide loss to the Democratic choice, Lyndon Johnson.

Just a few days before Martin Luther King, Jr., was assassinated in 1968, Democratic president Lyndon Johnson had faced the television cameras and announced, "I shall not seek, and will not accept, the nomination of my party for another term as your president."

That opened the door for the Republicans to try again. For the third time, my father campaigned hard for Nelson Rockefeller. I suppose that he liked Rocky's refined sophistication. The wealthy heir of the Standard Oil fortune had come from a family of philanthropists whose financial support of African-American cultural and educational institutions, such as several historically black colleges, had directly benefited African-Americans. He was clearly in support of civil rights and integration.

The Republicans bypassed Rockefeller, however, for the "law and order" candidate Richard Milhous Nixon. Still mindful of the landslide rejection of Goldwater's overt Southern Strategy segregationist stance in '64, Nixon's more pragmatic strategy was to use code words that were racially tinged. The "silent majority" was obviously noninclusive of the minorities in America. His speeches referred to "welfare cheats," people who were "culturally deprived," who had a "lack of family values," and took to "crime in the streets." I still wonder if my father recognized this Nixon as the same one who had accepted his invitation to speak in Seattle for a Lincoln Day celebration in the 1950s.

So before the national convention in Miami Beach, Florida, Daddy campaigned for Rockefeller at the Washington state convention in Seattle. I remember that time well, because of the paper dress.

One day when Jon was visiting me and we were slouching around looking at TV, Daddy approached us and asked if we wanted to help campaign for Nelson Rockefeller. "Not really," I replied, and turned back to "The Dating Game."

"What if I gave you each twenty dollars?"

Jon sat up and answered quickly. "Where do we sign up?" I just looked at him. A few minutes before, he had said he was going to have to cut out soon to meet his friends on the basketball court.

"What do we have to do, Dad?" I asked skeptically. I had been through this campaigning bit before.

"Just a minute, and I'll show you," Daddy replied, and left the room.

When he returned, I realized that he had already planned for us to perform this task, whether we had wanted to or not. In his hands were the "campaign uniforms" we were to wear. More accurately, they looked like campaign costumes. Jon was to wear a straw hat with a red, white, and blue Rocky slogan on the band. He would have to go home and put on slacks, a shirt, and a tie.

For me, Dad held up a yellow dress in a print of simulated campaign buttons with Nelson Rockefeller's face all over it. I recognized the A-shaped style. But I couldn't figure out what material it was made out of. As I was examining this most hideous garment, my mother came in the room and said with amusement, "Steph, that dress is made of paper!"

"Oh my gosh! I can't wear this!" I exclaimed. "What if somebody *sees* me?" When you're sixteen years old, the worst thing that can happen to you is public humiliation. "What if it *tears?*"

"Calm down," Mom said. Fashion was her expertise. "Just wear a real dress under it."

I took the paper dress upstairs to my room as Jon drove home to change. Mom soon appeared next to me and together we scoured my closet and pulled out a green, cotton, short-sleeved shift that I had proudly made myself in sewing class. I slipped it on. Then I put the sleeveless paper dress on top of it. It looked like I was wearing a gunny sack. Mom said it looked fine and left the room.

Standing in front of the full-length mirror on the back of my closet door, I wondered how I was going to get away with wearing this contraption. It was not only made of paper and tied around the back of my neck, but it was practically covering my knees.

Then, for the first time, I realized that there was an advantage to the dress being made of paper. I could cut the bottom of it to make it as short as I wanted to! No sewing was required to "tailor" the dress to my own specification, which was, of course, micro-mini. I grabbed the scissors and whacked off several inches from the nonexistent hem of the garment. The gold belt in my closet was made of big, round chains about the size of each of Rocky's faces, so I fastened it around my waist. Finishing the look with my gold, flat ankle-strap sandals, I was ready to roll!

Jon came back with his straw boater on, and Daddy drove us down to the Seattle Center Arena. There, our assignment was to stand near the registration tables and give out to the many conventioneers one-inch-round, navy blue buttons with white letters that spelled simply, "Rocky!"

When the event was over, Dad did indeed hand over our twenty-dollar bills, which instantly became disposable income. But that paper dress hung in my closet between my old ballet tutus and Halloween costumes for years and years to come.

Nelson Rockefeller lost for the third time, and that was the last time I ever saw my father actively campaign for a Republican presidential candidate or attend a political convention.

Yet, I'm sure he voted for Richard Nixon, since the former vice-president had once come to Seattle and, as was the custom, the party threw their support behind the nominee in a show of unity.

I wasn't old enough to vote, of course, but from what I saw on television, Minnesota Democrat Hubert Humphrey seemed to be more supportive of the nation's youth and of its antiwar activists, a cause for which I was a sympathizer. As usual, Daddy, André, and I debated these politics and party platforms. During Nixon's presidency, my father defended him by saying that at least he had given an executive order in 1969 to establish the Minority Business Development Agency within the United States Department of Commerce, specifically to encourage the creation and growth of minority businesses. "So, see? Nixon did something for you colored people," Daddy would tease us.

Both my parents were staunch supporters of black businesses. We went to a black dentist; we were regulars in the office of an African-American eye doctor. The architect and interior designer of our house were black. If anything needed fixing in the house, my parents sought out black plumbers, electricians, and handymen. Enterprise was not only a source of black pride, but it was compatible with the Republican tenet of self-sufficiency.

In 1972, Nixon took his support of black businesses further by pushing through the Minority Enterprise Small Business Investment Companies (MESBIC) Act. In a letter to a congressman, President Nixon had asked for support of the legislation, writing:

Not only will the MESBIC legislation expand available capital to give minority businessmen a greater "piece of the action," but it will in turn stimulate the employment of minority individuals and provide inroads into the unacceptably high unemployment rate for minorities.

Like most black men, that's what my father wanted—a piece of the action. As an attorney, he was pretty much a self-employed, black-owned business himself. And he knew that a law practice and politics alone would not a Rockefeller fortune make. So, as my mother said, "He tried all sorts of money-making schemes."

With some other partners (including Uncle Hayes, the brother of my mother's first husband), he invested in the first black-owned jazz radio station in Seattle, KZAM-FM. But it was too early in the infancy of the FM band, and the station didn't fly. He owned a barbershop, and took me with him to collect the rent the barbers paid for the chairs there. Real estate was another investment. As the landlord of several houses, he increased our family's net worth with these assets. However, he probably made little profit from the rentals. I was always asking why he didn't raise the rent on one particular house in which an older couple lived.

"Listen here," he snapped at me. "Those people pay that rent on time, every time, year in and year out. So I'm not going to turn around and up the rent." He tried to put an edge in his voice, but I knew he was really just saying that he was an old softie at heart. The 250 dollars they paid had more than covered the mortgage, which had long since been paid off, so he was content with the situation. And that's what the tenants paid, month in and month out, for the thirty years they lived there.

Presidential politics aside, I also disagreed with my father on civil rights tactics. He and my mother were staunch followers of Martin Luther King's nonviolent movement. As an impatient youth, I leaned toward Malcolm X's philosophy that we should defend ourselves by "any means necessary." But then again, when it came to the war in Vietnam, I was a pacifist. Not one to miss a trick, my father was quick to point out my contradictory stances upon cross-examination, as if he were in court instead of at the dinner table.

Daddy admired Edward W. Brooke, the only black United States senator at the time, a Republican from Massachusetts. He and Mom hosted the handsome and elegant Senator Brooke once in our home when he was visiting Seattle. My idea of a politician on the national scene was the boyish and brilliant Julian Bond, a state senator from Georgia. My cousin Gloria had a crush on him, and we both wished that at age twenty-eight he hadn't been too young to accept the nomination for vice-president at the 1968 Democratic National Convention.

Only one time, though, did I feel I really won a debate. Daddy was talking about how black people shouldn't risk alienating white people. He said he felt that we shouldn't publicly criticize whites, as militants H. Rap Brown, Eldridge Cleaver, and Huey Newton did. How would we get jobs if we did that? How would we get the support of whites in Congress and state legislatures to pass civil rights laws? When black folks rioted and burned down white-owned stores, he characterized them as "biting the hand that feeds you."

"You became a judge last year, right?" I asked him.

"Right," he replied, wondering what this had to do with the topic at hand.

"You were the first black district-court judge in this state, were you not?" I prodded, with a little Perry Mason attitude.

"Correct."

"At sixty-five years old, which is retirement age for some people, did you *just* become qualified to be a judge? Did it really take you almost forty years as a prominent attorney to get enough legal experience to be a judge?"

"Well . . ." I could tell he was seriously thinking about what I was saying.

I butted in. "The reason you weren't made a judge before is because of *racism*. The reason why you weren't considered until last year, 1968, is because to make things change people had to riot, people got water-hosed, people had dogs attacking them, folks got put in jail, people *died.*" I was getting emotional, but I could see that he understood and appreciated it as the only way I knew how to say that I was proud of him, and that he probably would have gone even higher if he hadn't been born in a country that considered its black citizens second-class. I felt that whites didn't want to share power or even consider us equally for positions we were qualified for, such as judgeships. So we had to make social change happen by committing revolutionary acts of civil disobedience.

As a man who respected the law, Daddy was against breaking it, even for our freedom. But he knew a change had to come, and he had identified with the struggles of Fannie Lou Hamer, Rosa Parks, and Viola Liuzzo, and had mourned Goodman, Schwerner, and Chaney. As he had said on many occasions, he may not have been one to be on the front lines himself, but he "dern sure" would have defended in court anyone who was.

"If we have an equal education and an equal chance, why does anyone else have to 'feed us'?" I asked rhetorically. "Like James Brown says, 'Open up the door, and I'll get it myself.' " I tried to add something funny at the end of my soliloquy so he wouldn't ask me who I thought I was talking to in that tone of voice.

But he didn't. He just looked at me for a moment, and then spoke softly.

"I guess you're right."

= 17 =
Pomp and Circumstance

I WAS NO VALEDICTORIAN as my maternal grandfather had been, but for my high school graduation, I was asked to deliver the invocation and a poem. I did not tell my father I would be doing this, and kept it a secret between my mother and me.

My mother was pleased to see that the summer of "choral reading" classes she had enrolled me in when I was nine had paid off. But I would not be reciting what I had learned there, such as, "The owl and the pussycat went to sea, in a *beautiful* pea-green boat." Instead I tried to persuade my Caucasian English teacher, who was serving as my oratorical coach, to allow me to recite a "revolutionary poem" by Don L. Lee or Sonia Sanchez. She gently but firmly refused, explaining that such a poem would not pass muster with the principal or the parents.

ABOVE: *My high school boyfriend, Jon Bradford Massey III, and me at my prom.*

So I compromised with Langston Hughes's "I Dream a World." It was a poem by one of the few school-approved African-American poets, yet it had a racial message with a hopeful ending. Like Martin Luther King's "I Have a Dream" speech, the "dream" aspect made it acceptable to whites. With growing militancy, more than a few black kids felt that if anyone in the country thought our racial problems would be solved nonviolently, they could "dream on." But those thoughts were better expressed at Black Panther meetings than at a public school graduation.

I was looking forward to surprising my father, who was a big fan of Langston Hughes's poetry. He had once won a much-publicized death penalty case by practically bringing the jury to tears with his closing argument that featured the poem "Mother to Son."

> *Well, son, I'll tell you:*
> *Life for me ain't been no crystal stair.*
> *It's had tacks in it,*
> *And splinters,*
> *And boards torn up.*
> *And places with no carpet on the floor—*
> *Bare.*
> *But all the time*
> *I'se been a-climbing on,*
> *And reachin' landin's,*
> *And turnin' corners,*
> *And sometimes goin' in the dark*
> *Where there ain't been no light.*
> *So boy, don't you turn back.*
> *Don't you set down on the steps*
> *'Cause you finds it's kinder hard.*
> *Don't you fall now—*
> *For I'se still goin', honey,*
> *I'se still climbin',*
> *And life for me ain't been no crystal stair.*

Around the house, Daddy often repeated just that last line of the poem: "Life for me ain't been no crystal stair." I was never sure if he was talking about the lives of his clients or his own.

During the weeks that I practiced for the graduation address, anti–Vietnam War activity on college campuses accelerated. Like most students in my class, I bought a "Senior Scene" scrapbook/workbook to document my final year of high school. In it, on the page titled "News Worth Remembering," I wrote these notes in bright green ink:

DEMONSTRATIONS! PROTESTS!

Four students were killed at Kent State University in Ohio, May 1970, by National Guardsmen in confrontation between police & students during a protest demonstration to end the war in Vietnam & President Nixon's proclamation to "clean out sanctuaries" in Cambodia, thus furthering the war in Indochina.

University of Washington closed May 8, 1970, in commemoration of the four students killed at Kent State as a day of mourning. Many students participated in demonstrations in support of freeing Bobby Seale (Black Panther leader) because he was not judged by a "group of peers" before he was jailed.

Within one week of the Kent State killings, police killed 2 students and wounded 8 others at Jackson State College. The difference between the two events was that these students were all BLACK!

My point was that "campus unrest," as the media called it, was occurring among students of all races. On the facing page was a newspaper photo of a demonstration with protesters holding a sign that read PEACE NOW. Under it was my own caption: "Rally & demonstration to end Vietnam War, April 1970."

Unfortunately, another death was soon to hit closer to home for me. My fifth-grade boyfriend, Waymond Joseph Miller III, whom we called Butchie, drowned on May 31. The brother of my close friend Renee, Butch had been swimming in a backyard pool with a cousin of mine. I found out when Renee called me that evening and said simply, "Butchie's gone."

I was home alone that evening. When my parents came in together, they found me in shock and tears, sitting at the top of the steps leading to the basement, where they had to enter from the garage.

Just the day before, as I was driving toward the intersection of McClellan and Thirty-first, near my school, I had seen Butchie's big bomb of a car heading toward me. Making a quick left turn in front of him, I had cut him off as a little prank to get his attention. When I looked in my rearview mirror, I thought I would see him in mock anger with his middle finger pointed in my direction, but instead he was calmly and slowly driving by, smiling and waving. Little did I know that it was not only a hello, but our last good-bye.

In my "Senior Scene" I pasted his obituary from *The Seattle Times* that was appropriately headlined "Drowned Youth Known as 'Positive Force.' " It said that "Butch was known by the faculty and administrators at the multiracial [Rainier Beach High] school as a "positive force . . . a good boy . . ." and as "a strong potential leader."

My mother allowed me to miss school and she accompanied me to the funeral, held just across the street from our house at the St. Clement's Episcopal Church. The memorial program went in my scrapbook too, where I wrote: "NEVER TO BE FORGOTTEN . . . Waymond Joseph Miller III, age 17 for all eternity."

The same day that Butchie died, *The Seattle Times* published a story about seven of my school's "students of the month," described as a "cross-section of Franklin's student body—two are black, two white, three Oriental; two girls, five boys." I was included and interviewed for the story, in which it was announced that I was "headed for Howard University in the national capital." I was quoted as saying, "What's a 4.0 grade average if you don't use it to work with the people?"

Of course, my father and mother were pleased that I had been chosen for this story, entitled "Franklin Students Reflect a Good Image." In view of all our political debates, hairstyle disagreements, and the "generation gap," I wouldn't be surprised if they weren't always sure I would shake out that way.

At last, the day I had waited for came. On June 8, 1970, I arrived early at the Seattle Center Arena, on the grounds of the former World's Fair in the large multipurpose hall where I had recently seen James Brown in concert. I was known more for arriving on CP Time, which was short for "Colored People's Time," in other words, late.

But this evening I was right on time, ready and excited to do my thing onstage. My father had remarked that it was rare for me, the person he had to yell at just about every morning to get up for school, to be so early. He, my mother, my brother, my aunt Katie, and Uncle King had their choice of seats. I still had not disclosed to Daddy that I had to be there early to get stage directions for my part in the program.

The school band began to play "Pomp and Circumstance." As the students marched out onto the floor of the arena, Daddy looked for me among the four hundred teenagers. I was not to be found.

Fifteen minutes after the procession ended, he leaned over to Mom and whispered, "Where's Steph? See her?"

She played along, stalling him until she could finally say, "There she is." She pointed to the stage.

After the principal, Mr. Frank Hanawalt, greeted the crowd, it was my turn to rise to my feet and walk to the podium. To my own surprise, I was not nervous at all. The weeks of coaching had been helpful.

"We the Benjamin Franklin High School Class of 1970 are concerned about the problems which face our nation today," I began, speaking into the microphone. "Hate, mounting racism, injustice in our courts, pollution, the never-ending war. We share a dream with Langston Hughes of a world of peace, love, and understanding. To the world in which we are emerging tonight, we dedicate his poem, 'I Dream a World.' "

I took a deep breath, then glanced up and to my right, in the direction of my parents. The stagelights were too bright on my eyes for me to see them. I stared straight ahead into the faces of my classmates, for whom I served as spokesperson, and then began to recite from memory.

> *I dream a world where man*
> *No other will scorn,*
> *Where love will bless the earth*
> *And peace its paths adorn.*
> *I dream a world where all*
> *Will know sweet freedom's way,*
> *Where greed no longer saps the soul*
> *Nor avarice blights our day.*
> *A world I dream where black or white*
> *Whatever race you be,*
> *Will share the bounties of the earth*
> *And every man is free,*
> *Where wretchedness will hang its head*
> *And joy, like a pearl,*
> *Attends the needs of all mankind—*
> *Of such I dream*
> *Our World!*

The poem really ended with "my world," but I had changed it to "our" for the sake of the graduation. After I finished, I paused, then continued slowly and deliberately. "Our prayer tonight is that this dream will come true—*soon!* Thank you."

To the thunderous applause and the approval of my peers, I sat down, relieved I had gotten through it without either tripping and falling flat on my face or forgetting my lines.

Our class was proud that a female student, Laura Chin, was named valedictorian, having maintained a straight-A average throughout high school. She was headed to Seattle University. Our student body president, Vince Mitchell, who was not only totally fine in his full-blown Afro, but smart enough to get accepted to Bowdoin College in Maine, also made us smile. One student who made the top ten of our graduating class was Brian Gorelick, who served as pianist and president of our Bel Canto choir. Little did we know then that he had a younger brother who was musical as well. In a few years, Kenny Gorelick would be known to the world as saxophonist Kenny G.

After the ceremony, my family managed to find me among the hundreds of people in the hallway near the arena's exit. My father approached me feigning anger. "You buttonhead," he said, giving me a hug. "Why didn't you tell me you were going to get up there and give that extraordinary speech?" Someone eavesdropping might have wondered what he was talking about. You'd have thought I had been the keynote speaker. As Daddy planted a mushy kiss on my cheek, I looked over his shoulder at my mother and we both smiled at our success in keeping the secret.

Soon the "Senior Scene" book would be filled with notes and mementos of all I had gone through that year, from the sad passing of my childhood friend to my joy at being named the fashion rep for the hip, teen clothing store Jay Jacobs. In the colorful scrapbook, I collected the calling cards of my classmates with their names embossed in sophisticated script. My Polaroid camera captured my sister, Vicki, visiting with her two daughters from Los Angeles, and my brother, who had transferred from Wesleyan to graduate from Reed College, in Portland, Oregon, and was on his way to the University of Washington Law School.

I even had a picture of the puppy my assistant choir teacher, Mr. Bishop, had given me my junior year. After carrying the tiny beige fox terrier with a stump for a tail around to classes all day in my book bag, I got her home and put a box in the kitchen for her to sleep in.

But my parents didn't come home to notice until late that night. Unfortunately, January 26, 1969, would mark the assassination of one of our most prominent local civil rights leaders. The executive director of the Seattle Urban League, Edwin T. Pratt, was shot and killed right in his own doorway in the Shoreline neighborhood he and his family had integrated. His murder was sadly reminiscent of that of NAACP field secretary Medgar Evers in Mississippi a few years before. Upon hearing the news, like other concerned and outraged African-American Seattleites, Mom and Daddy had gone to express condolences to the family.

Also saved for posterity were news clippings from the white papers and the black ones covering the Jack & Jill Ball, an annual formal event that my mother had helped to found for our Seattle chapter in the mid-1960s when Gloria and André graduated from high school. In July 1970, the ball was held at the opulent Olympic Hotel. Escorted by Jon (who would soon be leaving for Washington State University), and standing among the ten debutantes and the one male honoree, I'm hardly recognizable in the photos. That's because I'm wearing a Gibson Girl wig, a compromise I made with my mother so I wouldn't have to straighten my own hair. I'm dressed in a pink lace empire-waist bridesmaid gown. The affair, attended by Jack & Jillers and their invited guests, was a rite of passage that the black community held in the same high regard in which the white folks held their debutante balls. I danced with my father in a much-rehearsed and choreographed waltz, and was "presented to society."

My favorite scrapbook photo shows my Afro full and my exuberance unbridled. The moment frozen forever pictures six young women—Franklin classmates Dawn Murray, me, Pat Seay, Geneva Mills, Pam Crallie, and from Garfield High, my grade school classmate Karen Yates—dressed in white, smiles bright, spirits high, diplomas in hand.

The graduates (from left to right): Karen Yates (front), Dawn Marie Murray, me, Patricia Seay, Geneva Mills, Pamela Crallie.

= 18 =

I'll Be Somewhere Listening for My Name

THE LEGACY I LEFT HOME WITH that August of 1970 was one of pride in my community, my country, and myself. In 1971, during my sophomore year at Howard University, I voted for the first time when the age for suffrage was lowered that year to eighteen. It happened that my father was up for re-election in his judgeship, and my mother had made sure that I received an absentee ballot. And so the first time, I voted for a Republican.

Many years later, at the age of ninety-three, my father voted by absentee ballot, as well. As I always told people, it seemed that when he hit sixty-five, he stayed that age, looking good, blessed with robust health, until he turned ninety. He was intent on longevity—never smoking,

ABOVE: *Charles M. Stokes in his judicial robe.*

rarely drinking, always starting the day off on his stationary bike, eating raw vegetables, consuming "brown bread" when the rest of the family preferred Wonder white, and following the prescriptions in *Prevention* magazine. Although we kids teased him about his eccentric health habits, we never knew him to have had a cavity, much less surgery or illness. But in 1996, old age tapped him on the shoulder. He was succumbing to Parkinson's disease.

Throughout my own life, I could not recall my father ever admitting to voting for a Democrat. I assumed he had supported his neighbor and Sigma Pi Phi fraternity brother, Norman Rice, in his successful 1989 Democratic bid for mayor of Seattle, the first African-American to win that race. But since my teen years, I had been waging a friendly battle to get him to admit to voting for just *one* Democrat. My parents believed disclosing for whom they voted was taboo. Daddy had officially become nonpartisan when he became a judge. Plus, he said, he had a Constitutional right to privacy, in the voting booth and in my personal "exit polling" of him.

But this evening in November of 1996, in a long-distance phone call, I got a different answer. My teenage niece Alexis was caring for Daddy while Mom went to church for choir rehearsal. Lexi called me and said Daddy wanted to talk with me and my daughter, Anique. On the telephone, after asking him how he felt ("Oh, I'm still perpendicular," he replied), I reverted back to our normal course of conversation, politics. From his previous comments, I was sure that he had voted for George H. W. Bush for president in 1988 and '92. The Christmas card from President and Mrs. Bush was still prominently displayed in the house, although it was no longer Christmas or even the same year in which the card was sent.

But I noticed that whenever I talked about how much I liked President Bill Clinton, he didn't argue me down.

Because I knew he wouldn't tell me whom he voted for, I asked a roundabout question.

"How do you like Clinton?"

"Oh, I like him!" he answered with an enthusiasm that his illness usually prohibited. "Yeah, he's all right!"

I asked no more; I had my answer. As my mother later confirmed, it was likely that there were several times he had crossed over to vote for Democrats, just as the majority-Democratic black community had elected him in his successful Republican bids for office. "He voted for who he thought would be the best person for the job," my mother said.

In my last conversation with Daddy, he was still teaching me. From him, I learned that there was something more essential than whether one voted Republican or Democrat. I learned that it was important not only to vote in every election, but to vote with my heart.

But before the greatest loss of my life occurred, at the end of the 1986 interview between family friend Mary Henry and my father, Mrs. Henry sat up in the red leather chair in front of his law-office desk and prepared to click off the tape recorder.

"In your political life, what do you think was your greatest contribution to both the black community and the total community?" she asked as her last question. Daddy answered with typical honesty and modesty.

I didn't do anything spectacular. I wasn't a Martin Luther King or anything unto that ilk — or approaching it. I do think there's enough of me that people could look upon and say, "Well, there's a guy that I may want my child — daughter or son — to pattern after."

And I also feel there's definitely nothing much detrimental about me that would make people say, "For God's sake, don't do that — what Stokes is doing!"

In other words, I think the best thing I leave, and which I tell my kids, is that I give them my name. And a name, to me, is worth more than gold.

If you've got a good name, you can borrow money without a dime. If you've got a good name, your word is your bond; you don't need to sign a thing. From a purely personal standpoint, I think my good name — or rather my name (strike the first) — is the thing I cherish most. And I hope it has some salutary effect on others.

✳

A good name is rather to be chosen than great riches;
to be esteemed is better than silver or gold.
Rich and poor have this in common:
The Lord is the Maker of them all.

—Proverbs 22:1–2

EPILOGUE

Mine Eyes Have Seen the Glory

2003

On a snowy Saturday in January, I allowed myself to procrastinate when I should have been working on this book. Blaming it on writer's block, I lounged around on my comfy king-size bed in an old black velour hooded dress. With the remote, I switched channels from my HGTV addiction to see what else was on. *The Wizard of Oz*, starring Judy Garland, was just beginning on one of the networks. I had seen it many times, but this time, I watched with new interest, focusing on every

ABOVE: *My paternal grandparents, Josephine (my father's stepmother) and Rev. Norris J. Stokes, were married in Paola, Kansas, in 1909.*

shot of Kansas, every mention of Kansas, Dorothy's accent—was that how Kansans spoke?

Ironically, I had recently mentioned to a few of my coworkers at *Lifetime* magazine that I wanted to go to Pratt, Kansas, to see where my father had grown up. They listened as I explained that February 1 would be my late father's one hundredth birthday, and since it fell on a Saturday, I thought it would be a good time to go over the weekend. They knew I was writing about my father's life, and were supportive of my project.

"I really think I want to go to Kansas," I explained, "but I'm not exactly sure how to get to Pratt, which is in the middle of the state, far from a big-city airport."

"Click your heels together!" someone cracked. Everyone laughed.

If you were to tape a big map of the United States on a wall and then try to throw a dart smack-dab in the middle of it, your target would be Pratt, Kansas. The locals call the area, equidistant from the west coast and the east coast, "mid-continent." If you're from somewhere else, you might call it "the middle of nowhere."

This is where I decided to go for my father's birthday. If he had been alive, I thought, I would have been flying out to Seattle for a party, as I had done with my husband and daughter ten years before when my mother gathered us all for his ninetieth birthday. But now, I had to celebrate him in a more spiritual way. There would be no party in Seattle, no family reunion in Pratt.

My mother, who had been to Pratt many times with my father whenever they drove to midwest cities for conventions, had said that she would accompany me if I wanted to go visit my father's hometown, say, sometime in the summer. But when I decided to go in the dead of winter, when it was possible that we could encounter a snowstorm, she declined my invitation.

I had been there myself once before, as a youngster, on one of those cross-country trips to a convention in New York. But we were there less than twenty-four hours, so I don't remember much more than visiting with Daddy's stepmother, Mrs. Stokes.

She died in the 1970s, and then her youngest son, Maurice, moved back into the family home after retiring from his professorship at

Savannah State College. He lived there until his death in 1996, the same year as my father's passing. The little house on the corner of Eighth and Jackson, a stately, tree-lined, cobblestoned street, had been sold and torn down.

I had received an inheritance of many wonderful family mementos, including a large, oval, framed, turn-of-the-century sepia portrait of my grandparents. These cherished possessions gave me a new appreciation for anything with historical value. With regret, I recalled giving away the antique doll my step-grandmother had presented me with when we visited Pratt. But now, as the family archivist, I was determined to reclaim anything I could find of our family history there.

That is why when I called the Pratt office of attorney Michael Johnston, who had handled the family estate in the last years of my father's younger brother Maurice's life, I was happy to hear that they had some family papers and other belongings for me. That clinched my decision to travel to Pratt.

"You could fly into Wichita," the law office secretary, Kathy Wood, told me on the phone. "Then drive one hour and fifteen minutes to Pratt."

That sounded doable. I logged on to MapQuest and found that it was a straight shot from Wichita on Highway 54. Make a left out of the airport and just drive seventy-two miles until you get there.

I drafted my husband, Reginald, to go with me and to drive the rental car. He had known and loved Daddy too, and was down for some adventure in a part of the country he had never visited. We had the good fortune to find a cheapie airfare on Expedia.com and a reasonable rate at the Pratt Holiday Inn. We were going to Kansas!

As the day approached, I began to have trepidation about the weather. Tales of how my father had to "follow the snowplow" in April of 1949 to get to his father's funeral haunted me. I didn't want to get stuck in the Kansas plains in a rented car in a blizzard. I logged on to Weather.com. The temperature in Pratt was 27 degrees—cold and windy, much like the east coast weather at the time. But as I scrolled down the page for the seven-day forecast, I thought there might be an error. On Friday,

January 31, it read 55 degrees. For Saturday, February 1, the forecast was 67 and sunny. How was that possible?

With God, all things are possible, I remembered, and took it as a sign that I was doing the right thing.

Friday, January 31, 2003

At the Newark Liberty Airport on the Friday morning we left for Kansas, I sauntered down the long terminal after having endured the airport security check. Reggie was parking our car in a remote long-term lot. As I entered the Northwest gate area, I noticed an African-American man with a large Afro perched on the shoeshine chair, taking advantage of the service. Well dressed in a suit and tie, he looked dignified yet friendly as he bantered with the man polishing his shoes. He looked my way, but with my chronic nearsightedness, I couldn't tell if he was looking at me. Slowing my pace, I tried to look at him in a nonchalant way that wouldn't make him think I was staring. I immediately recognized the signature goatee in contrast with his fair skin tone and the black Malcolm X glasses.

"I just saw Cornel West," I said, as soon as Reggie sat down in the gate area next to me.

"Where?" he asked with instant interest, looking around for the renowned Princeton University professor and social activist.

"He was getting his shoes shined, but he's gone now."

"Which way did he go?"

Oh, no, I thought with amusement. *Reg is going to stalk Cornel West.*

"He walked in front of this counter," I said pointing to the vacant check-in area before us, "heading that way. I'm sure he got on that flight they just called before you got here."

Reg got up wordlessly and started walking in the direction I had indicated. I looked around, wondering if Dr. West had indeed gotten on the plane to Chicago or not. Our flight was heading to Memphis, where we would change planes for Wichita. I didn't see Dr. West in our boarding area, so I figured I was probably right. He was on that flight that just left for Chicago. Shortly, Reg returned, and shook his head no when I asked if he had seen him.

After we munched on muffins from the concession stand, our flight was called. Reg was among the first to board, before they called our row. Always the Proper Polly, I waited until the gate agent made the announcement that gave me permission to board.

When I stepped onto the plane and turned the corner into first class, there was Reg chatting gregariously with Cornel West. Reg later described their initial meeting.

"How are you doing, brother?" Dr. West had greeted him warmly when it was obvious that he had been recognized.

"I'm not doing so great," Reg said with a mischievous smile. "This threat of war has me all worried, man." Allowing nearby passengers to pass in the aisle, Reg stepped into the seat behind Dr. West and shook his hand. His greeting had been an attempt to see if he could get an opinion from the scholar on the impending war on Iraq.

"Yeah, the world is a scary place, isn't it?" Dr. West replied diplomatically.

"Oh, here's my wife." Reg gestured toward me as I approached. I shook my head and smiled in mock disapproval.

"Is he talking you up?" I asked Dr. West, and extended my right hand to shake his. Grabbing the shoulder straps of my heavy carry-on with my left hand, I became momentarily preoccupied with preventing the bag from dropping in his lap and embarrassing myself.

"How are you, my sister?" he asked me, flashing a generous gap-toothed smile that melted me, making me forget where I was or what to say in response.

I attempted to come back with how nice it was to see him, and how much we appreciated his work. But I didn't want to bother him, or fawn over him as some people do to public figures; plus, passengers were in line behind me waiting to board the plane. In making eye contact with Dr. West, however, I didn't look down before I moved along. So I didn't realize that the man stowing his belongings in the compartment over Dr. West's head had left his black computer case in the middle of the floor. As I moved away, I almost tripped over it. And then, to compensate for the awkward moment, I impolitely pushed the passenger aside, scurrying to my seat in the first row of coach, mumbling about how if people would just move into their row, others could get by, and we could all board the plane for an on-time takeoff. Good grief!

As we settled into our bulkhead seat, requested to accommodate Reg's long legs, I could see the back of Cornel West's head. His signature healthy, vibrant brown mane made a semicircle over the top of his seat that struck me as having a halo effect. I made a mental note of it as another good omen of the trip.

I caught myself grinning throughout the entire approach and landing in Wichita. With my forehead pressed to the window, I observed that Kansas really did look like the land of *The Wizard of Oz.* Flat, geometric parcels of land were bordered by arrow-straight roads. Some of the wide-open spaces I saw from the air formed patterns of spectacular concentric circles. It all looked like a comforting patchwork quilt.

At the airport Avis rental counter, the young, thin white guy handed us the key for the car and pointed to the parking lot nearby.

"You'll find the car in space number thirty-three," he said, and I didn't hear another word. I looked at Reggie with my eyes wide. He knew immediately what I was thinking.

Thirty-three was my father's lucky number. He had a thing for threes—3, 13, and 33 were his favorites. Our telephone number was once 323-3373. The license plate of his own car, the one he drove in his last years, was number 33. For my mother's car, he secured the number 13. People often stopped them at red lights or in parking lots to ask how they got them, assuming the low numbers would be reserved for VIP plates, and not understanding how a black person could rate that. The truth was that when personalized plates were offered for the first time in Washington state in the late 1960s, Daddy was one of the first to request them. He was not able to get number 3, because the city of Seattle had already reserved that tag, but he got 13 and 33. It was that simple.

When we got to the rental car, an Oldsmobile Alero, I noticed that it was red. After I remarked to Reg that this was Dad's favorite color, we both kept saying as we packed up the trunk with our bags, "This is deep!" Reg summed up our feelings when he stated, "This is like Stokey saying, 'Welcome to Kansas!' "

"It is *gorgeous* outside—fifty-four degrees!" we heard the DJ exclaim with exuberance on the Wichita radio station KDYN as we traveled west on Highway 54. The sun was bright and pleasant. We couldn't have asked for better weather in the dead of winter.

Leaving Wichita on the four-lane highway, I began to see signs for a town called Goddard. That got my attention because Daddy's first wife Eva's maiden name was Goddard. I had told Vicki about the trip, and she had wished me the best. Although Vicki worked for a major airline, she didn't like to travel by plane, so she didn't volunteer to leave her home in Los Angeles to meet me in Kansas. But seeing the sign, I thought of her and all the fun summers I spent with her at Eva's house in my teen years. Eva, who had passed away about seven years before, had always been good to me, just as my mother had been a caring stepmother for Vicki. Seeing the road sign made me miss being able to call to tell her I had passed through a town with her maiden name in her home state. As we drove on, I noticed more signs indicating that we were entering Goddard, Kansas. I suddenly realized that today, January 31, was Eva's birthday.

"Reggie, guess what!" I exclaimed. "This is Goddard, Kansas, and today is Eva Goddard Stokes's birthday." She and Daddy had met and married in Kansas, and had lived there for most of their fifteen years together. This whole trip was getting amazing.

About halfway to Pratt, there was a sign for Pretty Prairie. I looked around at the flat horizon and thought about the Laura Ingalls Wilder children's book series about frontier life that I had enjoyed so much as a youngster. One of the books, *Little House on the Prairie,* on which the popular television show had been based, was set in Independence, Kansas, which is just twenty-five miles south of where my father was born in Fredonia, Kansas. Having known Daddy only as a Seattle city slicker, it had never occurred to me that the topography of the region in which he had grown up may have had more in common with the plains and prairies mentioned in my favorite children's books than the urban setting of my own childhood. My father was born about thirty-five years after Laura Ingalls (whose birthday was February 7, 1867), so it was hard to determine how much had changed in that time. But my grandfather Norris J. Stokes, who also grew up in Kansas in the 1880s, would have been just slightly younger than Laura. With amusement, I considered that maybe he could have written *The Colored House on the Prairie.*

If he had, the book could have included some interesting facts about Kansas history that I didn't recall reading about in the *Little House* books. For example, Grandpa could have told the story of how white radical abolitionist John Brown moved from North Elba, New York, to Osawatomie, Kansas, in 1855. Following five of his twenty children, Brown went to Kansas to join the effort to keep Kansas from becoming a slave state. The next year, he and his sons defended Osawatomie from violent attack by racist factions, allegedly murdering five proslavery settlers.

A staunch antislavery revolutionary, Brown gave his life for his beliefs. In 1859, he was hanged after he and eighteen followers attempted to carry out a thwarted plan to invade the south by distributing weapons from the United States arsenal at Harpers Ferry, Virginia (now West Virginia), to arm slaves to revolt.

When the Civil War began a few years later, Union troops sang "The Battle Hymn of the Republic," originally written as a tribute to Brown. "John Brown's body lies a-mouldering in his grave/His soul goes marching on." The lyrics were later rewritten by antislavery poet Julia Ward Howe and ended with the words, "As He died to make men holy, let us die to make men free." This song had a strong affinity among Kansans, because of its origins as an ode to a local hero, and its double history as a call for black freedom and an American Civil War rallying cry. And it was a favorite of the Kansas native son who was my father, long after he had left the state. He had even requested that it be sung at his funeral.

The Colored House on the Prairie also could have told of how, as the gains of Reconstruction were violently stripped away, groups of African-Americans sought to leave the south to settle in places where they could experience freedom and self-determination. Benjamin "Pap" Singleton, who had escaped slavery in Tennessee, led a migration of blacks from Kentucky and Tennessee. In 1877, the same year my grandfather was born, the Nicodemus Colony in Graham County, Kansas, was established with three hundred people. The town, located in the northwest part of the state, was named after a legendary slave.

Daddy claimed that his father, Norris, had been born in Kentucky. So after I had learned about the African-American migration from there, I wondered if my great-grandparents had been part of it. I had read in my grandfather's obituary that he had been taken to Kansas as a child by his parents. There is no evidence that the Stokes family of the late 1800s settled specifically in Nicodemus. But, I thought, maybe they heeded the flyers that proclaimed

> *All Colored People*
> *That Want to*
> **GO TO KANSAS**
> *Can do so for $5.00*

Or perhaps their group just got as far as Fredonia, in the eastern part of the state, a small town with a name that celebrated freedom. At some point, Grandpa also lived in Paola, less than ten miles from John Brown's Osawatomie. What is clear, however, is that after the 1830 Indian Removal Act that resulted in the settlement in Kansas of more than ten thousand American Indian tribes, and after seven years of "Bleeding Kansas" border battles over whether the territory would be slave or free that left fifty-five dead, Kansas had entered the Union triumphantly in 1861 as a refuge—if not a haven—for freedom-seeking Americans of all races. It was here, in Fredonia, Kansas, where my father, Charles Moorehead Stokes, had been born in 1903.

I began to feel as though I was time-traveling. On one hand, I was looking at land that probably hadn't changed much since frontier times, yet in the car on the road between Wichita and Pratt on this sunny winter day of 2003 we were listening to National Public Radio's "All Things Considered" just as we did at home in New Jersey.

"There's a real ranch house—complete with a ranch," Reg remarked, as we passed one cattle ranch after another.

Driving through the town of Cunningham, I noticed a sign for Norris Street. That was another sign all right—Norris was both my grandfather's name and the name of his eldest son, my father's older brother.

We rose over a hill upon entering Pratt. The first thing I noticed, on our left, was McDonald's golden arches. There was a Wal-Mart. The town seemed more modern than I had anticipated, until we made the left turn onto Main Street. Angled parking gave the town an immediate old-fashioned feeling. I expected to see board-planked sidewalks, like in the TV westerns. But instead, we got another sign.

On Main Street, we passed a corner retail store as we looked for Attorney Johnston's office. In black letters on the white background, the name of the store was displayed in capital letters: MAURICE'S. Maurice was the name of my father's younger brother. Reggie and I just looked at each other in awe.

In the next block, we had our choice of angled parking spots in front of the law office of Johnston & Eisenhauer. Reggie noticed that unlike New York, Seattle, or even our suburban town, there were no parking meters in Pratt.

It was already after four o'clock on a Friday afternoon, when the office might have closed early for the weekend, but Kathy, the secretary who had given me the directions, greeted us warmly and allowed me to give her a hug across the reception counter. I thanked her for speaking to me over the phone and for advising me how to get there. She offered to call Attorney Johnston, whom she called Michael, and added that he might be home playing his guitar, and so may not hear the phone. But he did pick up, and in no time he was there at the office.

I don't know why, but I had assumed that the law firm my Uncle Maurice had hired to handle his estate before he passed away at age eighty-five in 1996 had been African-American. I hadn't realized before I researched the town on the Internet that there were only sixty-three black folks out of a population of 6,000 living there nowadays. So I was just a bit surprised to see that the attorney was not only white, but of my own generation. He came in casually dressed and welcomed us to his wood-paneled office, which ironically reminded me of the style and size of my father's street-level law office of his retirement years. While we exchanged pleasantries, Kathy walked from the reception area to a back office and returned shortly with several delicate and dusty items.

There were two copies of an academic book Uncle Maurice had written while serving as a professor of education at Savannah State College in Georgia. Entitled *An Interpretation of Audio-Visual Learning Aids,* the slim hardcover volume had an impressive book jacket of bold type, with his name, MAURICE S. STOKES, printed at the bottom. I felt pride that Uncle Maurice had actually written a book, and I also noted with chagrin that before that moment, I had assumed I had been the first in my family to become a published author. The title page featured a 1956 copyright held under the name Edward K. Meador of The Meador Press in Boston. The price on the inside cover was two dollars.

Also found among the belongings were four copies of a self-published, spiral-bound volume of writings of Uncle Maurice's world travels called *Educational Travel: Africa, Asia, Australia, Europe and North America.* I had known that Uncle Maurice, an eccentric, lifelong bachelor, had enjoyed the summer vacations that were a benefit of working in academia.

But I had not realized the extent of his travels, and that he had gone around the world several times with groups organized by the National Education Association. In his travel writing, he provided minute details about the history of his destinations, the political climate, and landmark places to visit. He mentioned going alone ("The group did not go") to attend a Sunday Mass service of a Roman Catholic church in Kyoto, Japan, in 1983. And in writing about Australia, he discussed an issue that African-Americans often debate about traveling there: Are we welcome?

As an "American Negro," who visited Australia for a brief period of time, my candid attitude and feelings are that national antipathies and racial prejudice are at a minimum in Australia. I was given a friendly, genuine, and cordial welcome in practically every place visited, by most of the people contacted while there.

When the cynic, skeptic, sardonic, and pseudo-critic presents insidious remarks about Australian people and ethnic relations, tell him that "Life can be beautiful." Tell him that I received, in general, a royal reception while in Australia.

I was especially interested in his many visits to Africa, the Motherland that my father never stepped foot on. Uncle Maurice documented the racial makeup of each country in Africa, such as

Gambia: Chief tribes—Mandingo, Wolof, Serahali, Sula, Jola
Liberia: Mainly Negroes

He acknowledges, however, that "Technically speaking, the word 'Negro' is not included in the African racial classification."

Of Nigeria, he wrote that it "has the largest population of any country in Africa." And that "Ancestors of most American Negroes came from here or nearby . . ."

Although there are many black-and-white photographs inserted in the book, I could find only one in which he was included. I was delighted to see him standing in front of a safari lodge at Kenya's Tsavo National Park. At age 77, he looks slightly stooped and elderly. But he is clean-shaven and just plain "clean"—well dressed in a dark single-breasted jacket with white shirt and gray slacks. With one hand in his pants pocket, he looks the part of the sophisticated traveler.

Not all the places of interest in his missive, however, are foreign ports. There is a chapter on Pratt, his hometown. Bookmarked with a personalized blank check from a long-closed bank account of his, it begins, "If a person wishes to know and understand the United States of America, it would be difficult to locate a more typical community." He also mentions that the state of "Kansas has a rock in it that is supposed to be the geographic center of the United States." As evidence of the modernity of his own town, he cites the First National Bank's drive-in feature and its "Automatic Teller Machine located on the Gidson's parking lot."

Sandwiched between sections about the Pratt Public Library and the Santa Fe passenger train is one that definitely caught my attention:

Pratt, Kansas, Negroes

For a period of years the total population remained under four hundred for the county. The County Extension Agents interview indicated that recently there has been a decline. Annually Negroes enroll in public schools and usually graduate from high school. A few of us have completed college and done advanced graduate work; also competed in athletics, cultural, social, and other values have been received. The most lucrative and pecuniary values have been in teaching and farming. Pratt has always had a few skilled and semi-skilled workers, such as automobile workers, tailors, musicians, carpenters, plasterers, and dancers. A few Negro domestic workers have served wealthy families for approximately fifty years. Prominent Pratt County families include such surnames as James, Williams, Buckner, Martin, Bright, Ganaway, Fleming, and Minnis. Sometimes family reunions have sixty or more people.

Two churches have been dominant in the history and progress of the Pratt Negro: namely, the Second Baptist Church and Bethel African Methodist Episcopal Church. They have had other churches. The present Baptist structure was constructed under the leadership of my father, Reverend Norris J. Stokes. At one time a lady evangelist conducted a revival at Bethel A.M.E. Church. Historically, about six families have controlled farms of 320 acres or more. Many of the farms have from 40 to 160 acres within a radius of 7 miles from Pratt. A number of farmers in Pratt County have been, historically, recipients of the Homestead Act of 1882.

I was glad to read that in Kansas, at least, some black folks got their forty acres and a mule.

The item I treasured most from those Kathy presented me with was a hand-painted piece of unframed artwork, long torn at the edges, but still beautiful and vivid in its watercolor. The picture was of the church, Second Baptist, which as Uncle Maurice had mentioned in his volume, had been built under my grandfather's pastorate. The year of its completion, 1919, was indicated in bold, black numbers painted on the bottom.

"I think this church is right down the street here," Kathy said, pointing to her right as she faced the street. "And the house your uncle lived in was around the corner, but it's torn down now."

As we gathered our things to leave, I told them both how much our family had appreciated their help when my uncle died. My father had been on his own death bed at the time, and no one in the family had been able to get to Pratt from Seattle, Los Angeles, Hawaii, or New Jersey to bury him, take care of his financial affairs, or clean out and sell the house. I could tell that these two people had gone beyond the job of providing legal advice to care for Uncle Maurice in his last days. Michael told us how my uncle, after he could no longer get around well, had asked him to buy some groceries for him one day.

"I didn't say that it wasn't my job as an attorney to go grocery shopping," he told us. "I just said, 'Well, Mr. Stokes, I charge 125 dollars an hour.' Mr. Stokes just looked at his watch and then looked at me and said, 'It's four-fifteen now.' " Michael knew those were his marching orders. We all laughed.

After getting a recommendation to eat dinner at the Café Bourgeois, Reg and I thanked them and left the law office. But before checking into the Pratt Holiday Inn and freshening up for dinner, I wanted to drive down Main Street in the direction of the church before it got dark.

"There it is!" I yelled at Reggie, immediately recognizing the corner brick building with stained-glass windows.

"Are you sure? How do you know?" He couldn't believe we had come up to it so quickly, just a couple of blocks from the law office. We were still getting accustomed to small town nuances.

"I can tell by the corner steps," I said. Several years before my father had passed, he had shown me the heavy black Bible that had belonged to his father. In it, Daddy had placed a souvenir journal of a 1936 Baptist convention, which featured the first photo I had ever seen of my grandfather. The caption read:

REV. NORRIS J. STOKES
PASTOR AND CHURCH BUILDER

On the same page was a drawing of the church; under it was printed:

SECOND BAPTIST CHURCH
PRATT, KANSAS
"STRANGERS' HOME"—ALL WELCOME!

That was all I'd had to go on, but as soon as I saw the church, I knew it was the same one as in the journal and in the picture I had just been handed. I was a stranger no more. I was home.

Reg pulled over to the curb and I jumped out of the car. I climbed those steps that ascended from both corners of the street and met together at the double doors. At the top of the steps I noticed a cornerstone embedded in the stately brick. The engraving took my breath away.

SECOND BAPTIST
CHURCH
1887–1919
N. J. STOKES, PASTOR

Here, in the streaming light of the sunset, was the church where my grandfather had preached eighty-five years ago. This was the place where my step-grandmother had worshipped, and the grounds on which her three boys had roamed. I was no longer gazing at the picture in the journal or even at the painting I had just been given. I placed my hand on the actual house of prayer that had been the religious center of the lives of my ancestors. I felt as though I was standing on hallowed ground.

Saturday, February 1, 2003
"This feels like when I went on pilgrimage to Mecca," Reggie remarked as we got dressed, wondering what we would see and experience on this special day—my father's one hundredth birthday—that we felt blessed to be spending in his hometown.

In 1970, Reggie had accomplished the spiritual journey of a life-time by traveling to Saudi Arabia and embarking on the most holy of rituals of his Islamic faith. He had been just twenty-three years old, six years before I met him.

Pratt was a long way from Mecca, but I appreciated his sentiment. I knew it felt like a spiritual journey to me. I responded by telling him how grateful I was that he had accompanied me. Daddy would have been tickled to know that Reginald Oliver, the native New Yorker, had gone to visit his little ol' hometown in Kansas.

Daddy used to enjoy watching "The Tonight Show" with Johnny Carson. Frequently, Johnny would interview centenarians on his show. We always laughed at the spry, clever, and witty men—and I mainly do remember just men—who belied their age.

"That's what you're going to do when you turn a hundred," I would say to Dad, once he started getting up in age. "I'm going to get you on there with Johnny Carson."

"That would be good!" he would always agree. Everyone always told him that he was a natural humorist. If you asked him a question on any subject, he could come back with a witticism. I thought he'd be great on TV. Reggie said that if he was alive nowadays, he could have had a perfect retirement career meting out justice on television, like Judge Joe Brown.

Around the time Dad turned ninety, Jay Leno took over "Tonight." I would engage Daddy in banter over the phone about whether Leno would continue having one-hundred-year-olds on the late-night pro-gram.

"Even if he doesn't follow the tradition, I'm going to write him to say he should make an exception for you," I said, playing Dad's agent. "And I'm going to get you on 'The Today Show' too," I added. "I can just see Willard Scott now, announcing your name and showing your photo. We'll have to make sure we send in a good one. Those snap-shots they show look tired."

"Ha, ha! You think so?" Dad would answer, indulging me.

I said, actually it would be even better if we showed up in person.

"Why is that?"

"Because then I could meet Bryant Gumbel," I shot back. And we laughed. Everybody in my family watched Bryant. Even though we were scattered six thousand miles from our Seattle hometown, from as far away as Hawaii (where André settled to practice law and surf), to Los Angeles (Vicki's base), to New Jersey (my house), we watched the same folks on TV.

I took this thing of making sure Daddy made it to one hundred quite seriously. I sent him humorous books by George Burns on living to be a hundred. For Christmas of 1993, I gave him the Delany sisters' book *Having Our Say*. If they could write a book at 103 and 101 years old, so could he. I reminded him that he was born the same year as Bob Hope, and that I fully expected both of them to make it to a hundred. I wanted him to feel that becoming a centenarian would be another achievement he could look forward to. I wanted him to live *forever*.

But, of course, that was asking a bit much. His time came in 1996, at age ninety-three.

So now, I spent his one hundredth birthday not accompanying him to Hollywood to appear on Jay Leno's late-night talk show, but standing on the land of his childhood home, gazing across the neighboring park where I could see his father's church standing majestically a block away. It was not my original fantasy, but it still seemed like a dream come true.

Reg and I left the rental car in front of the cleared plot of land where the Stokes family home once stood at the corner of Eighth and Jackson. We walked up the brick-lined street in the astonishing sixty-seven-degree sunshine—weather, we had been told, that was totally unusual for Kansas at that time of year.

At Fourth and Jackson, we came to a modern structure that we were pleased to find was the Pratt Public Library. Going inside and introducing ourselves, we met a librarian named Sandy.

"I knew who your uncle, Mr. Stokes, was," she said, referring to Uncle Maurice. "He visited here often, and when he couldn't visit anymore, he called." She smiled ever so slyly, and I smiled back, realizing that she was acknowledging both his scholarly nature and his high-maintenance eccentricity. That one sentence told me that she really did know who he was and had respected him.

Sandy led Reg and me to a back room where we could look through the microfiche tapes of *The Pratt Union* newspaper. I wondered if there might be a story on the dedication of Second Baptist's new building in 1919. As Reg sat nearby reading a book he had taken from the stacks on one of his heroes of Kansas history, John Brown, it took me at least forty-five minutes or more to scan every page of the daily newspaper until I got to a small item on April 24 that caught my eye. It was titled, simply, "The Colored Baptists." Never naming the church or the pastor's name, it told of a fund-raiser that resulted in 5,400 dollars for the building of a new church.

Scanning more headlines and pages of dense small type and surprisingly few photos, I found an untitled story, published on July 31, 1919.

> The annual session of the Southwestern District Association will meet at the Second Baptist Church. . . . Rev. Stokes is cor. secty. [sic] of the S.S. department and has worked up a gold medal contest which will be given on Wednesday evening. Don't miss the meeting for it will be worth going to attend. For further news, phone N. J. Stokes, 3398.

I had never done a genealogical search before, but now I knew how those who had and discovered unexpected nuggets of information about their foreparents must have felt. It was just amazing to see the name of the person I had heard about in oral history, documented right there in black and white in the local newspaper. In 1919, Grandpa even had a telephone! Surely, that was rare for most citizens so near the turn of the century, much less an African-American. Whether it was his personal phone or belonged to Second Baptist, it enabled him to do church business.

I decided to look through the *Pratt Daily Tribune* of 1949, knowing only that Grandpa died in April, but not the date. Considering the other inch-long column items, and the one that called the church the

"Colored Baptist" instead of its proper name, I was astonished to come across a long, front-page story on April 6:

REV. STOKES IS STRICKEN
SUDDEN HEART ATTACK THIS MORNING
CLAIMS LIFE OF LONG-TIME PRATT MINISTER

For most of my life, I had heard the story of how my grandfather was sitting in the Pratt train station reading the newspaper and waiting for the train to go to a Baptist convention. It was said that he "just slumped over and died." The story was always told with a tone of admiration, followed by comments of "That's the way to go," or "I hope I die like that." There was never any talk of a heart attack, just that he was happy and healthy one minute, and gone the next.

I was grateful to see that the newspaper article treated him with respect and seemed to support the oral history. When Reg and I had arrived in town the day before, I noticed the long-abandoned, brightly colored, single-story stucco train station, just across the way from Second Baptist. I couldn't believe I was seeing the place described in the family tale. It looked almost exactly as I had envisioned it, as though my own imagination had come to life. I just stared at the structure bathed in the light of dusk, and said to Reggie, "That is where my grandfather died."

Reg drove me up to the building and sat in the car meditating in the graveled parking area, while I got out and circled the place alone. I said a prayer of gratitude. But before my emotions turned to tears, I recalled that my father's funniest stories had taken place at the railroad tracks near the train station. It was there in the railroad yard where he had sneaked behind his brother and found out Norris's secret place for gathering the bigger stash of coal in their nightly competition. My mind saw the young boys playing, and I wondered how many times at sundown almost a century before had they played tag, thrown footballs, or counted train cars going by right where I was standing. I thought about the fact that all three sons had probably left from this station to go to college. Hugs and kisses hello and good-bye between my own family members—those I knew of, and other relatives I didn't—may have taken place here. I took pictures of the tracks as far as I could see in each direction, hoping maybe, just maybe, the film would capture the Stokes spirit.

Reg and I pulled ourselves away from the microfiche after another of the helpful librarians, who introduced herself as Rochelle, promised to mail us copies of the articles we found. Walking quickly, we reached the Pratt Historical Museum a few blocks away, getting there just before closing time. In the main lobby, I stood looking around, and to my far right I saw a glass enclosure with the title of the exhibit cut out of black construction paper on a white background: SECOND BAPTIST CHURCH. I walked closer and saw photos of a group of people standing on the front steps of the church, probably taken at the dedication of the church in 1919. And sure enough, there was my grandfather in the center of the crowd. I searched the young and old, trying to find someone who looked about sixteen, the age my father would have been, but I couldn't say for sure that he was in the pictures. I had seen only one childhood photo of my dad, one taken when he was four years old. So perhaps I didn't recognize him, but I did know the face of my grandfather, which resembled the journal photo I was carrying with me.

"Would it be possible to get copies of these photos?" I asked the founder of the museum, Mr. Rose. "It happens that you have more pictures here of my grandfather and his church than I have ever seen in my lifetime." He graciously obliged me, and disappeared behind a door to make photocopies.

While he was gone, I walked up to the framed drawing of Celeb Pratt, the person for whom this Kansas town and county was named. Under the intense gaze of the young, dark-haired white man was a write-up about his life: He was born in Massachusetts. In 1854 at the age of twenty-two he joined a group of members of the New England Immigrant Aid Company, who moved to Kansas. "This organization aided Free-State Advocates to become settlers in Kansas, so that it would not become a pro-slave state," the poster read. I liked this guy already.

"In 1861, he became a second lieutenant of Company D and served with General Lyon at the Battle of Wilson's Creek in Missouri. He was killed in the battle on August 10, 1861, at the age of twenty-nine."

Soon Mr. Rose returned with the copies and it was closing time. The docent who was with him when we arrived left, but Mr. Rose offered to stay to show us all of the museum, which extended far back into rooms we could not see from the entrance. There was a chapel upstairs, a replica of a nineteenth-century post office, a library, a blacksmith shop, a real caboose. There were Ford Model T cars and a soda shop. It seemed that most of the folks of Pratt had donated family relics and treasures to the historical museum, and that they took pride in preserving their history.

We left the museum and walked down Main Street, and decided to eat dinner—our first meal of the day—in a bar and grill that brought us back to the present. We were the only black folks in there. We hadn't seen any other African-Americans all day, except for one older woman I noticed driving down the street near the family home. Where were the descendants of the black community that had been there in my father's day?

Driving back to the Holiday Inn, we pondered this question. But we didn't stay up long. Each of us had carried one of a pair of my father's exquisite jeweled cufflinks during the day, as a way of connecting with him on his birthday. We walked into our room and laid them on the dresser. I glanced at the zebra-patterned flannel shirt of Daddy's that I had brought to wear that day, but had changed my mind because I felt we already stood out as newcomers in town. The black Sunbeam clock radio next to the bed showed the time in red digits as 10:46 when I— who usually stayed up late to watch "Saturday Night Live" and "Show-time at the Apollo"—turned off the light and drifted to sleep. Reggie was already out for the count. The words to an old church anthem came to mind as I ended the day on which my father had been born a hundred years before: *Wasn't that a mighty day?*

Sunday, February 2, 2003

Reg opened the blinds in our ground-floor hotel room, but no light streamed in. We looked out the window for glimpses of sunlight, but saw only gray. It was more cloudy and cooler than the previous two days, which had welcomed us to town with warmth and brilliant light. "Now we have Seattle weather," I remarked as we put on our jogging clothes.

The hotel was on Highway 54, so we asked the folks at the front desk where we could power walk away from the speeding cars and trucks. They pointed us to a road behind the hotel, and we cut over the grassy grounds to get there.

I'm always looking at real estate. Everywhere I go, I notice the architecture, the neighborhoods, and imagine choosing a house that I could live in. On our walk down the suburban Pratt streets without sidewalks, a brown, two-story home that looked like a new construction caught my eye.

"Let's turn down this way." I motioned to Reg.

"Nice house," he said, as we kept moving past it.

That street led to a dead end and we had to make a left turn onto another road. I looked at the street sign: Eighth Street. "Hey, if we keep going down this road, we'll get back to the church!" I yelled over to Reg.

Sure enough, as we kept walking, we came up on the side of Second Baptist. It was about 9:30, and there were no cars parked outside yet. Any minute, I thought, church members would be there for Sunday School.

I ran up the back steps and tried the door. It was unlocked! Not wanting to scare anyone who might be inside, I closed the door and walked around to the front entrance. That door, too, was unlocked. Quietly, we went in.

In the vestibule were bulletin boards with photos of what seemed to be church picnics and other festive events. Immediately, I noticed that there were white people mixed in among the blacks. It appeared that Second Baptist was no longer segregated by custom, as it had been during my father's childhood. Now it was a place of worship where the doors that had always been open to all actually received "whosoever will."

I hesitated to open the vestibule doors, because I figured they probably led to the sanctuary. Dressed in a navy blue Polo Sport hooded sweatsuit with sneakers, I didn't feel properly attired to enter the House of the Lord. I had never been in a church without being dressed appropriately. But now clothes seemed inconsequential as curiosity embraced me.

Gently pushing the wooden door, I peered in. A sudden peacefulness and stillness overcame me. Seeing or hearing no one, I opened the door wider and Reggie and I stepped inside the sanctuary.

It was beautiful! The church was not an expansive or elaborate place, but its simple elegance was stately and lovely. The royal blue carpeting complemented the twenty-five pews that were divided into three sections. Two side aisles, rather than a long center one, led down an incline toward the raised pulpit. The church looked like a miniature version of the church I had grown up in, Mount Zion, in Seattle. I could envision where my father might have sat, based on where he always perched himself at Mount Zion—in the front row under the balcony at the right of the entrance.

I looked at the table prepared with a white sheet over it in front of the pulpit, and I knew it signified something I had forgotten: Today was First Sunday. Communion would be observed today at Second Baptist, as it would be at Mount Zion, and at Baptist churches around the world. The monthly Communion, which signifies the Last Supper of Christ when He broke bread and drank wine with his disciples, "in remembrance of Me," before the Crucifixion, is the most sacred tradition of the Baptist Church. One can participate in Communion only if one has been baptized.

My heart began to race. The one thing I felt I was missing in my journey to Pratt was a ritual. Because there was no birthday celebration, I felt a void. But now I knew that I was going to experience something spiritually special, something that would fill my heart with both the love of God and of my family: I would have Communion in the church of my ancestors.

Reggie stood in the back of the church, keeping watch, as I slowly made my way to the front pew, directly before the podium. I looked around and pondered every little thing. *My grandfather stood at that*

podium and delivered sermons. . . . There is the pastor's study in which he
wrote them. . . . My father attended Sunday School here, and learned all those
church songs he hummed around the house, that we never sang at Mount
Zion. . . . My uncle was probably baptized in the under-floor cavity behind the
pastor's chair. . . . My step-grandmother may have played that organ. I sat on
the edge of the pew, and began to pray. Feelings of joy welled up in
me. *My cup runneth over.*

We walked more briskly back to the hotel to shower and change for
church. Now that I had seen how lovely the church was, I regretted
that I hadn't brought a dress. I had gotten accustomed to wearing
pants to my Unity Church in New Jersey. Since I didn't know how the
women dressed here, I shouldn't have brought just a pantsuit, I
scolded myself.

Reg drove back to the church, where we had our choice of parking
spaces. There were maybe five or six cars. Not many at all.

Arriving a bit late for the start of the eleven o'clock service, we
expected to have to maneuver through a crowd. When we gingerly
opened the doors and stepped into the church again, this time we saw
a minister and two other pastors on the pulpit, and two deacons standing in front of it. About twenty people were seated.

I made eye contact with one of the deacons, who nodded that we
should enter. We picked up a church bulletin for the order of service
from the table at the door. Seeing an empty pew near the door, we sat
down. The service was already in full swing, and the elderly, fair-skinned,
African-American minister, Rev. Marion Crockett, was leading the
devotion. When we rose to sing a hymn, I noticed that both of the two
white women in a pew in front of us were wearing pantsuits. Relieved, I
was further soothed by the song, "Just As I Am."

Every song sung and every hymn played were not just familiar to
me, but etched on my soul from childhood. Rev. Crockett asked a
small, brown-skinned lady to come from her seat in the congregation
to sing a solo. No one had to tell me that the song she chose, "Near
the Cross," was one that had filled that sanctuary countless times since
the day the church was built. I felt at home.

Eventually, the minister asked if the visitors would stand. We did, as well as the family that included the women in the pantsuits. A man in that group introduced themselves first. Then I introduced Reginald and myself, mentioning that I was the granddaughter of Rev. N. J. Stokes, and that we had traveled from New Jersey in celebration of my father's one hundredth birthday. After all the guests were welcomed, one of the deacons remarked, "I knew the Stokeses very well, and so we are glad that you joined us today."

In the middle of the sermon, two young African-American women with two black children and one white child entered the church. The youngest one looked about two. She caught my eye, and I was amazed at how remarkably she resembled my sister, Vicki, at that age. After the group seated themselves, the little one would not stay settled and began to inch her way toward me, smiling adorably. Instead of paying attention to the sermon, I winked at her, and she blinked both eyes back. I held out my arms and she came without hesitation. She sat quietly on my lap like a good girl for several minutes, first playing with my watch and having no luck snatching it off, then lifting the red crocheted sleeve of my sweater to find with delight a bracelet underneath. After she decided not to break the beads with her pulling and grabbing, she went back to Mommy.

When it was time for Communion, a deacon came up the aisle and stopped in front of us with one shiny silver platter of tiny cracker squares and another one specially made to hold thirty or forty individual miniature glasses of grape juice. I was surprised that Reggie took both the bread and the cup, as I had never seen him do so before in all our twenty-five years of church-going together. But in silence I understood and appreciated the gesture. This day, for both of us, was like no other. As he said to me later, he just didn't feel he should have defied the expectation that he would take Communion at the church of my ancestors. He was a black man, sitting in a black Baptist church. What else would one assume, except that he was a Baptist who would be taking Communion?

My own attention drifted back to the memory of my father, and the many times I had seen him and my mother take Communion at Mount Zion. As my head was bowed in prayer, I tried to imagine him here, in

this sanctuary, following the ritual under the ministry of his own
father.

The pastor began to recite the passage of I Corinthians 11:23–26
that I had heard all my life.

For I have received of the Lord that which also I delivered unto you.
That the Lord Jesus the same night in which He was betrayed took bread:

And when He had given thanks, He brake it, and said, Take, eat: this is
my body, which is broken for you: this do in remembrance of Me.

After the same manner also He took the cup, when He had supped, say-
ing, This cup is the new testament in my blood: this do ye, as oft as ye
drink it, in remembrance of Me.

As sure as one could be without having personally witnessed it, as sure
as I believed in anything I had not seen, I knew that Rev. Norris Jefferson Stokes had uttered those very words in this very church on many a
First Sunday, many years ago.

The congregation sang softly, "It is well . . . it is well, with my soul."
And it was.

After the service, congregants welcomed us personally and the deacons invited us back to the pastor's study. It was a small, compact room
behind the pulpit in which the antique desk and the brand-new copier
took up most of the space. Looking around, I was amazed to think that
the room probably hadn't changed much since my grandfather had
written his sermons there. It was likely that he had chosen and used
the very furnishings I was seeing. The only wall hangings were early
black-and-white photos of church members gathered outside the
building that resembled those we had seen in the Historical Museum
the day before. As Rev. Crockett spoke about how things had changed
in Pratt, and how few were in attendance at church these days, I looked
for my family members in the photos and found Grandpa in them all,
and a pubescent Uncle Maurice standing front and center in one.

Although I had met Mrs. Stokes, I couldn't identify her. Was she this pretty woman? Or was she this other one?

"So, you're a Stokes?" Rev. Crockett asked me.

"Yes, sir," I replied.

"Your grandfather, N. J. Stokes—he was *somebody!*"

I wanted to ask if I could interview him to find out more, but I thought at the time it would be inappropriate. There's a time to be a journalist, and a time to be holy.

Fortunately, one of the elderly black women of the church approached me after the service and whispered, "I am the only person here today who actually attended the church when your grandfather was the pastor."

She introduced herself as Billie Bright, and invited us to join her, her husband (who was one of the deacons talking with Reggie in the study), and two other parishioners at Don's Servateria, a buffet brunch place on East First Street. I gratefully accepted.

We went through the buffet line and piled our plates with mashed potatoes, turkey, and dressing, and made sure we got layer cake. As the six of us dined, I asked Mrs. Bright what she remembered of my grandfather. She had been a young girl during his ministry.

"I remember that he was my Sunday School teacher," she said. "He was the pastor, but he also taught the children."

I was delighted to hear that the Brights had been married in 1946 by Rev. Stokes. "He married us in the kitchen of the parsonage. It was so cold in the church, and we had a problem with the furnace, so he married us right there in his house," she said. This was fun for me to hear. As a judge my father had enjoyed marrying people, and sometimes opened our house to couples who didn't want the ceremony performed in his chambers, in the cold, austere government offices. I hadn't thought about the fact that his father, as a minister, had also performed weddings. Daddy liked to ask couples he met years after their wedding if they were still happily married, and took pride in marrying couples "for keeps." I looked at Mr. and Mrs. Bright, amazed that they had been married longer than any of the people my father had married. His father, who had died just three years after the Brights got married, had obviously performed a ceremony that stuck.

"Rev. Stokes was a leader," Mr. Bright went on. "He had courage, because back then there was nothing to back you up but your mouth. It took courage to stand up for right."

Reggie and I understood that he was talking about how vulnerable black people were in my father and grandfather's day. Saying or doing what was perceived by whites to be the wrong thing could result in your death—even here in "free" Kansas.

Mrs. Bright said, "He was also our lawyer." She explained that as one of two black ministers in town (the other one was Methodist), he was highly regarded by the town's white power brokers and was often called upon when things got rough. "He got a lot of kids out of trouble. He had a car and a phone when the rest of us didn't. So he helped us."

"Just his presence was helpful," added Mr. Bright. "You know, he didn't have to help us, but he did."

They also remembered my father, who left Pratt for Kansas University in another part of the state probably before they were both born. "Charles would come to visit and stop by to see Mom and Daddy," Mrs. Bright said. "He was closer to their age. Didn't he play in a band?"

I began to laugh, and nodded my head in agreement. Daddy had told us that he played the drums in a combo to make extra money for college. When I was a child, he had taught me how to beat out a drummer's cadence with my hands and feet.

"And your Uncle Jay," she began. Jay? She must have meant Daddy's older brother Norris, whom he called Jake. The reason why was a private joke between the brothers that they took to their graves. In recent years of Bible reading, I wondered if the secret ribbing had anything to do with the two preacher's kids relating to the Old Testament story of Jacob and Esau, brothers in rivalry for their father's favor. But as Mrs. Bright spoke, I considered that Norris's initials were N. J., like his father's, so if everyone else had called him Jay that would have made sense.

"Jay—that's what we called him," she said, sensing my puzzlement. "Every time he came to visit, he would sing at the church." I did know that Uncle Norris had made a living as a traveling gospel singer. Bingo!

"One time he came to visit, he was going up to sing a solo and slipped going down the aisle in the church," she said.

"Oh dear, I hope he wasn't hurt!" I exclaimed.

"No, he wasn't," Mr. Bright said. "But that's when we had wood floors. We raised money and got carpeting real quick after that!"

Mrs. Bright mentioned that she had been a nurse and that she had cared for Mrs. Stokes in her last days in 1970. She said she had wondered what had happened to the many precious family heirlooms that Mrs. Stokes had kept stored in a trunk in the home, but she hadn't known that there were any living relatives after Uncle Maurice's passing in the mid-1990s. She was glad to hear that Attorney Johnston had sent many of the heirlooms to my father, before his passing the same year, and had given me on Friday the rest of the things they had salvaged.

"I wondered where the blueprint of the church was," Mrs. Bright said. I told her that I thought she must have been talking about the painting of the church that I had been given. She seemed relieved to know that it would stay within the family. I felt a warm sense of her sincerity and was grateful for her concern.

I had mentioned to the Brights that I wanted to visit the graves of my family members before Reggie and I left for the Wichita airport that afternoon. Could they please tell us how to get there?

"We'll take you there," Mrs. Bright offered. "Just follow us when we leave the parking lot."

The sun had broken through the clouds after church, but now after brunch it was overcast again. Reg and I followed the four of them in the car in silence. After a few blocks, we made a turn that took us through the quiet, clean neighborhoods of Pratt.

It didn't take long before the road that passed well-kept homes led into an expansive cemetery. Like every place in Kansas, it was spread out on a prairie. We followed the Brights' car to the end of the curving one-car road inside the cemetery gates. Before I got out of our car, I saw two towering headstones side by side, each about five feet high. Beautifully designed with S monograms across the top, I knew they marked the graves of my grandparents.

On the left was the granite stone with these words engraved:

Mother
JOSEPHINE STOKES
1880–1970
Praise the Lord All Ye Nations

It was terribly disconcerting to see the same name as my own mother—who was very much alive, thank God—on a headstone. I moved my attention to the right, and saw my grandfather's identical tombstone with this inscription:

Reverend
NORRIS J. STOKES
1877–1949
Blessed Be the Name of the Lord

A smaller headstone had been placed to the right of theirs. It belonged to the person who had, most likely, ordered the larger ones in memory of his parents, Uncle Maurice. Or maybe all the brothers had decided together to order those monuments, so much taller and grander than others nearby; I didn't know. But Maurice's marker was decidedly more modest and lay upon the ground. I wondered if the kindly people at Johnston & Eisenhauer had been left to order it.

Maurice S.
STOKES
1911–1995

Uncle Maurice had been an elderly man the last time I saw him, at Uncle Norris's funeral in the late 1980s, but now as a mother myself, I thought of him as the baby of the couple in the adjacent graves. Here laid to rest were two parents and their baby boy—all of whom had lived long lives, made contributions to their world of Kansas, loved the Lord, and died.

Mrs. Bright pointed out that her own parents were buried there, and she showed us their headstones and graves nearby. She also noted that the family who had lived next door to the Stokeses was buried next to them. "Next door in life, next door in death."

Mr. Bright gestured toward all the surrounding graves and mentioned that this was the black section of the cemetery. He added in jest that if we really wanted to know where all the black folks of Pratt had gone, well, there's where they were. Right there in front of us was an entire former black community, now deceased and their descendants scattered in other parts of the country.

I was one of those descendants, I thought, and soon it would be time for me to return to where I had come from in another part of the country.

But first, as the wind picked up dramatically, reminding us ever so slightly that, after all, this was tornado country, we took pictures of Mr. and Mrs. Thomas Bright, the couple my grandfather had married and whom I felt fortunate to have met. Blest be the ties . . .

Reggie and I decided we would linger and sit on a bench near my family's plot for a little while after our gracious hosts left. As we walked them to their car, I gave Mrs. Bright an especially big hug. And in bidding me farewell, she said, "I didn't know you existed—but I'm so glad you do!"

In 2003, for my father's one hundredth birthday, I made a pilgrimage to his hometown of Pratt, Kansas, and paid homage at my grandparents' graves.

GRATITUDE

This book is a praise-song, but it's not a solo. Homage is due to the choir. The author would like to express abundant appreciation to:

Josephine Stratman Stokes, for *everything*—from marrying Dad and giving me life, to providing clear memories that brought more accuracy to these childhood remembrances, as well as support and encouragement in the writing of this memoir.

My siblings, **Vicki S. Stokes** and **André Stratman Wooten,** for shared history and sharing Daddy. My cousin, **Gloria Ratliff Leonard,** who was a part of it all.

Reginald Oliver, my husband, for making the pilgrimage to Kansas with me, as well as the journey through life.

My girls, **Anique, Amena, Aleeyah,** and **Ahmondyllah Oliver,** who have heard the stories *ad nauseum,* and still laugh.

This book was the brainchild of my literary agent, **Victoria Sanders,** to whom I am humbly grateful for her leadership and commitment to making it happen. Special thanks also to her staff, **Imani Wilson** and **Benee Knauer,** and to **Diane Dickensheid.**

Malaika Adero, my editor, whose belief in the book brought it to life. **Judith Curr,** publisher of Atria Books, for the green light. Publicist **Audra Boltion, Jeanne Lee,** the book's cover designer, and **La Marr J. Bruce** for his editorial assistance.

Mary Turner Henry for the invaluable two-day interview with Daddy, the audiotapes of which are now a family treasure.

Rev. Dr. Samuel B. McKinney whose recollections added richness to the story.

In memoriam of **Rev. Dr. F. Benjamin Davis,** who gave me his remembrances and his blessing just weeks before his passing.

Arthur Fletcher, former Assistant Secretary of Labor, for sharing his memories of the young Black Republicans of Kansas.

Former Washington State governor **John D. Spellman** courageously appointed my father to his judgeship and graciously recalled the story to me.

Hettie Jones accepted me into her renowned memoir-writing class at New York City's 92nd Street Y and transformed a writer into memoirist. I am grateful for the honest feedback of Hettie and the members of that class: **Daisy Barringer, Frank Beachman, Claire Cayson, Elizabeth Koster, Martha Maesaka, Molly Ness, Rosemarie Pettet, Sharon Schneider, DeeDee Sprecher, Judith Veder,** with special acknowledgment of memoirists **John Dillon** and **Judy Abrams** for hosting us when the class became the Hettie Jones Memoir Writers' Group.

Frank Lalli, former editor-in-chief of *George* magazine, for being the first person to encourage me to tell the story in print.

Victoria L. Valentine, editor-in-chief of *The Crisis,* for publishing the essay "Daddy, Me and Grand Old Party."

Susan Anderson Wooten for the long-ago gift of the cherished photo that inspired the cover design.

Janet Hill, my first book editor, for her continuing friendship and support.

Sally Koslow, Pamela O'Brien, and the editorial staff of *Lifetime* magazine, for encouragement in the beginning of the writing.

Edward Lewis, Michelle Ebanks, Harry Dedyo, Diane Weathers, Marlowe Goodson, Patrik Bass, the staff of *Essence,* and the *Essence.com* Web team for support at the end of the writing. Abundant, sisterly gratitude to **Susan L. Taylor** for always keeping the door open to my corporate home.

Cheryl Mayberry, Sheryl Huggins, and the *NiaOnline* staff for my monthly column, "On Purpose," in which they have always graciously allowed me to promote my books.

My sister circle of friends and writers: **Alycia Long Allen, Daphne Barbee-Wooten, Shelia Baynes, Iqua Colson, Audrey Edwards, Joyce**

Harley, Jill Hayott, Helena Mitchell Lindsay, Benilde Little, Cathy Ranieri, Michele Rawls, Teresa Ridley, Olivia G. Shaw, Geraldine Smith-Thomas, Brenda Yearwood Stone, Linda Villarosa, Susan Long Walsh, Marlene F. Watson, Nina Wells, Erlene B. Wilson, Valerie Wilson Wesley.

The lovely people of Pratt, Kansas, who made my trip there so memorable: **Billie and Thomas Bright, Dorothy Adams, Rev. Marion Crockett,** and the members of **Second Baptist Church; Atty. Michael Johnston** and **Kathy Wood; Rochelle Westerhaus, Sandy Hazlett,** and **Christine Mattal** of the Pratt Public Library; and the founder of the Pratt County Historical Museum, **Eugene Rose.**

Nancy Dehlinger of the Republican National Committee, who patiently researched and provided me with the documentation of my father's participation in the Republican National Convention.

Tom Healy of the Seattle Public Library, who helped with my long-distance researching of delicate newspaper clippings.

Horace Silver, jazz pianist, for the title inspiration, and for the music that I shared with my father years ago, and that accompanied the writing of the book now.

Thank **You,** every reader of this book.

CREDITS

ABOUT THE AUTHOR

Stephanie Stokes Oliver is the former editor of *Essence* magazine, where she worked for sixteen years before becoming the founding editor-in-chief of *Heart & Soul*. She has published two books, *Daily Cornbread* and *Seven Soulful Secrets*. Most recently, as president of SSO Communications, she consulted on the launch of *NiaOnline* and *Lifetime* magazines, and served as editor-in-chief of *Essence.com*. She lives in the New York City area and frequently visits her hometown, Seattle.

For more information or to contact the author, visit:
www.StephanieStokesOliver.com

SSocom@ad.com